ESCAPING HITLER

ESCAPING HITLER

*A Jewish Boy's Quest for
Freedom and His Future*

PHYLLIDA SCRIVENS

Skyhorse Publishing

Contents

List of Plates

Ida and Alfred Stern on their wedding day, August 1922.

Nickenich Village School Class of 1931.

Hintergasse, Nickenich 1930s.

Ploughing the fields around Nickenich

Stern family group 1936.

Günter in his fashionable sailor suit.

Wuppertal Suspended Railway. 1929.

View over Cochem to the castle overlooking the Mosel, 1919.

Günter's *Kinderausweis* (passport).

Passport reverse dated 29 November 1938.

Deustches Eck (German Corner), Koblenz, 1930s.

Allsopp family group in Lydney 1940.

Margaret Free aged seven.

The Allsopp house in Spring Meadow, Lydney (photographed in 2014).

Lydney Tin Plate Works

Factory floor at The Briton Brush Company, Wymondham, 1920s.

Jean Skitmore at a munitions exhibition in 1945.

Wedding group, 21 May 1946.

Joe and Jean on their wedding day in Attleborough.

Hazel Allsopp and Jean in Southsea, summer 1946.

Ernest Skitmore in his First World War uniform.

Lucy Skitmore (née Leach).

The King's Head, Worstead, Norfolk.

The Skitmore daughters, Joan, Jean and Marjorie.

Gordon Skitmore aged about twelve.

Gordon and Beryl on their wedding day, 5 November 1947.

Dedicated to Alfred and Ida Stern who brought up their son to be courageous, resourceful and generous.

Acknowledgments

I would like to thank the many people who have helped to make this book happen. Firstly, the people whom I interviewed, who were so generous with their memories and anecdotes of Joe Stirling: Brenda Dawson, Kathleen Bidewell, Michael Bidewell, Roy Blower, Hazel Brown, Graham Creelman, Julia Creusson, Ann Godfrey, Doreen Hardy, David and Heather Jack, John Jones, Joyce Knight, Nick Little, Judith Marjoram, Phillip Meakings, Jane Neville, Roger Rowe, Gail Scott, Paul Skitmore, Ian Stirling, Johanna Stirling, Martin Stirling, George Turner, Barbara Vedmore, Shirley Wilcox, Tom and Margaret Wooldridge.

So many others, both individuals and agencies, also played their part, sending me photographs and documents, acting as guides and translators, offering hospitality and above all sharing my fascination with the life of Joe Stirling. I apologise if I miss anyone: Jacqueline Amos, Johannes and Rosey Andernach, Beverley Andree-Bazerman, Avril Anderson, Archant Limited Historical Newspaper Archive in Norwich, Army Personnel Centre Glasgow, Hubert Becker, Maria Becker, Rosemary Dixon, East Anglian Film Archive at the University of East Anglia, Christopher Green, Jessica Hansen, Jütta Hansen, Friedhelm Henn, Anne Howarth, Margaret Kimberley, Pete and Stella Loewenstein, Nigel Lubbock, The National Archives, Norfolk Heritage Centre, Margit, Jörgen, Marie and Sophie Scholz, Jürgen Schumacher, Gerald Stern, Marijohn Trösch, Wiener Library, World Jewish Relief and the archivists at Somerville College and St. John's College Oxford.

My gratitude to Shirley Williams, Baroness Williams of Crosby, for generously agreeing to write the foreword. And above all I wish to record my gratitude and love for the two most important men in my life for the past four years, firstly to Joe for his co-operation, enthusiasm and remarkable memory and also to my husband Victor. His love, encouragement, support, inspiration and meticulous proof-reading have been invaluable throughout this incredible experience.

Illustration Credits

Running Boy courtesy of Alison White
Family Trees designed by Gill Blanchard of pastsearch.co.uk
Map of Europe from Pen and Sword Books

Plates Section 1

Horse and plough courtesy of Hubert Becker
Lydney Tin Plate Works, courtesy of Geoff Davis, sungreen.co.uk
Briton Brush Factory courtesy of Richard Fowle, Wymondham Town Archive

Plates Section 2

Advertisement for Tom Watts courtesy of Peter Goodrum
Advertisement for Stirling Holidays courtesy of Archant Publications
Stirling Holidays shop Magdalen Street courtesy of East Anglian Film Archive
Cat 640, Norwich, Norfolk 1960 – Magdalen Street Commercials.
Photograph of Marion Barron with kind permission of Roger and Deanna Millward

Plates Section 3

Lions Jacket 1979 with permission from *Eastern Evening News*
Civic Coach, with permission from *Eastern Evening News*
Norwich Civic Association with permission from *Norwich Evening News*/ Denise Bradley
Joe Stirling with Shirley Williams with permission from *Norwich Evening News*
90th Birthday Party photographs with permission from Daryl Fraser

Plates Section 4

All photos copyright of Phyllida Scrivens 2013

Other photos kindly supplied by Joe Stirling and family members.

Foreword

Phyllida Scrivens' enchanting book *Escaping Hitler* rang so many bells for me. Joe Stirling's life, from his childhood escape to Britain to life as a refugee in a strange country with a kindly family he had never met before, his education in unfamiliar schools and his ability to adapt to working as a professional in the politics of his adopted country, all have echoes with my own experience. But the sensitivity of Mrs Scrivens' account, her remarkable capacity to convey the significance of each small detail, make this biography of an outstanding British local politician, volunteer and businessman special. The early extracts from Joe Stirling's interviews with his biographer Phyllida Scrivens, with which every section starts, convey a chilling reminder of Germany's descent over four years from a reasonably tolerant, respectable, decentralised society into the intense nationalism, brutality and fascism of the Third Reich.

The young Jewish boy, Günter Stern, was well treated by his teachers, his parents inviting his schoolfriends to play with him. A few years later, the teenage Günter, isolated and excluded, set out on his own to walk from Koblenz to England, with little money and only a creased official letter from the English Jewish Committee telling him when the next *Kindertransport* would leave Cologne, in July 1939. It was his last chance.

My brother John and I were evacuated to the US to live in Minnesota for three years with a family we had never met. We were not fleeing the Luftwaffe's Blitz in British cities, but primarily the likely prospect of a Nazi invasion of Britain. My parents, though not Jewish, were both on the Gestapo Black List of people to be killed immediately in the event of a successful invasion. They felt this was a risk they should take, but could not impose on their children.

The story of Joe Stirling's successful integration into British life says a great deal for his determination, his resilience and his courage; the openness of his mind. He worked as a Labour Party official and organiser after his service in the British Army, in one of the most rural regions of England, East Anglia, at the grass roots, often in partnership with the Agricultural Workers Union, battling to end tied cottages and to challenge traditional, sometimes near-feudal, employment practices. He was one of my agents in the 1953 Harwich Parliamentary by-election.

A 23-year-old candidate, I recall the excitement of convening with Joe two or three meetings a night, hurtling down muddy lanes in the dark, looking for small halls, each with its audience of a dozen or so. Joe mobilised a handful of supporters from a score of villages to come. The boy from the Rhineland had become a Norfolk man.

Joe Stirling has made this his own country and the country has properly honoured him. Secretary and Agent for Norwich Labour Party, councillor and Sheriff of Norwich.

Joe Stirling has contributed to our public life for over sixty years.

Shirley Williams

Author's Introduction

I first met Joe Stirling quite by chance in November 2011. I had completed my Open University degree in English Literature and was temporarily working as a secretary at the University of East Anglia. If my walking companion had turned up as arranged that lunchtime, I doubt I would ever have spent the following four years increasingly absorbed in one man's life story. Joe was volunteering as a 'Human Book' at a Human Library event in the Student Union. The catalogue of available titles for loan was propped up against the legs of a metal table. The list was intriguing. *'Piercings and Tattoo Addiction'*, *'Gay and Proud'* and *'Confessions of a Self-Harmer'*. I was particularly drawn to *'I was a refugee from Nazi Germany'*.

The Human Library Movement came to Great Britain from Denmark in 2008. Our National Library Service immediately adopted the concept, setting up events in libraries, colleges and schools, in order to facilitate respectful one-to-one conversations, in the hope of increasing understanding and tolerance between the public and individuals who face discrimination and prejudice. At any one event there might be Human Books representing Goths, drug addicts, the LGBT (lesbian, gay, bisexual, transgender) community, recovering alcoholics, people with disabilities or mental illness, ethnic minorities, offenders, the homeless, religion, immigrants and refugees. The librarian looked at his clipboard to check if the refugee was free. 'Come back in five minutes. He's been popular all morning.' This was my opportunity to give up and leave. But no, I was curious. I would wait my turn. The refugee certainly didn't fit the stereotype. He was just an old man in a grey suit one size too big for him. I noticed a slight tremor as he poured water into a paper cup. But his handshake was firm. By contrast his voice was soft, hardly audible in the cavernous space. 'My name is Joe Stirling. I'm pleased to meet you. Do take a seat.'

My journey had begun. The following four years included studying for a Master's degree in Biography at the UEA, at the same time regularly visiting Joe in his home, recording our conversations while taking tea from a floral bone china cup. I interviewed nearly thirty others, each generously sharing with me memories of Joe Stirling. I transcribed thousands of words, researched books and websites, sent emails, made telephone calls. Joe allowed me access to his unpublished memoirs, written during the 1980s. I listened to Joe's appearances on BBC Radio Norfolk. He invited me to attend civic events. I visited archives, fascinated by the personal testimonies from a distant past. I wrote to local newspapers across the country, appealing for information about people who may have shared a moment of Joe's life.

Joe Stirling was born Günter Stern in the Rhineland. In September 2013 my husband Victor and I embarked upon a week-long 'footstepping' journey to Germany. With the help of some kind people we were able to see for ourselves many significant locations from Günter's early life. In pouring rain we arrived in his home village of Nickenich, meeting ninety-year-old Johannes Andernach, a lifelong resident of the village. Exploring the beautiful city of Koblenz, twinned with Norwich since 1978, we identified the place where the Sterns had lived for a short period in 1938–9, now a clothes shop in a busy shopping street. We stood on the platform at Cologne Station, later driving to places of significance in Joe's story; Meudt, Montabaur, Cochem and Vaals. Our suitcases swelled with additional research material. We had taken hundreds of photographs. In July 2014 I was ready. I submitted my book proposal. Pen and Sword Books offered me a contract. Now all I had to do was write it. Unless otherwise stated, all opening quotations are from Joe.

Escaping Hitler is not a traditional history book. I simply wish to tell Joe's story.

Phyllida Scrivens, April 2015

Stern / Stirling Family Tree

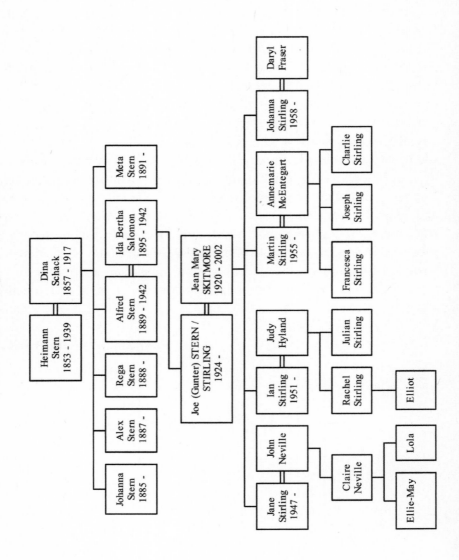

Skitmore Family Tree

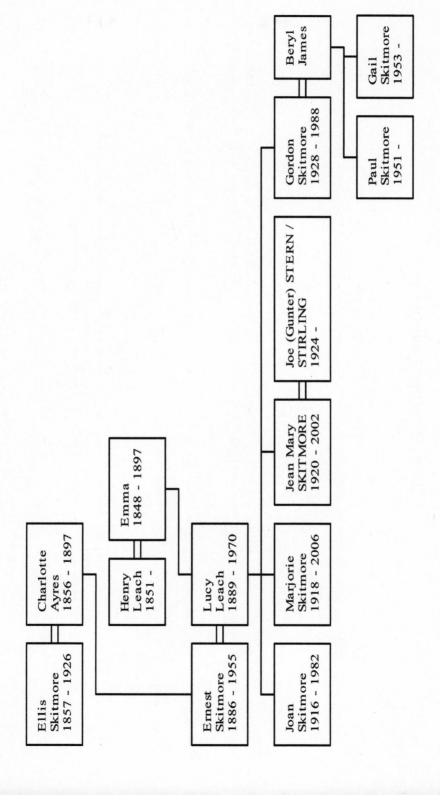

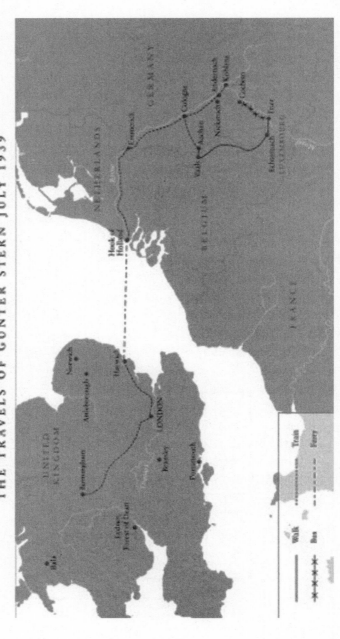

THE TRAVELS OF GÜNTER STERN JULY 1939

Prologue

Visitors

It happens so quickly. Loud hammering on the door at around four in the morning. Günter instantly awake. His father's heavy footsteps on the wooden stairs. The boy creeping from his body-warm bed, joining Mother at the top of the staircase. More banging. Raised angry voices. The door swinging open, rusty hinges straining under the force. Three or four men bursting over the threshold. Uninvited. Invading their home. Strangers, from Andernach or even Koblenz, clutching cudgels and brandishing revolvers.

'Alfred Stern? Get dressed. You're arrested.'

'Arrested? What have I done?'

Günter flinches as his father takes a violent blow across the face. Two men climb the stairs, pushing past woman and child. Roughnecks turning out drawers and cupboards, throwing contents to the floor, trampling over china and glass. Ida and Günter stunned, silent, shaking. Her husband pushed through the door and onto the cobbles of the *Hintergasse*. Ida's throat opens and she screams out:

'Where are you taking him?'

No reply. Just the muffled sound of Alfred's anguished objections to being treated as a criminal. He fought bravely for his country. He was wounded four times. He was awarded the Iron Cross. Soon his cries and the marching feet are no longer audible and the night is still once more.

Chapter 1

Child, 1924–1939

Innocence

'I was very keen to learn to read and we had lots of books. Shock-haired Peter *was one of my favourites. In a way these stories are very frightening. I used to enjoy learning to read them.'*

The powerful smell of tanned leather, sweetly scented woodland flowers, a suitcase full of banknotes and *Der Struwwelpeter*; the profound, personal blend of memories defining Günter's early childhood. Aged three or four, he sat on his bedroom floor hiding amongst hundreds of scraps of paper, each stamped many times over with an ever-increasing value. A little older, on days when the sun warmed the air, he met with other youngsters in the fields and woodlands around the nearby volcanic lake, *Laacher See*, to shape posies of blueweed, oxeye daisies, yellow archangels and phlox. These they proffered for sale to wealthy tourists who drove through the countryside in their Opel *Laubfrosch* convertibles and shiny Stuttgart limousines, looking for the nearby medieval abbey of *Maria Laach*.

Young Günter's formative summers in the Rhineland village of Nickenich were spent running errands or playing his mother's 78s, mainly Johann Strauss, on the windup gramophone. Günter loved to play football on the *Hintergasse* outside his home, the boys using a tin can for want of a ball. From a very young age, encouraged by his parents, Günter learned to read and in his quieter moments enjoyed discovering new worlds inside the covers of books. Along with timeless fairy stories of the Brothers Grimm, his favourite was *Der Struwwelpeter*, a fuzzy-haired character created in 1845 by storyteller Heinrich Hoffman. This collection of morality tales includes striking illustrations of Shock-Headed Peter, the naughty, unpopular boy who refuses to wash or comb his hair.

After his father, Peter was Günter's earliest hero.

Nickenich

'Lots of people were small farmers, who all lived in the tightly packed community, working narrow fields scattered all around the village. Each morning they would set off in their carts, drawn by a horse or more likely one or two oxen, to which of their strips required attention. The objective was to produce enough potatoes, rye, wheat, hay, oats and maize to feed their animals, and sufficient eggs, chickens, pigs and calves to feed themselves.'

Alfred Stern married his sweetheart Ida in her home village of Kettig on 5 August 1922. The couple had met whilst Alfred, a *Viehhändler* (cattle dealer), conducted business with her father, a supervisor at the main cattle market in Koblenz–Lützel, less than 10 miles from Kettig. The newlyweds chose to settle in Nickenich, a relatively large community of around 2,000 people, in the mountainous Eifel region, bordered by the Mosel River in the south and the Rhine Valley to the east. Two other cattle dealers were already serving the local farmers. However, Alfred knew that they were both nearing retirement. The farmers lived in the village; a close-knit community, each owning a cow or two, providing milk for the families, wives proficient at making cheese. This tradition, along with the close proximity of the cattle market in Koblenz, should ensure Alfred a decent living.

But at that time mere survival was a serious challenge. In the summer of 1923, whilst Günter was still the longed-for issue of a young bride, Germany suffered from a severe case of hyperinflation. Following defeat in the Great War in 1918, the terms of the Treaty of Versailles had crippling economic ramifications. The German standard of living fell to about half of what it had been before the conflict. Over the next five years the situation escalated into an unprecedented catastrophe. At the peak of the crisis the German currency included a note valued at 50 million marks. By November 1923 the mark was dead, all existing banknotes declared invalid, resulting in mountains of lower value notes burnt in place of logs or given to children as playthings. Years later Alfred would regale his son with stories from those desperate days. Once, having sold a cow, he gave his wife all the proceeds. Within hours she spent every pfennig on a much-needed new apron.

Having established his reputation, his list of clients growing, Alfred spent busy days transporting cattle, poultry and horses to market on hired trucks. He bought and sold the animals, having first washed and groomed them, skillfully trimming overgrown hoofs to make the valuable livestock more appealing. Meanwhile, Ida kept house in a rented one-bedroomed flat at the foot of the *Hintergasse*, a steep cobbled lane. The narrow houses formed a patchwork of black basalt volcanic stones from the region, the large smooth pebbles underfoot creating a sombre feel to the unlit streets. Most homes had a cellar for storing root vegetables, a large backyard, stabling for horses, cows, pigs, chickens and of course, a steaming pile of manure to enrich the fields and vegetable plots. The families sold any excess produce to help pay for basic necessities. On Saturday, 18 October 1924, Ida gave birth to a boy. It was a difficult labour. There would be no further babies.

A short time later, in need of more space, the Stern family moved up the lane to Number 183 Nickenich. At that time dwellings in villages and small towns were simply given a number, often without any apparent logic. It was not until some years later that their home became known as *Hintergasse* 10. It was common for the modest houses and flats to have outside toilets and no running water or heating. Günter's new home was a two-bedroomed flat above the workshop of Herr Doll, a saddler living in a nearby hamlet. He cycled every day to Nickenich to craft saddles, harnesses and collars using simple hand tools. Significantly for his tenants, the workshop boasted a boiler. The Sterns now benefitted from access to hot water, a real luxury, carried up the stairs in buckets to fill the metal tub for bathing in front of the fire.

Winter arrived in November, invariably holding on until mid-March. Günter and his village friends looked forward to waking up to a magical fall of snow, arrived silently overnight. Before the grown-ups could sweep it away with their shovels and brooms, the youngsters found their wooden sledges and tin trays, slithering fearlessly head first down the incline of the *Hintergasse*, before serious snowball fights broke out amongst the boys. An open log fire on the first floor of the flat provided warmth for Günter and his parents until they retired for the night. There was no heating in the bedrooms. But cotton bedcovers resembling large envelopes filled with real chicken feathers kept them snug.

When a little older, Günter enjoyed spending more time with his father, occasionally accompanying him on business trips to the cattle market in Koblenz, exploring the fenced-off animal pens, strolling hand in hand with his maternal grandfather, beloved *Opa*, from whom Günter learnt chess, cards, Nine Men's Morris and the importance of caring for others. At home Alfred acted as unofficial village vet. Günter watched fascinated, as his father felt the bellies of cows to confirm they were in calf. The boy marvelled as Alfred calmed nervous horses, a technique developed during his time in the Army. Occasionally the pair would walk together to a neighbouring village. Alfred would buy a cow and allow Günter to lead the creature, a string around its neck, along the road to the next community where he might sell it on at a modest profit.

Along the route Alfred impressed his son with tales of the Great War.

War Veteran

'My father told no end of stories of the horror of the war with all the battlefield names that became familiar like Ypres and the Somme.'

Alfred enlisted in the Imperial German Army in 1913, seeing active service only a year later. Initially he joined a Foot Artillery regiment, driving heavy horse-drawn guns, later transferring to the cavalry as a mounted messenger. Telephone wires laid under the ground were frequently broken and disconnected by constant shelling, necessitating the transfer of intelligence between command posts and front-line troops by a soldier on horseback. Pigeon post had to be abandoned when the birds, disoriented by shooting and explosions, ended up flying the wrong way.

Alfred was wounded four times. He spent the rest of his life with a piece of shrapnel in his neck, too near the spinal cord to be removed safely. This would later provide opportunities to tease his young son with weather predictions courtesy of 'shrapnel twinges'. He was rewarded with an Iron Cross for courage in the face of enemy fire. For many years Alfred continued to have nightmares, later relating horrific tales of combat, including having two horses shot dead from under him. A favourite tale was of the strange British troops who, despite at times wearing 'skirts like women', were fearless fighters. In the German trenches the men anxiously listened as strange wailing sounds signalled a British attack. Some soldiers were so terrified of this weird 'music' that they tried to desert, frequently resulting in execution by their own officers. The conflict over, Alfred returned to cattle dealing.

At nearly thirty it was time to settle down.

Lessons

'It was an all-age school. We learnt mainly reading, writing, nature study and arithmetic. And history. Remember it was in the early years of Hitler so it was history as Hitler wanted it taught. It was totally politically censored. You only learnt German history and the great things that Germans had done, which was fair enough, but also how awful nearly all of the rest of the world had been towards us.'

Just before his seventh birthday Günter joined the local school, a two-minute walk up the hill, turn left at the top opposite the catholic church dedicated to Saint Arnulf and into the school yard. On that first morning, the schoolmaster

Herr Weinand welcomed his new class of attentive faces. There was a message chalked onto the blackboard: '*Aller Angfang ist schwer.*' (Every beginning is difficult.) Günter had no notion of how many times in life he would have cause to recall that piece of wisdom. Addressing his young charges the teacher said, 'Stand up if you can read that'. Günter, grateful to his mother for patiently teaching him his letters, stood up along with about five others. Consistently attentive and quick to learn, the young schoolboy particularly enjoyed nature rambles and outdoor lessons under the trees when the days were still and mellow.

Some afternoons, instead of going straight home, he would visit a house just three doors down. By day this neighbour worked as a painter and decorator but in the evenings he played his violin in the local pub and was quite a celebrity in the village. Alfred could not afford to send his son for professional music lessons; instead Günter learnt the basics on a child-sized violin. Günter's enthusiasm for learning did not stop at music. A conscientious student at most subjects, it wasn't long before he could recite his tables. In class tests, some children endeavoured to copy his work, confident that Günter Stern would know the answers. Ida and Alfred dreamed of their son attending the *Gymnasium*, maybe going to university and becoming a doctor or a lawyer. But to be a student at the Grammar School in nearby Andernach required rather more than being top of the class. Your parents had to be able to afford the fees. But these were adult concerns. Günter simply enjoyed his books and being with his special friends, Rudi Pauken, Toni Fuchs, Alwin Bous and Heinz Becker. Heinz was the son of Hermann Becker, the village cobbler whose family lived in *Kirchstrasse*, at the top of the *Hintergasse* and opposite St Arnulf's Church. The only difference between them was that his friends went to church on a Sunday and Günter went to synagogue on a Saturday.

Günter was the only Jewish child in the school.

Observance

'*Every Spring on the Jewish holiday of Passover we would take gifts of matzah to the houses of our friends in Nickenich. These disks of flat "bread" were very brittle and quite tasteless, a bit like water biscuits. Our best friends got six rounds and quite a few others got two. Friends coming to play would ask if they could have a piece of "that funny stuff, like you bring round at Easter time". But if the request came "out of season" I had to disappoint them.*'

Alfred Stern was born on 9 December 1889 in Meudt, a small community in the Westerwald, a region of low mountains on the right bank of the Rhine, renowned for its relatively high proportion of Jewish families. Before 1810 the Jews used Patronymic names, derived from the given name of a father or male ancestor. Many generations of the Stern family can be traced back to one couple, Jakob, Son of Moyses and his wife Sara, both born around 1736. During the period 1810 to 1840 the dukedoms that would become Germany, forced the Jews to take family names. Names were chosen for a variety of reasons, many reflecting a profession or place of birth. Consequently, there are five different family names emanating from the descendants of Jakob and Sara, including Heilberg, Lahrheim, Löewenstein, Cahn and Stern, all originating from the village of Meudt.

Shortly before the Great War, Alfred's devoutly orthodox father, Heimann Stern, relocated his tailoring business, along with wife Dina and five children, Johanna, Alex, Rega, Alfred and Meta, to the nearby shoemaking community of Montabaur. It wasn't long before Alfred joined the Army, possibly in an effort to escape the restrictive religious rules ardently enforced by his father. During the conflict he was given special dispensation by the Army Rabbis and advised that God would forgive him for deviating from the observance of dietary laws. No Jew expected to be given Saturdays off or to receive any special food. These dispensations meant that Alfred would find it difficult to return to any form of orthodoxy in his civilian life.

After his son was born, once or twice a year and possibly out of duty, Alfred took Günter to visit his paternal grandfather, widowed since 1917, 40 kilometres to the east of Nickenich. As he grew older, Günter continued to be transfixed by the sight of the elderly man, in his white shawl and black brimmed hat, sitting at the rear of the family shop, Hebrew Bible on his lap, rocking back and forth, back and forth, quietly chanting, deep in prayer. Unbeknown to the boy, living in Montabaur was his father's namesake, Alfred Stern, known as Freddy, third cousin to Günter, one year younger and also an only child. The two boys shared a great-great grandfather in Alexander Leser, born in 1765. Freddy's branch of the Stern family had set up home at 24, *Bahnhofstrasse*, living over the shoemaking workshop. Like Günter, Alfred enjoyed a happy childhood. However, Montabaur was a much larger community than Nickenich. As the Nazi threat increased during 1938, Freddy felt compelled to carry a truncheon to school to ward off bullies from the Hitler Youth.

In Nickenich, Ida was intent on raising her son to respect the rites and customs of his ancestors. Her husband didn't make it easy. Despite her disapproval, Alfred consistently disregarded the strict rules of his Jewish heritage, cycling with his son on the Sabbath to the nearby village of Kruft to attend prayers, despite the command against using transport of any kind on holy days. Father and son hid their bikes behind a hedge so that the other worshippers would be unaware of them violating one of the laws of Moses. Ida baked kosher honey cake and flatbread buttons for Günter and his friends, who regularly dropped by on the off chance of an oven-fresh treat. She loved to sing, favouring songs from popular Strauss operettas such as *Die Fledermau* (The Bat) or Franz Lehar's *Die Lustige Witwe* (The Merry Widow). Günter loved breaking from his studies to savour his mother's fine singing voice.

Her husband, less interested in music, preferred to spend some evenings in the village pub, playing hands of 'Skat', the German national card game, with his Catholic friend Peter Saftig. Peter was a farmer living in near-by *Wiesenstrasse* with wife Margarete, son Franz and daughters Maria and Elisabeth. Once in a while, the two men worked together. On one occasion Alfred heard of a farmer in the village of Niederzissen, some 20 kilometres away from Nickenich, with two goats for sale. But he needed a truck. Alfred asked Peter for his help. On arrival at the farm there were actually three goats available, Alfred paying for all three, giving Peter one of the animals in payment for the transport. Livestock and home-produced food were readily acceptable as currency in the countryside.

While the children were at school, Peter's wife Margarete helped her friend to make and mend Günter's shirts and trousers on Ida's sewing machine, while catching up with gossip. Fortunately for Ida, her brother-in-law Uncle Alex had his own clothing store in the city of Düsseldorf. He generously supplied his nephew with good-quality, hardwearing suits from the Stuttgart clothing firm Wilhelm Bleyle, which specialised in fashionable sailor suits. Ida was a woman of high ideals. These gifts ensured she could send her son to school looking smart and tidy, unusual for the child of a poor cattle dealer. Once Günter had grown out of the suits, Ida passed them on to Margarete for her son Franz, two years younger than Günter.

In the early 1920s the twenty-four Jewish residents of the nearby village of Kruft established an oratory in the home of Hugo Kahn. Worshippers included members of the Kahn family, cattle dealer Felix and the ladies' dressmaker, Heinrich. The Rosenberg brothers, owners of a gas station and motor spares shop were regular members of the small congregation. Günter's father often hired a truck from David Rosenberg to transport his livestock. Max Abraham, the owner of a clothing shop directly behind the Town Hall, also attended services when the local bowling league or the 'Glee Club' did not distract him. With too few worshippers at that time to merit dedicated synagogues, the Jewish communities of Kruft and Nickenich were officially under the care of the larger town of Andernach, where on 30 May 1933 the inauguration of a new synagogue took place. The rural families could now attend festivals such as Hanukkah, Yom Kippur and Shavuot, worshipping alongside others, despite the five-mile walk.

At home, Ida ensured that her family properly observed the holy days. Günter looked forward to sunset on a Friday evening when the Sabbath began, a customary time of family, stillness and rest, complete with candles, sweet wine and *challah*, rich bread made with eggs. At Passover, a spring festival lasting eight days, Ida retold the story of the Israelites' escape from captivity and how they survived by eating roots and leaves. To demonstrate their suffering, Ida served samples of bitter herbs such as slivers of fresh horseradish to be chewed and parsley, dipped in salt representing the tears of the Jewish race. The expression on Günter's face invariably matched the ghastly tastes.

Despite this Günter fostered an inkling of religious doubt from a very early age. With no peer pressure at school and his father's limited commitment, he became secretly sceptical about the literal interpretations of stories from the Old Testament. Aged about ten or eleven, during a service in the Andernach synagogue, he took a risk and broke a direct instruction from the Rabbi. The Angel of God was about to descend to blow the holy Shofar, a Ram's Horn and everyone was told not to look. For a split second Günter peered out of one eye and saw it was the Rabbi blowing the horn. The boy felt vindicated.

He knew Mr Goldstein was no angel.

Aunts and Uncles

'I was eight years old when I became aware of some sort of crisis. There had been a general election in Germany and somebody called Hitler had won and was now our Chancellor. It meant little to me but I did overhear grown-ups talking. If you didn't support Hitler then you were an enemy of Germany and he said he would fight the Communists and above all he would fight the Jews. "The Jews?" I asked, "but aren't we Jews?"'

Since 1933 when Hitler first assumed power, government at every level adopted hundreds of new anti-Semitic laws. Decrees and regulations increasingly restricted all Jews from leading a normal life, alienating them from Aryan friends, neighbours, employers and clients. Between March 1933 and December 1938 many professions were decimated. All Jewish doctors, civil servants, lawyers, newspaper editors, tax-consultants, army officers, vets, teachers in public schools, auctioneers and even midwives were forbidden to work.

In the countryside the changes were more gradual and for many years the three Jewish families in Nickenich, Stern, Egener and Marx, experienced very little, if any, anti-Semitism, continuing their lives as part of the farming community. During the middle of the decade, Günter gradually learnt that some of his relatives, increasingly concerned for their livelihoods and personal safety, were contemplating emigration to the United States, Britain or South America. Ida's sister, Aunt Martha was the first to leave along with her husband, a steel wholesaler. Having built up business contacts in the French industrial region of Alsace, part of Germany until the Treaty of Versailles, they decided to temporarily live in that French region, just until the political situation in Germany settled down. Ida's other two sisters, Nelly and Selma, both married to butchers, applied early to the American embassy for coveted 'numbers' given to those requesting a visa to enter and remain in the United States. They were amongst the lucky ones. But there were no guarantees; it might take years to make your way to the top of the queue.

In the early 1930s, Alfred's elder brother Alex had moved north with his wife and children from Montabaur to the city of Düsseldorf, starting up his own business selling curtain materials. By the time Günter was around ten Uncle Alex was doing well. Having first bought a small shop, he then bought the one next-door, knocking through to form larger premises. His business quickly expanded into a thriving department store in the busy and exclusive suburb of Benrath, where he introduced a lucrative line in men's suits. When responsible enough to travel alone, for three or four summers Günter took the train from Andernach to Düsseldorf, staying for two or three weeks at a time. Uncle Alex collected him from the station in the family car, something rarely seen in Nickenich, driving to their luxury two-storey apartment over the shop. Günter loved to relax on the upholstered chairs, wriggle his toes in the deep-pile hand-made rugs and best of all, revel in the privacy and comfort of an indoor bathroom. In Nickenich Günter's meals consisted of 'potatoes, potatoes and more potatoes' but in Benrath he devoured beef stews, pickled herring and schnitzel, at both lunch and dinner, always with the luxury of white bread. Here he didn't have to choose butter or jam, he could have both. His older cousins Erich and Ruth were away at University in Grenoble and his aunt, well aware of Ida's limited resources, enjoyed having a child to feed, spoil and fuss over.

Günter relished his freedom to explore the city on foot or riding the trams, with a little pocket money from Uncle Alex to spend as he pleased. He regularly strolled around the extensive grounds and man-made lake of *Schloss Benrath*, a late baroque 'pleasure palace' and hunting lodge, built during the eighteenth century for Prince-Elector Karl Theodore. A variety of wild plants grew beneath the canopy of tall trees and bushes, reminding Günter of the flower-filled meadows around the lake in Nickenich. From the western side of the park there was direct access to the Rhine, where he sat marvelling at the activities of passing craft, loaded high with cargo, navigating towards Rotterdam or the Hook of Holland.

On Sundays Uncle Alex drove his wife and nephew the twenty miles to the thriving town of Wuppertal, known for cotton weaving, dye making and calico printing. Günter tingled with excitement when riding the *Schwebebhan*, the oldest elevated electric railway in the world, its hanging cars speeding above the River Wupper. It was here that he first visited a Zoological garden, enthralled by the lions, elephants and camels. In less favourable weather, the impressionable boy spent much of his time stood behind the counter in his uncle's shop, watching as staff advised the Düsseldorf *hausfraus*, shopping for buttons, blouses and bloomers.

It was a lesson in customer service, to prove invaluable for his life yet to come.

Young Entrepreneur

'At ten years old I started going around the village seeing if people had any skins, or asking when they were next planning to kill a goat or a rabbit for dinner. I would offer them a couple of pfennig each for them – real money. When I had several I would take them on my bike to the Furrier man.'

German people were beginning to fear trading with or even associating with Jews. The penalties for consorting with enemies of the Nazis became increasingly severe and it was prudent to be cautious. Alfred's business began to falter. When Günter was ten years old, an incident one morning hinted at the developing mood. As he did most days, he climbed onto his bike outside his home, turning it to face down the hill. After a few early wobbles he gained a little speed over the cobbles. The door of a nearby house swung open. A well-known village lad, wearing his Hitler Youth shirt, stared out at Günter, slipping the lead from his dog's neck. Snarling ferociously the animal chased Günter down the slope. The boy was suddenly aware of threatening shouts behind him, the animal encouraged to attack. For the first time he felt real fear in his own street. Despite pedalling faster and faster the dog caught him, barking, baring his teeth, leaping up in excited fury. Günter fell heavily to the ground, his bike careering across the lane and crashing against the wall. Blood seeped from his knees. It hurt. He looked for the dog, fearing worse to come. But the youth called the animal back. He had made his point.

A year later Günter demonstrated his entrepreneurial spirit by starting his own small business to supplement his father's vastly diminished income. It was common in rural villages for people to keep goats for both milk and for meat. Rabbits were plentiful, kept in cages before being killed for the dinner plate. Günter went house to house around Nickenich and near-by villages, asking to buy any unwanted animal skins. Faced with an enthusiastic small boy most people agreed, Günter paying a modest two or three pfennigs for each pelt.

Father and son worked together to prepare them for sale. The goats and kids had already been cut open at the belly, skinned to produce a flat membrane. Günter hung these out like sheets, the wet side outwards. Special attention was paid to the legs. If the skins were not stretched wide apart then flies would get in to any folds, lay their eggs and spoil all their effort. Little pegs were inserted every couple of inches and checked every day that none had fallen out and that the skin was drying evenly. The rabbit pelts finished up as sticky tubes of pink shiny flesh, stuffed with straw and hung out on the washing line to dry. Günter had fun turning the skins inside out exposing the soft white fur within. The young entrepreneur then cycled to offer his wares to the Jewish owner of a near-by tannery. In the early days Günter took the first price offered but later, encouraged by his father, the boy learnt to bargain. On this particular day the businessman was stubbornly sticking to his price.

'That is the most I can offer. There will be no money left for dinner if I pay you that.'

'Go on, you can afford a bit more.'

Günter saw the man wink at his father before replying.

'I don't think so.'

The boy drew himself to his full height, stubbornly holding the man's gaze.

'Maybe I should take the skins back home again.'

'Oh, very well. You drive a hard bargain young man.'

Günter was honing his business skills.

Enemies of the Reich

'Gradually I lost all my village friends. Most of them joined the Hitler Youth, some because they enjoyed the camping and sports and some because they were bullied into joining. They were taught it was bad to have anything to do with Jews. They were told that in some places Jews would slaughter Christian children for food. Also that if their parents spoke against the Nazi party, it was the Youth member's duty to report them. I heard of one or two decent people arrested and put into concentration camps.'

The family's financial situation continued to deteriorate, Alfred barely able to pay the bills or feed his family. Despite terrifying stories of Nazi brutality coming out of the cities, Alfred continued to believe that as a German war veteran nothing bad could possibly happen to him, refusing to join the thousands of Jews desperately applying for exit visas.

Gradually even Günter's friends began turning away from him. He was no longer chosen for the football team. A loyal few continued to visit him for a game of chess, but only after dark with less chance of being seen entering the home of a Jew. His violin teacher withdrew his services. Günter was kept occupied with his skins business while his schoolmates, each wearing a swastika armband, set up camps in the woods surrounding the village, singing songs in praise of the Fatherland while their heads were filled with anti-Semitic propaganda. At school the teachers were divided. Older ones, who started their careers before the ascent of the National Socialists, remained supportive and encouraging towards their only Jewish pupil. However, new teachers assigned by the government arrived, openly manifesting a different view. Günter was frequently abused, humiliated and banned from sports, with his schoolwork cruelly and publicly criticised.

During 1937 and into 1938, the authorities again stepped up legislative persecution of German Jews in an attempt to exclude them from economic life. Organised boycotts of Jewish businesses led to bankruptcies with Jews required to publicly declare every aspect of their finances. This culminated in a programme of wholesale transfer of money and property from Jews to non-Jewish Germans. The Nazis forbade Jewish doctors to treat non-Jews and they revoked the licenses of Jewish lawyers. In the cities, anti-Jewish feelings were spiralling out of control with arrests, beatings in the street and even public executions becoming commonplace.

In Nickenich Alfred still believed himself immune from the madness.

Bar Mitzvah

'I had a very high unbroken child's voice, still pure. When the Rabbi tested me with a little whistle he blew into, he suggested we try it just half a note higher. He found the highest note that I could sing.'

Like all Jewish boys, Günter longed to reach his thirteenth birthday and become a Bar Mitzvah, meaning literally 'son of commandments', a rite of passage marking the transition from boy to adult. To mark this momentous occasion his *Opa* from Koblenz would present Günter with a valuable adult violin; his Grandfather from Montabaur giving gold cufflinks and a signet ring engraved with his initials. From the age of thirteen a young Jew is expected to take personal moral responsibility for his actions, coming with certain privileges. These included leading some prayers, inclusion in the minimum requirement of ten male worshippers to hold a service and being permitted to wear the *tallit*, a prayer shawl with fringes called *tzitzit* on each of its four corners. In accordance with tradition, it is likely that Günter's Rabbi chose the date for his bar mitzvah ceremony based on his birth date according to the Jewish calendar. Complex calculations would have confirmed the appointed day as 20 Tishrei in the year 5698 (Saturday 25 September 1937), three weeks before his thirteenth birthday according to the Gregorian calendar.

In the autumn of 1937 this day fell on the ninth and final day of the Festival of Sukkot, known as the 'Feast of the Tabernacles'. This was how young Günter found himself chanting the Story of Creation from the sacred handwritten scrolls in front of a packed synagogue. This assigned scripture is considered by many to be the most holy and demanding passage in the Torah. Each Friday after school, for three months before his ceremony, Günter cycled or took the bus to Andernach for his Hebrew lessons with the Rabbi. To avoid travelling on the Sabbath, it was important to reach his destination before sunset, when the holy day began. Alfred and Ida had friends in the town, with a son just a few months younger than their own. After his studies, Günter shared the rituals of the Friday evening meal with this family, spending the night and joining the prayers in the synagogue the following morning.

Hebrew is not easy. Letters are read from right to left and the ancient alphabet has no vowels, instead a system of marks to indicate how the text should be read. However, with his usual conscientious effort, by the time the three months were up, Günter knew his assigned passages off by heart. At his Bar Mitzvah Günter was called up to the *Bimah*, a Jewish lectern, where the scroll was laid. Taking hold of the special finger-shaped pointer known as a *Yad*, used to avoid touching the sacred parchment, he sang in Hebrew the familiar words:

'In the beginning, God created the heaven and the earth.'

Kristallnacht

'That same night as my father, both my grandfathers were also arrested, one in Koblenz-Lützel and the other in Montabaur. The older men were kept in local prisons and mainly released after two or three weeks. There was no suggestion of arresting me, I was not old enough.'

From 8 November 1938, the newspapers were full of inflammatory stories about a seventeen-year-old Jew, Herschel Grynszpan, whose family had been deported from their home in Hanover to a remote spot close to the Polish border. Here they were abandoned in no-man's land to fend for themselves. Herschel was living in Paris and on receiving a distraught postcard from his sister, resolved to take revenge. On the morning of 6 November he bought a gun and walked into the German embassy. Unable to find the ambassador he picked on a minor secretary, Ernst vom Rath, firing five shots into his stomach. Herschel was immediately arrested. The headline of the Nazi Party newspaper, *Völkischer Beobachter* on the morning of 8 November read: *'Jewish Murder Attempt in Paris – Member of the German Embassy Critically Wounded by Shots – The Murdering Knave a 17 Year-Old Jew.'* Hitler's Minister of Propaganda, Joseph Goebbels, seized his opportunity, instructing the national press to continue running this key story in order to incite further hatred towards the Jews.

On the evening of 9 November, as the news broke that vom Rath had died of his wounds, Hitler and Goebbels were enjoying a gala feast in Munich. Hitler is alleged to have instructed Goebbels: 'The Police should be withdrawn. For once the Jews should get the feel of popular anger.' A few telephone calls to local branches of Nazi stormtroopers throughout Germany and Austria ignited a domino effect of destruction. While officers at concentration camps and police cells prepared for a mass intake, organised groups of violent uniformed thugs roamed the streets wreaking havoc and destroying property. This pattern of subversive and hostile behaviour was to play out in villages, towns and cities throughout Germany and Austria.

On the afternoon of 9 November 1938, Nazi stormtroopers arrived in Montabaur in two vans, waiting for their moment beneath the tenth-century Castle and surrounding woodland. The pogrom began at 7.30 p.m., the beginning of a night to become known as *Kristallnacht*, reflecting the mountains of broken glass left outside Jewish shopfronts, businesses and homes. Orders from the top were to collect every Jew in Montabaur, some seventy in total, rounding them up in the market square. The 66-year-old Karoline Khan steadfastly refused to reveal the whereabouts of her three sons. She was seen being dragged by her hair down the Rebstock, still wearing her carpet slippers, screaming in protest, her face bloodied and bruised. In the square a crowd of townspeople had gathered, kicking, jeering and spitting on their bewildered Jewish neighbours. Günter's third cousin Freddy Stern was not in the town that evening, spared the sight of his father, tanner and leather merchant Willi Stern and mother Betty, forcibly dragged from their home and locked in the Town Hall. From here the women and children were marched to the neighbouring village of Kirchähr for three days of captivity. The men faced a 300-kilometre journey to the horrors of Buchenwald concentration camp. By the morning of 10 November the small synagogue on *Wallstrasse* was a smouldering ruin, the surrounding streets piled high with shards of glass, splintered furniture with the remnants of feathers from torn pillows still swirling in the air.

In the commercial city of Frankfurt nine-year-old Alex Halberstadt watched from his bedroom as groups of Nazi brown shirts marched through the Jewish area, singing songs such as *Das Juden Blut vom Messer spritzen*, 'Jewish blood will spray from the knife'. That evening a large gang burst into a neighbour's flat, the home of hat-maker Herr Rakov, his wife and sons. The hats were looted and every jar in Frau Rakov's larder smashed. She later showed Alex her wallpaper, covered in blackberry jam.

Further east in the artistic and intellectual Austrian capital Vienna, Harry Bibring was just twelve. Since the annexation of Austria of March 1938 his home had been part of Nazi Germany. On the same evening Harry's family saw smoke outside their window. It was the synagogue burning. The following morning his father, Michael Bibring told his family to remain indoors, leaving his home to open up his men's clothing shop. Once he was gone his flat was raided. Harry, his older sister Gertie and their mother were dragged out 'like three frightened rabbits'. Once outside they saw a crowd of people surrounding some Orthodox Jews being made to scrub the pavements. All around the Jewish shops were daubed with hateful slogans. The family was locked into a flat with thirty other women and children without food. They took turns to sleep on chairs. Harry's father never arrived at his shop that morning, snatched off the street and held in a tiny cell with eleven others. For ten days he could do nothing but stand, even sleeping on his feet. Finally Michael and his family were released, re-united on the street outside their flat. Harry recalls his father looking pale with the shape of a Nazi swastika shaved roughly into his thick dark hair, mockingly cut there by SS soldiers. His father scooped his children up into his arms and wept with joy. It was the first time Harry had seen his father cry.

In Koblenz, little Sally Kriss woke to the sound of Brownshirts beating her stepfather and uncle about the head. Her apartment was knee-deep in smashed glass and china, the kitchen reduced to ruins. The men were taken away into the cold wet night without their shoes or jackets. Frau Kriss took her two daughters to her sister's home in *Schlossstrasse* to find that her nephew Leo had been taken away. Sally's stepfather and Uncle were amongst the more fortunate; the officers in Koblenz prison were not as yet completely 'Nazified' and allowed them to return home a few days later.

Whilst the farming community of Nickenich slept behind firmly closed curtains, Ida Stern's husband was beaten and taken into the night. Once they were alone, Ida and Günter clung together, trembling with shock. There was no more sleep that night. At first light on the morning of 10 November, having heard a radio report on the unfolding situation, Ida packed a few personal items, closed the door of their home and took Günter on a bus to Andernach to catch the train to Koblenz. They would never return.

Ida and Günter fled to Brenderweg, a tree-lined street in the Koblenz suburb of Lützel, on the opposite side of the Mosel, the home of her father, Meyer Salomon and stepmother, Sabine. It was devastating to witness the smashed windows, smouldering buildings and hateful graffiti that welcomed them to the city. Grandfather Salomon was not home. He had been arrested during the night. As a seventy-year-old man he was spared internment in a concentration camp, instead locked up for several days in a local prison. Sabine, not much older than Ida herself, welcomed the two escapees into her home; they would provide company and support and most important of all, they were alive.

On that first Sabbath after their menfolk had been taken, the Jewish women of Koblenz and their children, including Ida and Günter, gathered in a local hall, discussing the night of 'Jew Action'. Where had their husbands and sons been taken? Would they see them again? How could they manage? It was always the men who made the big decisions. Would they be able to rebuild their homes and businesses? What would they do with their youngsters now they were expelled from school? Why had this happened?

In the centre of Koblenz, at Florinsmarkt 13, a marauding mob reduced the interior of the nineteenth-century synagogue to ruins, destroyed along with many of the precious ritual objects. In this Rhineland city alone, forty Jewish homes and nineteen Jewish businesses were wrecked and plundered, the cemetery desecrated and 100 Jewish men over sixteen sent to the notorious Dachau concentration camp near Munich. Ten miles away the new synagogue in Andernach was a smouldering ruin.

The sacred scrolls, from which Günter had read so confidently only fourteen months earlier, were no more.

Dachau

'My father was taken to Dachau [....] where he spent the bitterly cold winter with only thin cotton prison clothes and eating mainly cabbage water (which they called soup) and dry bread. A cruel regime was imposed which included frequent "security

checks", supposedly head counts, for which they had to parade, often in the middle of the night, sometimes standing for hours in freezing temperatures.'

Built in 1933 on the site of an abandoned munitions factory high in the German Alps, Dachau was described by Heinrich Himmler as 'the first concentration camp for political prisoners'. Following the arrests of *Kristallnacht* the camp held over 10,000 men. Those who could prove they were taking steps to emigrate from Germany were released after a few weeks. Dachau was a training centre for SS guards and the organization and routines became the model for all Nazi concentration camps. Cruel punishments were endemic, including an obligatory twenty-five lashes on the bare upper body. One of the thirty-two barracks was designated for clergy who opposed the Nazi regime. It was here where another Nickenich resident would be interned during the latter months of 1940, having already served five months in Buchenwald.

Pastor Johannes Schulz was the Catholic priest in Nickenich from 1935. It was he who preached the gospels to Günter's classmates on Sundays at Saint Arnulf's, opposite the schoolyard. He performed the confirmation service for Franz, Maria and Elisabeth Saftig. He regularly spoke from the pulpit, denouncing the Nazi ideology and preaching that 'this arrogant Nazi Germany is a new paganism'. On 27 May 1940 Pastor Schulz and a fellow clergyman from Trier enjoyed a coffee on the terrace of the *WaldfriedenI* restaurant, translated as 'Peace of the Forest', on the banks of *Maria Laach*. Field Marshal Hermann Göring and his entourage entered in celebratory mood. The German army had marched into France with hardly any resistance. Other diners raised their arms in salute to the officers. It was noticed that both priests refused to do the same. Göring walked over to the men, offering them the chance to honour their Führer. They declined the invitation and that evening they were arrested.

In Dachau the priests were humiliated, compelled to write hundreds of times on a blackboard, 'Every German is committed to greeting the Reich Marshal'. Metal rods were inserted inside their prison clothes, their right arms forcibly raised in a Hitler salute. They were put to work in a nearby bog, where insect bites gave rise to poisonous blood infections. This and the effects of starvation resulted in Pastor Schulz being admitted to the camp hospital in early August 1942, where both his legs were amputated. He died two weeks later at the age of thirty-eight.

His last words are said to have been, 'I die for my community so that all may be saved for eternity.'

Plans

'We had no idea what had happened to my father for some weeks. When eventually he came back we barely recognised him. He'd lost much weight and in every way he looked a broken man.'

During the frozen midwinter, six weeks after *Kristallnacht*, Alfred Stern knocked at the house of his father-in-law and was reunited with his wife and son. He was suffering from pneumonia. Although delighted to see his father again, Günter was deeply shocked at the physical and mental state of his hero. Alfred was despondent. His army service, his medals and his wounds in combat counted for nothing. His work and standing in his local community were worthless. He was considered an enemy of the state merely because of his racial background.

During his convalescence Alfred had time to think. Before his release from Dachau he had reluctantly assured the authorities he would immediately make arrangements to leave Germany. His official record completed by the Koblenz Gestapo, dated 12 December 1938, states that: 'Stern intends to emigrate to North America with his wife and son.' Two weeks earlier Ida, anticipating her husband's change of heart, made a trip to Andernach and applied for a passport for Günter, just in case.

But the decision for the family to leave Germany had been left too late. Immediately following *Kristallnacht* applications for exit visas rose dramatically throughout Germany and Austria. Alfred and Ida were now in a desperate race to get away. Other members of the family had more luck. Ida's youngest brother Otto made his way to Shanghai, a so-called Open City, requiring no visa to enter. Unable to afford his passage, he worked his way as a stoker on a freighter during an eight-week sea crossing. On arrival he found a job as a kitchen hand in a European-run hotel, registering with the American consulate for a 'number'. Some years later he joined family members in the United States. Aunt Martha and her husband had already left Germany. Her remaining two sisters, Nellie and Selma, received their emigration numbers and headed for America before the outbreak of war.

On Alfred's side, his youngest sister Meta had married Leopold Rosenthal in 1920. Leo spent six weeks in a concentration camp after *Kristallnacht*. Only a few days after his release Meta, Leo and their two children left Germany for Providence, Rhode Island. Uncle Alex also applied for a number for America, but the delay became intolerable and he managed to get a permit to enter England on the basis that he could afford to maintain himself and his family until it was their turn to board a ship. He sold his business and left. It must have appeared to Alfred and Ida that everyone, except from them, were making their escape.

Grandfather's house in Lützel was too small to accommodate three more people. Once Alfred was released, it was decided to find somewhere else for him, his wife and son to live. A Jewish contact offered them a two-roomed flat above a shop in the Old Town, just around the corner from the heavily-beamed *Altes Brauhaus*, a brewery and pub since 1689. Not that Alfred would be allowed across the threshold. The flat had few facilities and only a small stove for cooking.

The Stern family settled as best they could into *Görgenstrasse* 6.

Cross Countries

'I thought, "If war breaks out then I'll never get away." I was determined to get to England before the shutters came down. I would try and get over on my own. Of course I couldn't tell my parents. They wouldn't have allowed it.'

Günter's paternal grandfather Heimann died of a heart attack on 28 February 1939. At the age of eighty-five he never recovered from the shock of his arrest on *Kristallnacht*. His body was returned to Meudt for burial, grave number 36 in the Jewish cemetery. Although still recuperating from his illness, Alfred took his young son to attend the ceremony. As an orthodox Jew, Heimann was buried in his *tallit*, the neckband removed and one of the fringes cut off, symbolising that once dead a Jew is no longer obliged to observe the rituals and customs of his religion. Günter stood amongst the adult mourners, joining the traditional chanting of the *El Malei Rahamin*, a prayer reassuringly declaring that the deceased is now 'sheltered beneath the wings of God's presence'. The sensitive child shed a tear for his grandfather as the simple wooden casket lowered into the grave to the rhythmic beat of the spoken *Mourner's Kaddish*, the prayer for the dead.

After three or four weeks of recuperation Alfred received a visit from a member of the Gestapo.

'I think you are fit enough to work now.'

'But I've not found any work yet.'

'You don't need to. You'll be building the *autobahns*, and there is a lot of digging to do.'

Alfred was attached to a forced-labour unit living in caravans on the roadside miles from Koblenz. He was allowed to return home at weekends only if he could afford his fare, which wasn't often. Expelled from school, with no father, no friends and reluctant to venture out, Günter had little with which to amuse himself, apart from watching the endless columns of Black and Brownshirts marching through the streets below. To ease the tension he made music on his new violin, losing himself in the moment.

Rumours were circulating in the Jewish community that a group of people in Great Britain had successfully lobbied their government to allow the immigration of more refugees, specifically children between eight and sixteen, thought to be under threat from the Nazis. They would enter England on temporary travel documents and re-join their parents once the crisis was over. A £50 bond was required for each child and they would make the journey in sealed trains. Volunteer families and financial donations were actively being sought in Britain. Those children for whom sponsors could not be found, would be housed at Dovercourt, a holiday camp on the east coast of England, until a foster home could be found. Above all the refugees were not to be a drain on the British State.

Whilst there was no way out for Alfred and his wife, it was crucial to offer their son a future. They asked Günter if he would like a chance to go to England. The boy did not hesitate. His application was lodged and the wait for a response began. Sometime in February 1939 a brown envelope arrived from the Jewish Refugee Committee in London. The letter was brief and to the point: 'We can now confirm that Günter is on the list and you will be advised when a seat is available for him on a *Kindertransport* out of Cologne.' Günter read the letter over and over, excited at the prospect of escape. It became his 'special treasure' and lived permanently in his trouser pocket.

More waiting. March came and went. Nothing in April. No word by early May. Hardly able to afford to feed herself, never mind a growing fourteen-year-old boy, Ida asked her husband to find Günter a job with lodgings, maybe on a farm where he could eat plenty of fresh meat and vegetables. Alfred had an old business contact from his days as a cattle dealer, living in the vicinity of Cochem, a medieval town on the banks of the River Mosel, about 50 kilometres southwest of Koblenz. The farmer kept a small vineyard and although not Jewish, was sympathetic to the desperate plight of Germany's Jews. Günter would live with him and his wife in the farmhouse and work on the land for his keep. Relieved that her son would now receive hearty nourishing food, Ida turned away as her husband advised the boy, 'Eat whatever you are given, whether it be pork or whatever, it is not your fault.'

No stranger to feeding and mucking out chickens, horses and cows, as well as helping to harvest the crops around Nickenich, Günter fitted in well. He devoured the fresh farmhouse meals, regularly accepting second helpings. With good food, hard work and the outdoor life the boy began to thrive. Despite Alfred declining any payment for his son's labour, the farmer insisted on giving Günter a little pocket money every week to spend in the village, telling him, 'No need to tell your father.' Gunter occasionally hiked down the wooded hillside, pausing to admire *Schloss Reichsburg,* originally a twelfth-century castle stronghold destroyed by the French in 1689. A wealthy Berlin businessman rebuilt it in Neo-Gothic style in 1868. The castle still had the original *Hexenturm* or Witches Tower as well as the imposing four storey octagonal tower, which never failed to attract Günter's gaze. Then into Cochem, following the riverside road to the heart of the town with its hotels, restaurants and shops, swastika flags over every building. The farmer knew that Günter was a Jew. The people in the town did not. It was best to keep it that way.

As temperatures climbed during May 1939, so whispers of impending war became louder. Heated political discussions between farmer and his wife worried their young lodger. With still no news from London he had to do something. His cache of pocket money had accumulated and it could now be spent on something worthwhile. He bought a series of maps and studied them carefully in the privacy of his bedroom. In happier times, his parents had taken him to the ancient German town of Trier, not too far from the River Mosel, which formed the border with Luxembourg. In the middle of this long hot dry spell, Günter knew it was likely that the river would be little more than a stream. He could wade across with no problem. But it would have to be after dark. And as for walking to England; that would be a pleasure.

Early July and he was prepared. Once the farmer and his wife were in bed, he stuffed his small rucksack with maps, handkerchiefs, a few coins and his letter from London. He then wrote a short missive to his parents addressed to the apartment in Koblenz.

'Just to let you know that I'm afraid the war will break out soon so I am making my own way to England. I will write to you when I get there.'

Placing this on the kitchen table he added a brief note to the farmer asking him to post the letter. Well before sunrise Günter tiptoed from the house. The walk down to Cochem was familiar to him. The darkness proved no obstacle and he was soon standing at the bus stop, awaiting the early-morning bus through the winding valley to Trier. With mixed emotions he joined other early-risers on the bus. A confident lad, overly confident some might say, Günter was aware that he didn't look particularly Jewish. However, there was danger everywhere and the 100 kilometre journey could take three or four hours. As he scrunched low in his seat, attempting to remain invisible, he was nervous, yet buoyed by adrenaline as he watched the beautiful *Moselland* unfold through the bus window.

The view was dominated by hillside after hillside boasting a profundity of vines, predominantly bearing the traditional Riesling grape. Sunflowers proudly displayed their golden heads and mass of wide green leaves. Trees heavy with rich yellow apricots, apples and peaches lined the riverbanks. At first Günter was aware of the river being on his left. Looking across the water to the village of Bruttig-Frankel, the boy marvelled at the crashing waters of the enormous lock at the entrance to Ellenz-Poltersdorf. The river scene was lively; the tourist cruisers emitting towers of steam as they traversed the narrow waterway, followed closely by working barges carrying goods to the many riverside communities. Further downstream, the river resembled a sheet of glass in its stillness, apart maybe from a few discernable ripples as the wind caught the surface or a small boat left the trace of a wake.

Did Günter notice the ornate slate and gold church spire at Edeger-Eller? On arriving in the larger market towns to drop and collect passengers, Günter's heart beat just that bit faster when he saw Wehrmacht vehicles parked in the squares. Groups of men, displaying their Nazi armbands, shared morning coffee and cake at the pavement cafés.

The timber-framed houses lining the main street of each village blended into the next as the bus bumped its way through the community of Bremm, with its Lutheran church spire. Onward past the hamlets of Neet, Alf and Zell with resplendent floral window boxes and swathes of wild flowers painting the houses and riverbanks with a million different hues. Swans drifted silently through tall reeds on tiny tributaries, appearing from the road to sail on dry land. After Zell the bus crossed a small bridge so that the water now ran along the right hand side of the bus.

Entering the extensive town of Marienburg, the driver stopped for a scheduled break. Günter welcomed the chance to stretch his legs, intrigued by the bars and restaurants filling with shoppers, farmers, soldiers, vintners and genteel ladies, all needing an early lunch or relaxing *bier*. His stomach squeezed as he saw plates piled high with schnitzel, frankfurters and sauerkraut, served by *fräuleins* in starched aprons. Even if he could afford to eat, the Nazi symbols displayed everywhere he looked warned him to remain close to the bus.

Moving on through further vast expanses of vines, Günter's bus journeyed through Traben-Trarbach, set at the base of an enormous oxbow lake. An imposing metal bridge, *Brücke Wolf*, spanned the water, reminding the boy of the many bridges crossing the Rhine at Koblenz. Günter's imagination was stirred by the hilltop castles, some medieval, others neo-gothic nineteenth-century reconstructions, the magnificent Schloss Kues-Bernkastel reminiscent of the one at Cochem. Consulting his maps, he followed the road with his finger round an impossibly tight bend at Trittenheim. Passengers began to gather their belongings in anticipation of arrival and Günter felt his pulse quicken. The bus drove up two steep inclines, followed by a dip into Luiven, lurching on to join the long final straight into the Roman city of Trier, skirting the suburbs of Lorsch, Langen and Schweich, under the *Porta Nigra*, the impressive Fortress Gate and the end of the line.

Raised to be always polite, Günter thanked the driver before climbing down onto the street, feigning composure, totally relaxed, just another young boy arriving home from a day out. Early afternoon, the sun high in the sky, the wooden shutters on the houses closed to cool the rooms and prevent fragile fabrics fading in the intense sunlight. Now came his exit from Germany and illegal entry into another country. The River Mosel flows through Trier from its source in France to the south, but his plan was to turn northeast, following a tributary, the River Sauer, as it hugs the Luxembourg border. He would eventually cross the river after dark at Echternach in the north of the Grand Duchy, a charming and sleepy town with its thousand-year-old abbey. In the centre of the town a bridge marked the divide between Germany and Luxembourg, heavily guarded by armed soldiers.

The meandering waters of the Sauer did indeed lead him to the outskirts of the historic town, visible on the opposite bank. Having identified a likely crossing point, the water low and still, he waited for nightfall. Rucksack held high above his head, the boy scrambled through the reeds down the bank and into the river, the water almost at his waist, wading as fast as he could, anxious to leave Germany behind. As he pulled himself out on the other side, a voice called from the darkness. A policeman. Günter froze. For a moment the officer looked directly at the slight figure, by now shivering and dripping with slimy weeds, before waving him on. Günter had been given another chance. He was free.

From there it was a mere 14 kilometres to Belgium. Günter knew that by sticking close to the border there was more chance of local people speaking some German. For the next two days he continued to follow the path alongside the river, hiding in the shadows of the Black Alder and willow trees, catching glimpses of water as it rolled and spat over smooth rocks, until the river eventually dried up. Avoiding the prying eyes in the tiny hamlets of Vianden and Stolzembourg, his route took him through meadows, copses and fields of rusty cattle, down winding country lanes. He negotiated both hills and valleys, before crossing into heavily-wooded Belgium, this time unnoticed. The forests of beech and oak offered a welcome drop in temperature and a degree of privacy. Günter slept under the stars, no hardship for a country boy during a hot summer. At daylight he sought out small farms, knocking on doors and asking politely for a drink of water. His father had taught him not to beg.

However, asking for water was not begging. Water was free. The exchanges became well practised.

'Could I have a glass of water?'

'Would you like some milk?'

'Oh yes please.'

As the days went on and the boy's appearance deteriorated, the farmers' wives could not resist him.

'Could I have a glass of water?'

'Would you like a sandwich?'

'Oh yes please.'

Even if the fillings involved forbidden ham, the famished boy would simply recall his father's advice and eat the meat, relishing the unfamiliar flavour.

Vaals

'I was about three kilometres into Holland when a policeman on a bike overtook me. He looked back and stopped. I was scared because, of course, to me a policeman was a Nazi.'

After eight days Günter crossed into the Dutch border town of Vaals. Günter was alarmed as the policeman walked over to him, addressing the boy in a local dialect. Günter replied in his own tongue.

'I'm sorry. I can't understand you. I'm from Germany.'

Without hesitation the officer switched to perfect German.

'Germany? What are you doing here?'

'Heading for the Hook of Holland.'

'So you crossed illegally?'

'Yes. I need to get to England.'

'Have you an entry visa for England?'

'No, but I do have this.'

Digging deep into his pocket, Günter withdrew the by now crumpled letter from the refugee agency in London. He handed the paper to the policeman who took a few moments to read it.

'This won't get you into England. This isn't a visa.'

For a moment Günter did not know how to react. Then he told his story. The policeman was concerned.

'Even if I allowed you to go to the Hook, which I can't as you are now an illegal alien, you would not be allowed to enter England.'

Günter started to tell him about the *Kindertransport* trains but he already seemed to know, explaining that those children travel on a group visa and have pre-arranged families to meet them at the other end.

'I'll tell you what we'll do. I will take you to my house and explain to my wife, she speaks very little German and then she will let you have a good wash. I have to go and see my boss at the police station.'

The pair walked the short distance to the policeman's house and Günter was shown to the bathroom. Feeling much better after a good wash with real soap, he cautiously entered the kitchen. The lady of the house had laid the wooden table with a mix of cold meats, several cheeses, black bread and white rolls, tomatoes and boiled potatoes. She was smiling, like his mother always did, taking him by the hand and sitting him down. Günter was both reassured and embarrassed. Still filling his empty stomach, he looked up anxiously as the policeman returned. He told Günter he could stay at his home for a while, 'unofficially, you understand'. That evening he should write a letter to the Jewish Refugee Committee in London, explaining he was now in Holland and could they please send an individual visa to this temporary address.

The week that followed seemed like the longest of Günter's short life. From the third day he spent many hours sitting on the front step watching for the postman. By day four he was desperate and contemplated hitching a ride to the Hook. He dare not spend any money. He would need it for the ferry fare. Finally on the following Monday morning, just five days since posting his request, the postman thrust a letter into his hands. It was a handwritten note in German. Nothing else. No visa, no passport, no ticket. The note confirmed his worst fears; he could only get into England via the official channels and that meant travelling on his assigned train from Cologne with all the other children. He was instructed to return home and await his visa and travel details.

'But I can't go back into Germany.'

The policeman and his wife tried to calm him with words of advice.

'Focus on the good news. Go home and pack your bags.'

How could he possibly return home? He was terrified at the thought of facing the Nazi border police. What would he say? He had left the country illegally. But the policeman had a solution. He knew of a German farmer who hated the Nazis. He lived just on the German side of the border outside Vaals and had already helped people escape from Germany into Holland. This time it would be the other way around. The policeman left the house. On his return he had good news. The farmer was happy to help.

At midnight the policeman walked Günter to the border, lifting him over the waist-high fence into Nazi Germany. The farmer met him on the other side. He would just be like any other German boy travelling home on a train. It was only a three-mile walk in the darkness to Aachen railway station. The farmer bought him a ticket to Koblenz via Cologne and sat with him until it was time to wave him off. Although Günter was anxious, there was a comforting familiarity about being back in his own country with everyone speaking his language. The journey went without incident. Now he must face his mother.

Günter walked from Koblenz station to *Görgenstrasse*. He knocked on the door. Ida, who feared she would never see her only child again, hugged and hugged him without a word of admonishment. He was alive. He was home. Her son was safe.

Sea of White Handkerchiefs

'My mother's cousin lived in Cologne where the special train was to depart. They had twins about my age, a boy and a girl. The boy was very thin and the girl very fat. Their parents had asked them if they would like to go to England but the girl was terrified of leaving their parents. They hadn't even got themselves a number for America – they would just stick it out together in Nazi Germany.'

A few days after Günter's return to Koblenz, a letter arrived addressed to his parents. Finally, the long awaited confirmation of his ticket on the *Kindertransport* out of Cologne. Sunday, 18 July 1939, less than two weeks away. With typical German thoroughness, the timings were detailed to the nearest minute. The train was scheduled to leave at 15.29, due to reach Emmerich, the final station in Germany, at 17.39. Arrival at the Hook of Holland was 20.37 with the ferry arriving in Harwich, England at 06.20 on the morning of 19 July. The instructions were clear. Just one small suitcase, light enough to be carried without help. There was a limit on the cash he could take. No more than one *Reichsmark* and items of any value were forbidden. This ruled out Günter's two most treasured possessions, his paternal grandfather's signet ring and his violin. Günter loved the instrument and argued passionately to be allowed to take it to England. But Alfred and Ida felt sure that German customs officials would simply confiscate it.

Instead, Günter found himself encumbered by a heavy winter overcoat. Too large to fit in the suitcase it would need to be draped over one arm, despite sweltering July temperatures. Once the boy read the advice to take warm clothing for the English winter, he looked at a map. Discovering that England

Ida and Alfred Stern on their wedding day, 1922.

Nickenich Village School Class of 1931 (Günter is front row, far left).

Hintergasse, Nickenich 1930s.

Ploughing fields around Nickenich.
Alfred's friend Peter Saftig is second
from left.

Stern family group 1936. Ida and Alfred at top, Günter front row second from
left. Aunt Nelly far right.

Günter in his fashionable sailor suit.   Wuppertal Suspended Railway, 1929.

View over Cochem to the castle overlooking the Mosel, 1919.

Günter's *Kinderausweis* (passport) with photo.

Passport reverse dated 29 November 1938.

Deustches Eck (German Corner), Koblenz, in the 1930s.

Allsopp family group in Lydney 1940. Left to right, Günter, Alan, Doris and Hazel.

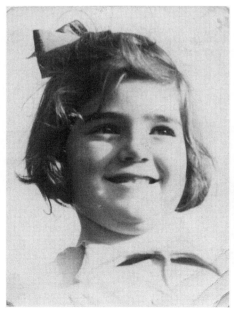

Margaret Free aged seven.

The Allsopp house in Spring Meadow, Lydney (photographed in 2014).

Lydney Tin Plate Works.

Factory floor at The Briton Brush Company, Wymondham.

Jean Skitmore inside shell casing at a munitions exhibition in 1945.

Wedding group, 21 May 1946. Left to right Gordon, Joe, Jean, Ernest.

Joe and Jean on their wedding day in Attleborough.

Hazel Allsopp and Jean in Southsea, summer 1946.

was further north than the Rhineland, he reasoned that it could be really cold, even colder than at home and probably foggy and wet most of the time. Uncle Alex helped out, producing from amongst his salvaged stock, a thick lined coat and a cloth suit with trousers to just below the knee, the ensemble perfected by white woollen ribbed socks and heavy soled, laced leather boots.

The day arrived. Alfred, on a rare visit home, was able to accompany his wife and son on the local train from Koblenz to Cologne. The *Kindertransport* was timed to meet the night ferry. But Günter harboured an irrational fear of crossing the sea. Shortly before he left Nickenich, he had learnt a long ancient poem at school telling the story of Dutch fishermen drowned whilst struggling to get into port during a great storm in the North Sea.

This would be his first time at sea and this concern, coupled with the exhilarating anticipation of escape, dominated his thoughts, distracting him from any real sadness at leaving his parents. The little family entered the vast station with its sixteen expansive platforms under the great glass canopy. Down into the underpass, up the steep staircase and onto the platform, they joined a steady stream of youngsters, aged between six and sixteen with their parents and extended families. Whispered stories passed between them, talk of parents clinging to their children, jumping onto moving trains and even pulling hysterical youngsters through open windows. Learning from the mistakes of earlier *Kindertransport*, the Gestapo were no longer allowing the adults to accompany their offspring to their seats.

Instead Günter and his parents gathered with the others behind a barrier. As so many of the children, he made promises to make arrangements, as soon as he was able, for his mother and father to join him in England. Fifteen minutes before the train was due to depart a rope was hung across the platform. An announcement came across the loudspeakers.

'Children only must carry suitcases to their seats. Parents stay where you are. You are forbidden to enter the platform.'

Placing a kiss awkwardly on his mother's cheek, Günter became aware of his father whispering into her ear:

'Remember what you promised me, no tears 'til he's gone.'

Despite the pain of separation, Günter was focussed. He had planned for this moment for months. Without looking back he joined the 300 youngsters following the organisers towards the carriages. As they boarded, volunteers placed cardboard signs around their necks bearing an identity number. Along with other older boys Günter helped the youngest children with their suitcases, finding their allocated seats. Many were confused and distressed, having been told they were simply 'going on holiday' and that their families would join them in a few days. The children sat eight to a compartment and as the train steamed slowly out of the station, they lowered the windows and took turns, two little faces at a time, to wave at the massed group of adults. Günter, consumed in guilt at his abrupt goodbye, wasn't able to recognise his parents amongst the multitude of pinched adult faces, his lasting image a sea of damp white handkerchiefs.

Just Five Cents

'At Emmerich, the last station in Germany, the train came to a halt. Frontier police climbed in at the first and last carriages. They worked towards the centre, checking passports. The customs officers asked us questions like: "How much money have you got?" and "Are there any valuables in your case?"'

A proportion of children were ordered to open their luggage for a thorough search. Günter was spared. This was rather galling; maybe he could have got away with bringing his signet ring. Inspection over, the German guards left the train to be replaced by sympathetic and approachable Dutch officials. The train rolled across the border into Holland. Retrospective accounts from Kinder speak of an abrupt change of atmosphere amongst the children once out of Nazi territory; smiles, laughter and shouts of elation punctuated with noisy profanities against the hated oppressors. It is likely that something similar occurred on Günter's journey, but his overriding memory is the acute thirst he and the others suffered that evening in the unforgiving summer heat.

With the little ones showing severe signs of dehydration, Günter alerted the guard, asking with a mixture of mime and sign language if refreshments were available. The guard explained in perfect German that no such facilities had been provided at Cologne. Günter tried again.

'Is it possible for the train to stop somewhere to take on water?'

'Well it's not on the schedule, but I'll see what I can do.'

It seemed an eternity before the train stopped, apparently in the middle of nowhere. The children watched as a guard leapt down and walked over to the base of a manned signal box where the men held an animated conversation. The guard then climbed aboard and announced that the train would be calling at Utrecht in about half an hour. As they pulled into the station the children were instructed not to disembark under any circumstances as they did not hold visas for Holland and could be arrested.

A group of young men appeared on the platform, each carrying a tray, much like an ice-cream vendor in a cinema. The trays were loaded with glass bottles of various drinks. The children leaned out of opened windows to make their choice. The cost would be 95 cents. But they only had one *Reichsmark* each, the equivalent of one Dutch Guilder. All the money they had for England. Most children handed over their precious silver coin, receiving just five tiny copper one-cent pieces in return. Other accounts tell of Dutch generosity with gifts of free milk, chocolate, fruit and sandwiches. Günter and his companions were not so fortunate.

How Deep is the North Sea?

'We queued at the purser's office and were given a little ticket with a cabin number. My cabin was two or three decks down. That was scary – what if we hit a rock?'

It was dusk when the train completed its journey into the Hook of Holland. Exhausted bodies, hushed and subdued, lifted gently down and led to the quay where the steam ferry was preparing to slip her moorings. Anxious about his first ever crossing, Günter sought the advice of a Dutch sailor, 'How deep is the North Sea?' The reply, 'Too big to stand up in!' Some *kinder* laughed, albeit a little nervously. For many this would be their first night away from home. Suitcases were placed on pallets and lifted by a large crane into the hidden depths of the boat while the children, obeying every command without question, clambered up the shuddering gangplank.

Günter shared a tiny cabin with three other boys, slightly older than him but all under 16. After that age the Nazis considered Jewish boys to be men and sent them to work camps along with their fathers, uncles and cousins. The bigger boys had chosen the top bunks but Günter was relieved to be in a bottom berth, fearing a rough sea would tip him out of bed. He chose to sleep in his sweaty shirt, maybe recalling *Struwwelpeter*, secretly pleased there were no grown-ups insisting he wash his face or brush his teeth. As the ship's engines lulled the travellers to sleep, Günter's eyes pricked with tears as he recalled the final words he had heard his father say.

At first light they woke to a loud knocking on the wooden door. Harwich was only an hour away. On being asked whether he had slept well, Günter confessed he had been disturbed by a horrible dream in which he had been crying. One of the boys replied, 'You *were* crying, we heard you.' Humiliated, Günter silently vowed never to cry again. He would have welcomed the chance to glimpse the North Sea but by the time the boys appeared on deck the ship was steaming up a huge estuary and the opportunity was lost. Disappointment gave way to hunger and he joined the crocodile of youngsters clambering up the narrow steel steps, their footsteps echoing through the ship, heading for the on board canteen.

The sizzling aroma from enormous frying pans posed a dilemma, particularly for those from more orthodox families. Over 300 Jewish children faced with plates of bacon. If the egg merely touched the rashers that too would have to be refused. They glanced at each other nervously. Whilst some flatly refused their hot meal, others began to nibble at the bacon, keeping an eye on everyone else. Once they realised that nothing cataclysmic was happening, more children tried some. Günter sliced through the pink meat. The salt stung his tongue but then as the juices squeezed through his teeth it tasted really good. He ate it all. With the ice broken the children's chatter swept through the space like a wave. They drank hot English tea from white pottery mugs, warming their hands and their hearts.

Before disembarking, every refugee was handed a small booklet, published by the German Jewish Aid Committee in 1933, offering helpful information and guidance to all refugees from Nazi Germany. The preface requested that the youngsters regard the suggestions as 'duties of which you are in honour bound'. The instructions included:

1. Spend your spare time immediately in learning the English language and its correct pronunciation.
2. Refrain from speaking German in the streets and in public conveyances and in public places such as restaurants. Talk halting English rather than fluent German – and do not talk in a loud voice. Do not read German newspapers in public.
3. Do not criticise any Government regulations, nor the way things are done over here. Do not speak of 'how much better this or that is done in Germany.' It may be true in some matters, but it weighs nothing against the sympathy and freedom and liberty of England, which are now given to you. Never forget that point.
4. Do not join any political organisation, or take part in any political activities.

The right-hand page of the booklet held the same information but translated into German. Günter and the others tucked the booklet into their pockets. They would look at it later.

For now they had a new world to discover.

Leave to Land

'We had to go through immigration, where we showed our passports, had our names ticked off a list and got a stamp with unreadable English words which said: "Leave to land granted at Harwich this day on condition that the holder does not enter any employment paid or unpaid while in the United Kingdom".'

Tummies comfortably full, the *kinder* collected their belongings from the enormous pile of small suitcases now unloaded on the platform at Parkeston Quay. Günter found his and helped some others. Bellowed instructions ensured that orderly groups of eight lined up ready to fill each train compartment. An empty train drew in and the signal was given for the first group to climb on board. To everyone's surprise, as soon as they were inside, they all spilled out again.

'What's the matter?' called the railway guard. One or two called to the other children.

'This can't be our train, it must be first class and we don't want to get into trouble.'

By now further groups of children were entering the carriages and immediately bounding out. The guard was frustrated.

'Get in, why don't you get in?'

One of the boys who spoke good English, explained.

'In Germany our trains have hard seats. This train has soft seats; it has to be for first class passengers.' The guard was relieved.

'In England all compartments on the boat trains have upholstered seats. Nothing less for our important guests. Now on you get.'

The journey to Liverpool Street involved much bouncing up and down on the springy seats, accompanied by wide smiles and laughter. By 10 a.m. on arrival in London, it was more difficult to remain positive. At least the police were not armed, but they would now discover what sort of life they could expect. The refugees were led in a crocodile into the cavernous ballroom of a railway hotel and told to wait. And wait they did. Names were read out, a child would approach the front desk and leave with a stranger. Günter listened for his name but it did not come. By 1.30 p.m. he was both anxious and hungry. When only thirty children were left out of the 300 who had arrived, he almost gave up hope. But then he heard a voice call out 'Cousin Günter'. He was astounded to be faced with his cousin Erich, Uncle Alex's son from Düsseldorf, whom he had not seen for three or four years. Erich was studying at Grenoble University but was now staying in Manchester with his parents, whilst they awaited final clearance to emigrate to America.

'I have to take you to the station, and then to a city called Birmingham.'

'But we're at the station already.'

'No, another station.'

'Are there two stations in London?'

'There are eight. We're going to Euston. Now, would you like to go by underground or on the bus?'

'What is the underground?'

'Trains that go through long tunnels. It's quicker but you won't see so much.'
'Then we will go by bus.'

At the bus stop the people were standing patiently in line. This amused Günter. He couldn't help thinking that at home there would be a scramble with everyone fighting to get on. His first-ever ride on the top of a double-decker bus was wonderful; so many cars and lorries, all driving on the wrong side of the road. Tree branches swept the windows, people hid behind open newspapers, a bell that had the power to stop the bus. Euston was a revelation with no fewer than ten platforms. Although they travelled third class on the London Midland and Scottish train, once again the seats were far more superior to those in Germany.

For Günter, the familiar presence and uncomplicated chatter of cousin Erich was a most welcome tonic.

Chapter 2

Schoolboy and Soldier, 1939–1945

Moseley

'Erich seemed to know where to take me. We took another bus to Moseley and walked down Yardley Wood Road, a street of solid-looking houses with small neat flower gardens next to the road. Erich knocked on a door and a lady opened it. She was obviously expecting me and I clearly remember that she had a smile on her face. I did what all Germans did, the way of greeting someone you don't know. You shook their hand, bowed your head and clicked your heels together. I had learnt a few words in English but I got things mixed up and as I shook hands with her I said, "Goodbye".'

Erich explained that his young companion was understandably nervous, thanked Mrs Free and, declining an invitation to take tea, left Günter to settle in. The boy was overwhelmed. The living room had deep armchairs and a large settee. There was a separate dining room with a shiny polished table. Upstairs he was shown into his own bedroom with a desk under the window and a wardrobe with a row of drawers down one side (not that he had anything to put in those drawers) and a bed of his own. The bathroom had a flush toilet, just like his uncle's home in Düsseldorf. From the window, he caught sight of gigantic silver barrage balloons, each attached to the ground by steel cables. Birmingham had acted quickly to prevent enemy planes from diving low and dropping their cargo of deadly bombs.

Günter was about to venture downstairs when he saw the door of another room was slightly ajar. On the bed sat a pretty, round-faced girl of about seven, holding her hands over her eyes, hiding from this stranger. Later he was introduced to Margaret, the Free's only child. She had been so looking forward all day to receiving her new brother, but when the doorbell rang she had fled upstairs, too shy to say hello.

A little later Oliver Free arrived home from work. Günter greeted him in the same respectful manner he had Mrs Free. Oliver was deaf. His hearing aid whistled when reacting to changes in volume, so he tended to leave it switched off, preferring silence to conversation. When Freda wanted to speak with him, she signalled to her husband to turn on his device. The evening meal was chicken salad, appropriate for the hot weather. Günter's only challenge was the beetroot. Mrs Free put several slices onto his plate. How could he tell her he hated the stuff? He watched in horror as red juice seeped onto the new potatoes. He had eaten nothing since that very early breakfast on the boat. Trying a tiny piece he found it to taste very different to the beetroot he had at home.

Surprisingly good, in fact.

Education

'My guardian, Mrs Free, took me by bus to Yardley and the large school. I was shown into an empty room but Mrs Free couldn't come with me. I wanted to shout "Help"! Then three elderly ladies walked in and took seats at the table after shaking my trembling hand. My well-rehearsed words "How do you do?" came forth three times and the ladies seemed pleased.'

The outcry following *Kristallnacht* prompted various agencies in Britain to launch a major appeal. Volunteers were needed to foster children escaping from Nazi Germany. Fortunately for Günter Oxford University graduates Oliver and Freda Free were amongst those who responded. This couple believed education to be an essential in any life and had no hesitation in nominating Günter for a grammar school place.

In the last week of July 1939, the formidable ladies of the Birmingham Quaker charitable committee would have scrutinised young Günter both diligently and objectively. Here was yet another child who might benefit from the bursaries on offer from the 'Queen Mother of British Chocolate', Elizabeth Taylor Cadbury. The committee noted that Günter had arrived in Birmingham just one week earlier on 20 July. They nodded sympathetically when learning that his father, a cattle dealer, had been interned in Dachau Concentration Camp following *Kristallnacht* on 9 November the previous year. At fourteen this boy was no longer required to attend school but he appeared bright enough to benefit from higher education. How lucky he was to have been allocated a home where they appreciated the value of a first-class education.

Günter could hardly believe his good fortune.

Freda Free

'Mrs Free was Jewish but Mr Free wasn't. They were a lovely couple. She was very warm and she explained to me at our first meal that they did not observe

Jewish dietary laws, however they didn't often eat pork or ham, but her husband did like bacon for breakfast.'

Freda Free was the eldest child of Russian Jews. As children, Solomon and Anna Salingar were most likely part of the emigration to England following the escalation of anti-Semitic pogroms in Russia from the 1880s. By 1901 the couple were married, with a baby daughter Freda, sharing the Liverpool home of Anna's parents. Freda's father worked as a Foreign Clerk at the Canadian Government Office and her grandfather was an insurance salesman for the Provident Association. Evidently, Freda inherited the family intellect, for in 1922 she graduated with a Masters degree in Chemistry from Oxford University. Here she met Oliver, the man she would later marry. Whilst at Somerville College she was a contemporary and friend of the writer, poet and pacifist Vera Brittain.

Freda felt great empathy with the plight of the Jews under Hitler. She was also aware that her comfortable suburban home, with the spare fourth bedroom and modern bathroom with hot running water, would be eminently suitable for a displaced child. Whilst gentle persuasion may have been required to encourage her quiet research chemist husband and daughter Margaret to share their home with a stranger, it seems she succeeded. Late on that warm summer's afternoon in 1939, Günter was made most welcome at 167 Yardley Wood Road, Moseley.

Mrs Free was a wonderful pianist and her brother Ernest Léon Salingar, recently qualified as a doctor, was an accomplished violinist. Günter spent the following two Sunday afternoons listening intently as they played beautiful sonatas for violin and piano by Brahms, Beethoven and Bach. Margaret and her father were less interested in music so Günter became their audience of one, the boy soaking up every note. Nearer to Günter's age than to that of his much older sister, Dr Salingar, affectionately known as Leo, was to prove an unwitting influence on the impressionable boy. These soirees served to stimulate his emerging appreciation of classical music.

They also rekindled memories of his mother's operatic voice.

North Wales with Oliver

'Mr and Mrs Free had a little bungalow in North Wales in the mountains. Of course I had never heard of Wales. Off we went by train, because like most people, the Frees didn't have a car. After a time Mrs Free said that the next station will be in Wales. I said, "Oh, do we need passports?"'

Oliver Free was born in December 1902 to Redditch residents William and Ann Free. This expanding Midlands town was renowned for the manufacture of needles and fishhooks. During the 1870s Oliver's grandfather, William E. Free built up a family business, firstly as a harness maker and later progressing to saddler. His eldest son William took over the business and at the start of 1903 was sharing his home with wife Ann, daughter Sybil and baby son Oliver. But his son's future was not to be in leather goods. Instead, in 1922, following his education at Redditch Secondary School, the Leather Sellers' Company offered him a scholarship to Oxford. With finances arranged, Oliver embarked on a degree course, reading Natural Sciences with Chemistry at St John's College; most probably the first child in the Free family to go to university, his intelligence and diligence leading to a First Class Honours Degree.

Günter was to spend the month of August with this man and his family in the remote Welsh hamlet of Talardd just outside the village of Llanuwchllyn, not far from Lake Bala, the largest natural lake in Wales. Günter was delighted that there would be no need for his smart new suit or heavy overcoat. Once the school term resumed, the family would return to Birmingham with Günter embarking on his grammar school education. The boy could hardly wait. August was traditionally Oliver Free's time for some annual rest and relaxation in his own holiday cottage, far away from his research career at Docker Brothers Paint and Varnish Manufacturers in Birmingham.

Günter was confused. How would they know when their train crossed into Wales if there was no frontier? Mrs Free told him that Ruabon would be their first stop on Welsh soil. But it looked just like England. Soon they could see mountains in the distance as the train followed a small river. Margaret told him, 'that's the River Dee and we follow that right to Lake Bala.' They were to disembark at Llanuwchllyn, translated as Village by the Lake. A car was waiting for them at the station. Driving along a very narrow road they passed a number of small farms before reaching a cluster of cottages. Then up a steep track to a small bungalow, grass below and dense bracken above. Behind were acres of grazing land, topped with rocky cliffs, rising to twin mountains, Aran Mawddwy and Aran Benllyn, at a height of about 3,000 feet.

For Günter it was like coming home.

Lakes and Mountains

'Mr Free said, "Time for lunch". I didn't argue. The sandwiches came out and I took the cheese and tomato. Eventually there were just two left, side by side. I could see one had white meat filling, probably chicken, and the other had pink. I quickly took the pink one and bit into it. Mr Free reached for the final sandwich

and he said, "Oh dear, did you take my ham sandwich by mistake? You don't eat ham or pork do you?" I replied, "I don't mind if you don't". Mr Free smiled. "I don't think it will poison you."'

The country boy, raised beneath the Eifel Mountains of the Rhineland, found the familiar landscape of meadows, forests and streams relaxing, an opportunity to bond with his surrogate father. Günter had always been a keen long-distance walker, demonstrated by his eight-day adventure across northern Europe. Was it only a month earlier? August was spent sharing long days filled with cloudless blue skies, hikes through meadows with hundreds of sheep and the occasional cow and languid lunches with a thermos of tea and a gingham tablecloth. As they ate, man and boy silently meditated, inspired by the spectacular views from the peaks of Aran Fawddwy or Aran Benllyn, down to the waters of Cardigan and Tremadog Bays.

Oliver enjoyed the novelty of having a boy for company. An expert climber, he was impressed by the boy's fearless approach to pulling himself up almost sheer rock faces, confidently finding secure crevices for his hands and feet. Oliver was also a keen angler, a peaceful activity not compromised by his deafness. But fishing did not appeal to Günter. He had never fished at home. How did Mr Free know the fish didn't feel any pain? He found excuses not to go and before long Oliver stopped asking.

Once confident that Günter would behave responsibly, and aware of his desire to wade in the sea for the first time, one exceptionally hot morning, Oliver and Freda allowed him to travel alone by train to the Welsh seaside town of Barmouth. Günter was astounded by the spectacular views of the Irish Sea from the cliff tops, reached after climbing hundreds of steep steps past slate-roofed cottages, placed one above another. Günter had never been on a beach before, quickly stripping to his bathing trunks, alternating invigorating swims in the briny surf with long leisurely sessions of sunbathing on the yellow sand. By the evening and the journey home, the boy was glowing like a beacon. The following morning he complained to Mrs Free of burning skin and of feeling sick. Mrs Free admonished him for not even having the sense to wear a hat.

Günter resolved never to suffer in that way again.

Lost Hope

'Mrs Free was greeted by the farmer's wife as an old friend and they chatted for a while. I became aware that I was the subject of their conversation although I couldn't follow it, especially when the other lady spoke. On the walk back Mrs Free explained that she had told her why I was with them. The lady had been

shocked that I had to come without my parents. Mrs Free had explained that adults couldn't come unless they had lots of money or had a guaranteed job and somewhere to live.'

Each morning Günter walked the two miles down a track to the nearest dairy farm to buy fresh milk for the family breakfast. Occasionally Mrs Free would join him. Unlike her husband, Freda spoke some German, but only used it when absolutely necessary. However, essential gossip about the possibility of war was full of emotional, complex language and Freda would patiently act as interpreter between the farmer and the inquisitive refugee. Once Freda explained the boy's situation and the plight of his parents in Germany, the farmer was full of sympathy.

The farmer told Mrs Free that the war could most probably be soon and his two sons would be called up. Would Günter's father be willing to work on the farm? With Mrs Free's help, Günter told him that his father was experienced in farm work and was especially good with animals. His mother could do housework, washing, cooking and ironing. Anything in fact. The farmer said he could not pay much but there was a derelict cottage, would his father be able to do the repairs? Günter could hardly contain his excitement. He would write to his parents immediately with the wonderful news.

But it was not to be straightforward. The visa forms stipulated that two additional guarantors were required in case the farmer changed his mind. Oliver generously volunteered to be one, but at first they doubted whether anyone else would take on the enormous liability. However, the farmer's brother in the next valley was persuaded to help and the application forms were despatched to the Home Office. The acknowledgement warned of a four- to six-week delay so there was nothing left to do but wait and hope. On the morning of 3 September 1939, families throughout Britain and the Commonwealth gathered anxiously around the wireless to hear the Prime Minister, Neville Chamberlin, speaking from 10 Downing Street.

This morning the British Ambassador in Berlin handed the German Government a final note stating that unless we heard from them by eleven o'clock that they were prepared at once to withdraw their troops from Poland, a state of War would exist between us. I have to tell you that no such undertaking has been received and that consequently this country is at war with Germany.

For Günter it was as though shutters came crashing down, cutting him off from his parents and smashing their hopes of escape.

Oliver's plans would now have to change. He would return to work in Birmingham while Freda tutored Margaret in the comparative safety of Merionethshire. Yardley Grammar School sent word that they would be evacuating to Lydney in Gloucestershire with immediate effect. Freda was not comfortable with Günter being uprooted again so soon. Demonstrating her tenacity she negotiated with the school, securing the promise of a deferred place after Christmas. In return Yardley insisted that Günter be sent to a local school in North Wales for the autumn term, in order to improve his English and help him prepare for the rigours of a more challenging education.

Arrangements were made for Günter to attend Bala Secondary School. For most children the school leaving age was fourteen but a small number usually stayed on to take School Certificate exams. It transpired that the Headmaster of Yardley Grammar School must have been unaware of the language policy in North Wales' schools. This was yet another culture shock for Günter. The other children were all Welsh speakers. Sometimes he learnt the Welsh word for something in English, but didn't know what either of them meant. There were compensations. The ten-minute scenic rail journey to the other end of Lake Bala was uplifting, the teachers supportive and the children certainly not hostile.

The German boy was a welcome curiosity.

Evacuee

'The lady in charge obviously had some problem finding a suitable home for me. When she met me at the station she said she was still working on that and meanwhile I could come and stay at her house. It seemed very grand to me; they even had a maid. I wanted to ask the lady why she needed to find me another family, her house would do nicely and they weren't short of rooms.'

It snowed in the Forest of Dean in January 1940. As a boy from the Rhineland, Günter was familiar with snow. Undeterred, he packed his winter clothes, bought for him by the Frees and donned his new school uniform. It took several trains to reach Lydney, a busy industrial town in Gloucestershire, on the west bank of the River Severn just over the border from South Wales. It was time to join his fellow pupils from Yardley Grammar School. He had come to England as a refugee, and was now arriving in Lydney as an evacuee. Mrs Carson, the chief billeting officer and wife of the local doctor, met him in her car. She and her committee had been tasked with finding homes for evacuated youngsters since they started arriving from Birmingham and other cities on 8 September the previous year. This one was a late arrival and a German, so it was proving more difficult to place him. As she drove the boy through the town to her house, he saw the wide strips of brown tape, pasted in crisscross patterns onto every window. Surely they weren't expecting German bombers here?

Dr and Mrs Carson lived on the High Street opposite the Town Hall. It was a grand detached house with curved bay windows and a covered porch. As the car drew up, the maid opened the door. Once inside Günter became aware of some giggling girls: maybe they were evacuees too. Less than a week later Mrs Carson finally found a sympathetic family with the requisite spare bedroom at 35 Spring Meadow Road, a ten-minute walk to the Grammar School. In return for a rent of 7s 6d per week, paid by the government, these working-class people would feed and nurture Günter for the next three and a half years. Günter offered the adults a strong English-style handshake.

His heel-clicking days were over.

Eddie Allsopp

'What wonderful people they turned out to be. The man was a great man. The lady came from Wales but spoke English with a very, very Welsh accent. They had two children. Allan was eleven and just starting at Lydney Grammar School and Hazel was only six.'

The 'great man' was George Edward Allsopp, known to his family and friends as Eddie. The youngest of three brothers, he was the son of George and Catherine Allsopp, born on 15 January 1901 in Lydney, at that time still officially in Monmouthshire, Wales. They lived with Catherine's parents, George and Ann Fisher at number five, Factory Street. Mr Fisher and his son-in-law worked together at the Lydney Tin Plate Works, owned by Richard Thomas & Company, a major employer in the area for many decades. George Fisher was a 'Scruff Melter' and George Allsop a 'Roller'.

Ten years later Catherine had borne five further children and the family now had their own home at No. 2, Factory Cottages. On leaving school Eddie trained as an engineer, but during the Depression had found it difficult to find work. He accepted his fate and joined his father at the Tin Plate Works. Eddie was still working there when Günter arrived in Lydney. The work was tough, labouring at the mouth of fierce furnaces, swinging hot bulky pieces of steel out of the flames and onto huge rollers. When setting out for his shift Eddie made sure he had a gallon or more of drink to replace the heavy perspiration that went with the job. In particularly warm weather, Günter would walk down to the Works with additional water, gawping through the huge doors into the Hell within.

During 1940, the British Government built a new factory on a 14-acre site on the Severn Estuary, two miles out of Lydney. Eddie was overjoyed to be offered an engineering role, where he could revisit his earlier skills and earn more money. The Pine End Works was a 'shadow factory', built in secrecy so as to keep manufacturing goods, vital for the war effort, secure from enemy bombing. Wooden panels were produced for the Mosquito fighter-bomber and the Horsa assault gliders used in the D-Day landings. Many local residents remained unaware of the actual activities within Factories Direction Limited, until after the end of the war.

During that time, Mr Allsopp remained a committed member of his local Labour Party and Trades Union movement. As Günter matured he watched, listened and learned about politics, occasionally accompanying Eddie to local meetings. Günter's growing interest in current affairs led to him becoming involved in the Lydney branch of the Federal Union, taking advantage of free membership as a student. There were people who believed that after the war, Britain and France should invite all European countries to join together under a single federal government, so reducing the chances of future European conflict. Although fascinated by the concept, Günter was unconvinced about the wisdom of allowing Germany to join.

But if it meant the end of wars he was all for it.

Doris Allsopp

'Mrs Allsopp was a traditionalist and highly patriotic. She made sure that her children attended Sunday school and the family regularly went to St Mary's Church on Sunday mornings, where Allan would sing in the choir. Somewhat emotional, she seemed at times to get heart palpitations and her husband would take over any domestic chores in need of being done.'

Mrs Allsopp was born Doris Ethel Trew in 1896 near Caversham in Oxfordshire, the first child of Allan and Jessie Trew. The family moved to Dyffryn Clydach in Glamorgan when her father took on the role of Farm and Estate Bailiff at Plasnewydd Home Farm, where Jessie would have three further children. Doris was thirty-one years old when she married Eddie Allsopp in Swansea in 1927, returning to her husband's home town to produce son and heir Allan in 1933, later completing the family with the arrival of baby Hazel. Doris was a disciplined and highly-organised housekeeper, very much in charge on the domestic front. Mrs Allsopp constantly worried about Günter. He took his school studies very seriously, immersing himself in his books, working all hours. Instead of her having to coerce him to do his homework, as mothers expect to, she was concerned that he might actually have a nervous breakdown and insisted he take breaks.

A stalwart of St Mary's Anglican Church, she was anxious to introduce Günter to Sunday services, as it would be good for him. She was also proud of Allan's place in the choir and insisted that Günter come to church and hear him sing. Their young lodger tried to explain that as he was Jewish he could not really relate to the Christian prayers and preaching, but out of politeness to his hosts he did go a few times before Eddie told his wife to leave the boy alone. Eventually Mrs Allsopp gave up.

The Jewish boy was almost certainly a lost soul.

New Friends

'He was a nice boy and I liked him. Everybody liked him. They knew what he'd been through and it was a terrible thing.' (Barbara Vedmore (née Hyde) speaking in 2014)

Life wasn't all about studies. The ancient forest gave Günter a welcome escape route and time to think. He joined a Saturday morning walking group, sometimes rambling the 12 miles to the historic market towns of Coleford or Cinderford; occasionally tackling the slightly longer hike to Chepstow, along the River Wye, evoking memories of his cross-borders epic walk. As he became more confident he would go out alone. Günter, in his unconventional trousers, finishing just below his knees and long white socks, was quite an oddity and the local children were naturally intrigued. Number 41, just two doors up, was the home of the Hyde family. Barbara and Derek Hyde were already close friends with Allan and Hazel and they invited Günter to join them in their early evening ritual of congregating around the lamppost outside Barbara's house.

Allan was never totally sure about Günter, an older boy usurping his position in the household pecking order. And he now had to sleep in with his annoying little sister, while this evacuee took over his room. As they tried to sleep, the children listened to the deep drone of German bombers following the River Severn upstream, the pilots navigating by the silvery thread as they drew closer to their industrial targets in the Midlands. This made Günter anxious for the safety of Oliver Free. Mrs Free and Margaret were still spending much of their time in North Wales, but Mr Free was in Birmingham and so surely must be in danger.

Most winters the forest was shrouded in a deep layer of snow. Günter, well versed in winter sports, enthusiastically joined in, whooping and laughing whilst sliding down the nearby hillside, using tin trays, wooden sleds and anything else that would do the job, exactly as in Nickenich. Before the end of that first winter, Günter received a letter from his mother. *Opa* was gone. He was the last of his grandparents to die.

Barbara was eleven when Günter arrived in her street, and over time grew very fond of the shy, dark-haired German boy. She thought him very good-looking, so different to the local lads. Her bedroom looked directly across into his room and she could see him working at his books every evening as she prepared for bed. Just before blackout when thick black curtains were tightly closed to hide the lights from enemy planes, Barbara watched Günter until he looked up and met her gaze. Then she would shyly wave, delighted when the young man raised his arm and waved back.

Günter once wrote in Barbara's autograph book,

'Remember who you speak to, of whom you speak and where you speak.'

This advice offered young Barbara a disturbing insight into the risks of Günter's earlier life, something she would never forget.

Studies

'I was with the twelve-year-olds for Science, a great big boy sitting in with them. But no-one was unkind, and I think some of the young ones thought it was fun – I was a funny guy!'

Life for everyone during wartime was challenging with rationing, air raids, blackouts and fire watching to contend with. Lydney had an influx of additional young people to feed and nurture. As with so many 'Evacuee' towns, the education authorities in the Forest of Dean devised a system to serve everyone. 'Lydneyites' would take classes in the Victorian building from 8.30 a.m. to 12.30 p.m., after which those children were instructed to spend their afternoons collecting seasonal wild fruit from the hedgerows and waste ground, returning their bounty to the canteen. The school cook then boiled up the fruit into jam for distribution to the families. The Yardley students studied from 1.30 p.m. to 5.30 p.m. Günter thrived under a routine of mornings in the village hall playing chess, Monopoly and table tennis, followed by afternoon lessons, some sitting in with the younger children. The teacher explained to them that Günter, as well as improving his command of English, had much yet to learn, including subjects he had never yet been introduced to, such as algebra, Shakespeare, chemistry, physics and Latin. He encountered the same problem as at school in North Wales. Learning the Latin word and English translation was one thing, but sometimes he did not know what either of them meant.

The two schools employed a number of extraordinary characters. Mr Burch, the Headmaster of Lydney, had a wooden leg. During the eighteen-month build-up to the War, he had the foresight to lay in huge stocks of basic materials, including chalk, paper, ink, soap and chemicals, ensuring the school never ran short. Amongst his loyal colleagues was 'old' Joe Ellison, who taught handicrafts and organised letters and parcels for Old Boys serving in the Forces. The Deputy Head of Yardley Grammar School was the indomitable Miss Rattray. Standing no taller than four feet ten inches and known throughout the school as 'The Rat', she drove to school in a black Austin Seven car whilst her colleagues arrived by foot or bicycle. Miss Rattray took young Günter aside. His accent was far too Germanic. Over several months she conscientiously helped him improve his English pronunciation.

By the end of the school year in 1940, with his sixteenth birthday only three months away, the school recommended that Günter skip an academic year, returning in the autumn to join Class 4A where the brightest pupils would work towards taking the School Certificate a year early. Although gratified that his hard work had been recognised, nonetheless it was a daunting prospect and the first term back was challenging. He sacrificed all morning leisure activities in favour of further study, concentrating after Easter solely on revising for the exams scheduled for June 1941. The absolute minimum requirement for a School Certificate was a pass in English, Maths and three other subjects. One of his subjects was German, but even that was a struggle. He had not spoken his native language for two years. Günter found it almost impossible to grasp Shakespeare and Chaucer. He did not hold out much hope for his English Literature result.

On 22 March 1941 the Home Office Regional Advisory Committee summoned Günter to Bristol for interview. He travelled by train from Lydney with his physics master, Mr Kenneth Gilbraith, for support. Günter was now over sixteen and officially an adult enemy alien. Fear of spies was escalating and many Jewish refugees were being interned in camps, the majority on the Isle of Man. The fact that they were unlikely to be followers of Hitler seemed to be irrelevant. Günter was nervous and distressed at this turn of events. After the interview was completed, the civil servant wrote his report, concluding that it was not necessary for Günter Stern to be called before a Tribunal. The entry reads:

This boy attained the age of 16 on 18 October 1940. He is a Jew. His father was a farmer and cattle dealer. Both his parents are living in Koblenz. The boy was forbidden education under the Nazi regime on racial grounds and was brought to England by the Inter Aid Committee on 21 July 1939. He is being educated at Lydney Grammar School. Mr Kenneth Gilbraith, a master at the school, attended as referee and spoke highly of the alien who, he said, is absolutely loyal to England. The alien tendered four very satisfactory testimonials from persons of repute and reliability. The Advisory Committee formed the opinion that he is to be trusted and is reliable from a security point of view.

Günter was free to live his life. That summer of 1941 was spent helping the war effort on a farm, gathering the harvest just like old times. With so many thousands of agricultural workers away fighting, everyone had to lend a hand to keep the country fed. During August the exam results were published. Günter's hands trembled as he opened the envelope. A distinction in German, a disappointing pass for History, fails in Art and English Literature; everything else solid passes with credit. It was only two years since he had entered England, unable to speak the language. The results were extremely satisfying. He wrote to Mr and Mrs Free, stressing his wish to stay on for the Sixth Form, hoping to qualify for a university place to read chemistry. Oliver and Freda could not have been more proud.

On the first day of the autumn term, Günter was appointed as a prefect, with special responsibilities for younger evacuees. He chose to study the sciences, learning chemistry from the Lydney Grammar School chemistry master, Joe Hotchkiss. This dedicated and meticulous teacher, admired by many for his sense of justice and generous nature, had a significant influence on Günter, grateful for the extra time and attention given to him in the laboratory.

Ever since his arrival in Britain, Günter had kept in touch, as often as possible, with his parents in Koblenz. The Red Cross could only cope with forwarding letters once every three months, but each one was a welcome reminder of his early life and in turn an opportunity to reassure Alfred and Ida how well he was doing at school. There was a real fear that the letters were intercepted and sometimes censored, so any mention of current affairs was taboo. During February 1942 a letter arrived. Günter tore open the envelope impatient for news. It contained an unusually brief message.

'We have just been informed that we are going to be resettled in Poland but we don't have an address there yet, so we will write to you as soon as we get there.'

It was the last letter he would ever receive.

Pressure

'I really wanted two or three weeks in peaceful surroundings so I asked Mrs Free if they were going to North Wales, and if so, could I join them? Yes, they were and yes, I could. It was good to be back in the Valley and see the Arans again. I was shocked to see that Mrs Free had noticeably aged and had trembling hands, occasionally dropping a kitchen implement or jar. Nothing was said and I felt it was not my place to enquire what was the matter.'

Having worked hard throughout the Lower Sixth, including extra tuition in the evenings to catch up with the others and master the mysteries of mathematics and physics, Günter completed the year with the honour of being awarded a copy of *The Seven Pillars of Wisdom* by T. E. Lawrence, the annual prize for Service to the School. He was exhausted, in real need of a break and had not seen the Frees for almost two years.

During his visit, with Mrs Free clearly so unwell, Günter resumed his 'milk run' to the nearby farm. The farmer and his wife remembered the German refugee and asked after his parents. Günter now had the language skills to thank them personally for their offer of rescue from Hitler's Germany. The farmer was very sorry that the plan had not worked out. With Oliver still working in Birmingham, Günter took a picnic and went hiking to the top of a pass called Bwlch-y-Croes leading to Lake Vyrnwy. The solitude and view from the top were both heartening and therapeutic.

Günter's final eight months in Lydney stretched ahead. During these he was made Deputy Head Boy, took dance classes, listened to popular jazz records by Duke Ellington, Artie Shaw and Harry Roy and his Band, worked up a sweat playing 'rugger' and hockey. He went swimming, devoured Professor Joad's *Guide to Philosophy*, learnt First Aider skills and despaired at Classical Greek Literature. The early months of 1943 were devoted to revision, revision and more revision for his Higher School Certificate exams in Chemistry, Biology and Physics. The physics master asked Günter and a few of his friends to make up the numbers in his evening sessions in Applied Mechanics and Electrical Engineering, held at Lydney Technical College. Günter found the lectures inspiring.

Then it was all over; time to shake the hand of the 'great man' and thank the Allsopp family for being outstanding hosts. Günter's early childhood had been played out in a world increasingly filled with hatred and prejudice. In Lydney the tolerance, charity and sympathy shown towards him, despite his enemy alien status, left him grateful, confident and self-assured.

Rivets and Relationships

'Mary floated like a fairy, but she kept a proper distance, except in the waltz where the final twirl was irresistible and I held her close to me. She said, 'That was nice, but look here, I don't want to come between you and Rita. Thanks for dancing with me anyway.'

Günter returned to the Frees' home in Yardley in triumph, with a much-coveted conditional offer to read Chemistry at Birmingham University. But the more Günter thought about it the more he felt drawn to do his bit for the war effort. As a German national he could not be called up but volunteering might be an option. The Army Recruitment Officer explained that at the time he could only offer the Pioneer Corps, the Army's unskilled labour force. Fortunately, the Sergeant was impressed by the young man's educational record and advised him to delay enlisting. Instead, perhaps he should use his scientific know-how in essential work, maybe at Baxter's Bolts, Screw and Rivet Works in Sheepcote Street. Their slogan 'We Make Millions Every Hour' proudly referred to their rivets destined for the aircraft industry. As a parting comment, he reassured Günter that the rules might be changing soon to allow aliens to sign up for the infantry. He could always apply again.

Günter was offered a position in the metallurgical laboratory, testing ferrous and light alloys for chemical composition and reliability. He loved his steam-pressed lab coat, powerful microscopes, the company of like-minded colleagues and taking home £3 10s a week. It was hard adjusting to the twelve-hour shifts but chemical analysis of coiled steel was absorbing and could save lives. After only a few days Günter made his decision. He would reject his university place and continue working at Baxter's until the Army offered more options. He was adamant that in time he would join-up and repay his debt to Great Britain.

After a hard day measuring with a micrometer, an eighteen-year-old boy needs distraction. The International Club was an established social venue for refugees from all countries, offering table tennis, cards and chess. There were young people from Czechoslovakia, escapees from occupied France and Holland, students from the colonies and a number of English. Günter found it easy to make friends, notably with two particular young ladies. Rita, lively, intelligent, talkative with a definite weight problem, seemed keen on Günter, asking him his plans, when would he next be in, was he going to any concerts? Where Günter was, Rita was there too.

One evening she made the classic error of introducing Günter to her rather more attractive friend Mary. Mary was not interested in classical music or politics. Rita must have felt quite safe. However, at a Club Dance a few weeks later, Günter could not fail to notice how stunning Mary was looking. Out of loyalty he first asked Rita for a dance. She seemed incapable of moving her feet, resulting in Günter stepping all over them. Mary had been dancing too, her partner holding on to her for a second go. When she was seated again she whispered to Günter, suggesting he dance with her so as to avoid further attention from the unwanted suitor. Compared with Rita, Mary was light on her feet and a joy to dance with. Three numbers later, during the final cords of a waltz, Günter gave in to temptation and twirled Mary around before holding her close.

The Army did change the rules. Günter handed in his notice at Baxter's. At the International Club, on revealing his plans to enlist, Rita cried a little. Mary discreetly slipped a note into Günter's hand, including her address and a message, 'Just in case you want to get in touch'. Faced with this moral dilemma he thought it best to make his situation clear. While Rita was distracted elsewhere he told Mary, 'You should know that Rita is just a good friend and nothing more. You don't need to feel bad if you ever wish to meet me away from the club.'

Mary smiled and squeezed his hand.

In the Army Now

'We would learn parade ground drill, general fitness exercises and disciplinary rules. After that a decision would be made and those selected to proceed in the infantry would be posted, depending on vacancies to one of a number of corps training centres. The course would last six weeks, at the end of which we would be "battle ready", with the ability to use a rifle, sub-machinegun, bayonet and grenade.'

On 15 May 1944 Günter returned to the recruiting office in Birmingham, declaring his desire to fight Hitler's Army. There was no argument from the Recruiting Sergeant on this occasion. He immediately enlisted him for six weeks' basic training with the Territorial Army at Budbrooke Barracks in near-by Warwick. His Army application form E531 was stamped, 'Desires eventually to serve in the Royal Warwickshire Regiment'. Having been allocated service number 14448059 and awarded the rank of Private, Günter underwent a medical examination. He was declared to be Grade A1 and 'fit for general service'. Before leaving the office Günter swore an oath to King George and his Heirs, witnessed by Major George Newman.

Günter had no idea what to expect at the barracks. On arrival he and the many hundreds of brand new recruits, were lectured on the traditions and battle honours of the local Warwickshire and Leicestershire Regiments. Then it was to the Quartermaster's Store to be issued with battle-dress, boots, underwear, shorts and tin hat. The men were laden with dog tags, mess tins, eating irons, basic first aid equipment and intriguingly a little fabric pouch known as a 'Housewife', containing a thimble, two balls of grey darning wool, fifty yards of linen thread, needles and spare brass buttons. In the dormitory Günter chose a top bunk this time, without fear of falling out in a rolling sea! Each young soldier was issued with three sack covers, to be filled with straw forming a mattress for his bunk. Then a further medical examination, Günter delighted to still be graded as A1, followed by inoculations and a blood-grouping test. Having collected his pay book, Günter knew he had finally made it.

He was a British soldier.

Tragedy and Loss

'I was downstairs with Mrs Free and we suddenly heard a shout from upstairs. I ran up, because by now she was having difficulty climbing the stairs. Mr Free was in the bath, lying back, not moving at all. Mrs Free asked me to go next door as they had a telephone and to call a doctor. An ambulance took him away.'

At the end of his first week in Warwick, Günter returned to Yardley on a day pass, looking forward to a home-cooked Sunday lunch and intent on showing off his khaki battledress to eleven-year-old Margaret. He found the family in a parlous state, with Oliver particularly poorly and due for hospital tests in a few days. It was fortunate that Günter was there to pull Oliver from the bath and raise the alarm. Once her husband was safely on his way to hospital, Günter made some tea with extra sugar to settle Freda's nerves. Once she felt calmer, Freda shared her family secrets with the young soldier.

In 1925 Oliver had been a Research Student, working under Nobel Prize Winner Professor Frederick Soddy, a pioneering scientist in the field of radioactivity. One afternoon Oliver and two colleagues were involved in an experiment dealing with emission of poisonous gases. There was some sort of explosion and he and one of the others were taken very ill. Günter wondered if that might have been the cause of Mr Free's deafness. Oliver had been laid up for six months before being able to return to his studies. Although by then feeling much recovered, doctors warned him that the gas might have caused serious lung damage. The effects could recur again, at any time within the next twenty years. Günter was horrified but there was more. Mrs Free went on to explain Margaret's delicate disposition. Although invariably lively and intelligent, her daughter had been born with a degenerative condition of her digestive system, needing to avoid certain foods. But she was now losing weight and the prognosis was not optimistic. Günter returned to barracks with a heavy heart. He would never see any of them again.

The hospital could not help Oliver and sent him home to rest. He died with his wife at his side on 7 July 1944. He was forty-two and had suffered cardiac failure. He left an estate worth £4,627 8s 8d to his widow and her brother, Leon Salingar. His death proved a turning point for Freda. Giving up hope and retreating into her own illness, she and Margaret moved in with her elderly mother, Anna Salingar, at 114 Salisbury Road in Moseley. Günter was never to return to Birmingham, by now very much the itinerant wartime serviceman. Consequently, he lost a number of personal belongings left with the Frees for safekeeping, including irreplacable family photographs and precious letters from his parents.

Sometime after Mr Free's death, Günter received a final letter from Freda. He replied, asking if he might visit her. A neighbour responded:

Mrs Free has asked me to say thank you very much, and please don't take this the wrong way, but you should forget about the Free family because you know that she has lost her husband, and Margaret is now in danger, and you know how ill she is, she can hardly move and may have to move in with her doctor brother, so please forget them. She doesn't want you to go through losing another family.

This was unbearable. He immediately wrote back, expressing profound gratitude for giving him a life and an education. If there was ever anything he could do to help she should just write. In the summer of 1946 Anna Salingar died aged seventy, mercifully spared watching the further deterioration of both her daughter and granddaughter.

Since May 1943, Margaret had been a pupil at the prestigious Edgbaston High School for Girls, a diligent and popular member of the school. However her health failed and she died in hospital aged thirteen on 6 March 1947. Her death certificate cites the cause of death as 'Atrophy of the Liver with Infective Hepatitis'. Five years later, on 1 May 1952 Freda Free finally succumbed to her own progressive condition at Selly Oak Hospital. Her cause of death was recorded as 'Disseminated Sclerosis'. In the 1960s a condition known as

'Wilson's Disease' was identified, a rare inherited liver disorder. Sufferers are unable to reject excess copper from their system and are advised to avoid certain foods. An adult form results in predominantly neurological features, including 'an asymmetrical tremor, difficulty speaking, ataxia and clumsiness of the hands'. It is possible that mother and daughter were suffering from the same inherited condition.

In her Last Will and Testament dated 8 July 1948, signed in an unmistakable shaking hand, Freda donated her beloved piano to the School of Music at the Birmingham and Midland Institute. In a nod to her Jewish background, she bequeathed a generous sum to The Hebrew University of Jerusalem for the furtherance of education. In addition Freda honoured her daughter by giving the sum of £1,000 to Edgbaston High School, the money 'to be devoted to the setting up of equipment and maintenance of a Library in Margaret's name'. In December 1956 the school magazine *Laurel Leaves*, carried a report from the recently-appointed Headmistress Miss Hopkins. She wrote:

> I want to tell you of a generous gift to the school in a legacy from Mrs Freda Free. She has left £1,000 for the equipment and maintenance of a library as a memorial to her daughter, who was at the school from May 1943 to March 1947. We shall use this for all the new equipment needed in our library, which will then be called the Margaret Free Memorial Library. I am told that Margaret was a brilliant girl.

Günter was completely unaware of this double tragedy until 1954 when, as a family man living in Norwich, he made enquiries about Freda and Margaret. A Jewish Refugee Agency contacted Freda's brother, Léon Salingar, by now a well-known surgeon, who broke the news in a letter.

The matter was closed.

Glasgow

'I had thought the Sergeants and Sergeant Majors who trained us at Warwick were a bit bossy but I was soon wishing I were back with them.'

After around three weeks in Warwick completing forms, discovering the meanings of 'fall in', 'fall out' and 'slope arms', exercising until he dropped, memorising the various ranks and practicing how to march like a British soldier, Günter considered himself an infantryman. Still disturbed by the shock revelations from his visit home a week earlier, Günter felt the need to see Mary and invited her to take the bus to Warwick on a Sunday afternoon early in 1944. They met near to the Castle, sitting close together on a park bench. Having told him not to be 'so serious all the time', Mary 'plonked' herself on his lap, put her arms around his neck and kissed him. Günter was smitten and the following weekend he returned the favour, visiting Mary and her widowed father at their Birmingham home. Her father proved to be most amenable, not even asking difficult questions about Günter's past. The two men enjoyed talking together, Mary later commenting that 'they would make a good pair'. She then added, whilst stealing a kiss, 'but then so would we'.

During the last week of June, Günter attended his passing-out parade, the Regimental band providing a rousing soundtrack and the senior officer taking the salute. Following the ceremony the troops were given details of their forward postings. It was not going to be easy to explain to Mary that he was about to be sent for six months to far away Glasgow, to undergo further combat training alongside the infamous Highland Light Infantry.

On 29 June, just one week before Oliver Free died, Private Günter Stern was 'Called to Colours', officially an infantry soldier in the Royal Warwickshire Regiment. Unfortunately he was unable to attend Oliver's funeral. Following a long and tedious rail journey north, Günter found himself outside the forbidding gates of Maryhill Barracks in Glasgow. This sprawling Victorian complex on the north side of the city was built in the 1870s to house 1,000 men. During May 1941, the notorious Nazi leader Rudolf Hess was held for a night in the guardhouse following his surprise arrival in Scotland. Günter would be training alongside men from the very regiment most feared by his father in the trenches of the Great War.

His first month was daunting. Day after day the men were led into forced marches with full kit on their backs, followed by the additional weight of a rifle and packs of ammunition. Other days they would face the assault course, crawling through pipes, crossing water on a single strand wire, climbing walls on a rope, abseiling down the other side or jumping from first floor windows. He learnt how to perfect his bayonet technique by driving the blade over and over into sacks stuffed with straw, not forgetting to twist the rifle when pulling it out. When not digging trenches the soldiers were trained in how to strip rifles and machine guns, putting them back together again – blindfolded. After several challenging weeks Günter once again found himself marching through scenic peaks and valleys, sleeping rough, this time not in Moselland but in the Scottish Campsie Fells.

Sunday afternoons regularly provided a welcome respite from the tough regime. Working-class families volunteered to give the 'boys' a cup of tea, groups of two or three spending time talking and sharing memories with the Sassenachs struggling hard to decipher the Glaswegian accent. Despite this language barrier, many families and soldiers developed close lasting friendships over drop scones and cups of tea. And sometimes a drop of the hard stuff.

Baptism

'I wanted to say that Stern actually sounded quite English. But you didn't argue with an officer, that much I had learned in the army.'

It was a sensible precaution for German nationals when joining up not to mention their origins. If asked, Günter told comrades that he came from 'The Rhineland', relying on the ignorance of most fledgling soldiers about the geographical regions of central Europe. During the evening of 19 July 1944 Günter was ordered to see the Adjutant. Knowing that this summons invariably meant a dressing down for some misdemeanour, Günter anxiously stood to attention in front of the Captain.

'Sir?'

'Right Stern. Instructions from the War Office. They strongly recommend that you change your name.'

'My name, Sir?'

'Something less foreign. In case of capture. The Germans could shoot you as a traitor, quite within their rights.'

'Sir.'

'They suggest that you keep the same initial. Well?'

'Can I think about it Sir?'

'Think about it? There's a war on Stern, get a move on lad.'

Günter was unprepared. This was a huge moment. Then inspiration came, how about 'Sterling' as in the British currency?

'Sir, could I call myself Sterling?'

The officer scribbled on the documents. However, being a Scot, he instinctively thought of the nearby city of Stirling and wrote the new name spelt with an 'i'. Günter made a declaration in accordance with army regulations and was dismissed. Surprisingly, the officer had not appeared unduly concerned about Günter's very Germanic given name. However, in the barracks, Günter's young comrades spoke up.

'But what about "Günter"? Jerry will spot that one right away.'

'No, he didn't mention changing that.'

'Joe. We'll call him Joe.'

And so Günter Stern became Joe Stirling.

Disappointments

'On the last week we faced some very tough manoeuvres, the real final test. I was standing at the top of a 10-foot wall with my rifle on my back, slung loosely as required, about to jump. I had done it a dozen times before. Next moment I was on my way down, although I hadn't jumped.'

With the gaps between meetings becoming longer, Mary began to have second thoughts about her young soldier. Correspondence dried up and eventually Joe found himself 'dismissed'. Although initially heartbroken at losing Mary, the country was at war and Joe focussed on preparing for his part in it. The talk in the barracks was of the continuing and successful movement of Allied troops through Nazi-occupied Europe and the heavy casualties on both sides. Everyone was keen to 'have a go'.

During his final week in early September Joe took part, once again, in assault course training. While soldiers climbed up a rope to the top of a high wall, the height of a two-storey building, others discharged small grenades beneath them, replicating the conditions of combat. As Joe was preparing to make a controlled jump from the wall, a grenade exploded dangerously close, knocking him off balance. He landed heavily; his rifle swung round, the butt smashing into his foot, fracturing three small bones. The pain was intense but he reacted instinctively to the shouted order: 'Come on, come on lad, keep moving.' A few moments later the foot gave way and he had no choice but to hobble back to barracks. Despite rest and a plaster cast the bones did not heal.

Joe was despondent as he wished his friends good luck. Operation 'Market-Garden', masterminded by that most celebrated of Royal Warwickshire soldiers Field Marshal Bernard 'Monty' Montgomery, was launched a week later on 17 September. A number of Joe's close colleagues were destined, as part of the British XXX Corps, to supply infantry back-up to the I Allied Airborne Corps. Had he not sustained an injury, Joe would most certainly have been amongst the 9,000 Allied troops at the Battle of Arnhem. Only 2,000 survived to withdraw across the Rhine. Broken bones probably saved Joe's life.

An orthopaedic surgeon sent Private Stirling for examination on the grounds that 'he has difficulty in carrying out normal training'. At 10.00 hours on 6 October the doctor warned Joe that he might have sustained permanent damage. He also pointed out that he had PES Planus (Bilateral), jargon for flat feet, hinting that this condition should have been diagnosed back in May before he was signed up to an infantry unit. The Sergeant Major ordered Joe to attend an assessment board and ironically on his 20th birthday, 18 October 1944, his medical records were endorsed with the words, 'Downgraded from A1 to B2 – unfit for active service'. Not a birthday gift Joe would have asked for. His official army records, however, make no reference to his accident or to broken bones.

Joe's comrades would face the enemy without him.

Bramley Camp

'There was a refreshingly different ambience at Bramley, with a great mix of personnel, ranging from near new recruits to professional soldiers, some of whom had seen front-line action.'

To assess Joe's future, he was first sent to Saltburn, a small seaside town on the northeast coast. Here the Army had commandeered a row of guesthouses where recruits and 'regraded' soldiers underwent a series of aptitude tests to identify skills and strengths. Private Stirling was well educated, he had studied chemistry. What about the Officer Cadet Training Unit? Maybe not. Or the Signal Corps? Hearing not sharp enough. The decision was made. Based on his science education he was assigned to the Royal Army Ordnance Corps. Not that Joe exactly knew what that meant.

He was to undergo training as a Storeman, Second Class, with a view to progressing to an Ammunition Storeman or maybe an Ammunition Examiner with the automatic minimum rank of Sergeant. On 22 December Joe passed his Certificate of Trade Proficiency Part 1. Next stop was Wellington in Shropshire where Joe was instructed in how the men in the Ordnance Corps tested, stored and distributed everything that the Army required in the way of weaponry, military equipment and munitions. His training included how to record stock, handle shells, grenades and small-arms ammunition and administer requisitions from other units. It was certainly not hand-to-hand combat or target practice, but it was important support work, back up for the real fighting men. He would do his best.

The very English village of Bramley in North Hampshire lies halfway between Reading and Basingstoke, close to the Berkshire border. There was a Saxon church, hotel, historic manor house and blacksmith's shop. In 1917 a prisoner-of-war camp was established at the southern fringe of the village. At its peak the camp housed 3,500 German prisoners. In 1922 the Royal Army Ordnance School of Ammunition arrived. At the beginning of the Second World War the camp was ringed with anti-aircraft defences with decoy concrete roads constructed in near by Morgastor Wood, along with 33 miles of railway track for the movement of staff and ordnance. The pathways were carpeted with bluebells and primroses, ferns and patches of dense woodland. When Joe arrived in Bramley during February 1945, 4,400 military and civilian staff worked at the camp, handling 35,000 tons of ammunition every month.

This was his new home.

Jean

'I found Jean very attractive. I think it was her diction that first caught my attention; no trace of a regional accent that I could tell, yet no affected la-di-da. I would take her to the NAAFI for a cup of tea and later a stroll to the village to visit the Silver Slipper, something short of a night club!'

At the camp the soldiers benefitted from a NAAFI (Navy, Army and Airforce Institute) with its shop selling cheap cigarettes and the ladies from the WVS (Women's Voluntary Service) serving tea, even homemade cakes if rationing allowed. The enormous Drill Hall served as a gym, boxing venue, cinema and theatre, as well as a dance and concert hall. A popular pastime was to visit the near-by village. Reverend Greenstreet organised nightly cocoa and cribbage evenings for soldiers at the old village hall overlooking Clift Meadow. The troops dubbed it 'The Silver Slipper' in honour of the notorious Regent Street nightclub opened by American actress Tallulah Bankhead in 1927, featuring a glass dance floor and painted Italian murals.

Having unpacked his bag in Hut 26, Storeman Stirling of 'B' Company, No. 1 Battalion, was destined to spend his days unloading, carrying, itemising and stacking shells bound for artillery pieces and tanks in mainland Europe. He dug trenches at the disposal ground, preparing for faulty or obsolete mines and grenades to be destroyed under controlled conditions. It was Ammunition Examiners who tested the shells before they were despatched to the front. Many of these were women, members of the Auxiliary Territorial Service (ATS), working alongside the men, but paid rather less. Unlike the men, who once qualified were immediately promoted to Sergeant, the women Examiners had to settle for one stripe as Lance Corporals, with only a limited number making it to full Corporal.

The evening chat in the NAAFI or local pub was dominated by updates on the situation in Europe. The Allied troops were making headway. It must be over soon. What sort of Britain would emerge from the conflict?

How would the occupation of Germany be organised? Most of the troops spoke little if any German. Knowing even a smattering of the language would be most helpful in the aftermath of war. Joe's plan was to volunteer to play his part in the reconstruction of Germany. He did not hesitate when asked to organise evening classes in the German language. He took his new role very seriously, visiting the Army Education Corps unit, 18 miles away in Aldershot, to collect appropriate teaching aids. He returned to barracks with an adult education language textbook entitled *Heute Abend* (This Evening).

The class proved popular, attracting about thirty men and women of all ranks. Joe demanded high standards of pronunciation from his students, believing it preferable to get it right from the start and avoid bad habits setting in. But he was also aware of the difficulties of learning a new language. The process took them through basic vocabulary to the mysteries of declensions and conjugations. It was the women who were more willing to study, some memorising lists of new words in advance of their next lesson. Regular attendees included a small group of women ammunition examiners. One of these, petite and slim with chestnut brown waves and a shy manner caught the eye of the young tutor. Norfolk girl Jean Mary Skitmore was four years older than Joe but at little over five feet tall in her stocking feet, she looked deceptively youthful. The couple began hanging back after class for more private discussions, followed by tea, a cigarette or maybe a stroll to the Silver Slipper Club in the village; the return walk along unlit country lanes proving quite delightful.

A devotee of classical music, Joe organised a visit to London for his students. Train tickets for uniformed personnel were subsidised by the Ministry of Defence, costing just one shilling each way. Discounted tickets for the concert at the Wigmore Hall were priced the same as the train. Despite the total representing a whole day's pay, twenty-two people signed up. Jean, although knowing little about chamber music, was keen to be there, her first trip away with her new special friend. The programme was *Die Winterreise*, a song cycle by Franz Schubert from 1828. The twenty songs, performed in poetic German, tell the tragic story of a solitary traveller during a bleak savage winter, whose heart is frozen with grief.

Joe and Jean sat close together.

Attleborough and the Skitmores

'If Jean's mum could produce the sort of meals served up that day, then I could only hope that Jean had learned a little of her culinary skills. I was sorry when it was time for me to leave and hoped I would be asked to return some time.'

A critical point in any romance is meeting with the parents. Jean cautiously explained to Joe that her family were simple country people who not only worked on their own smallholding, but that their home was actually two converted railway carriages without electricity or running water. She need not have worried. Joe was relieved. Jean's background seemed remarkably similar to his own. The toilet in Nickenich had been at the end of his garden. He reassured her that he would never judge people because of their circumstances. And anyhow, he thought to himself, people with a daughter as lovely as Jean must be special.

Jean's home was in Attleborough, 17 miles southwest of the city of Norwich. The rural town owed its existence to turkeys and cider. At the Thursday markets the stalls spread along the length of Church Street and into the open area by the Angel Hotel opposite the Griffin Inn. Every year on Michaelmas Day thousands of turkeys were sold to people arriving from all over Norfolk. South Norfolk was covered in orchards. Farmers sold apples and pears to Gaymers Cider works. This had stood in the centre of town since 1896 and boasted its own railway siding. Lots of locals relied on Gaymers for work. The parish church of The Virgin Mary was the largest in the region, not that Jean had ever been inside. It was only a few years earlier that the Old Post Office was sold and became the Doric Restaurant in Queen's Square. Since the Gas Works was built in Queen's Road late in the 1930s, gas was slowly being piped into homes and businesses, but sadly not yet into railway carriages.

Jean's parents both came from rural Norfolk families. Her father, Ernest William Skitmore, born on 29 May 1886 in the small village of Little Ellingham in the south of the county, was the third of six children. His father Ellis was a farm labourer. Jean's mother was born Lucy Leach on 5 October 1889, the youngest child of Henry and Emma Leach. Henry was the publican for ten years from 1890 at The King's Head pub in Worstead. The couple had five children, three of whom died before the age of twelve. Emma then died prematurely, leaving Henry to care for his son Frank, aged nine and his younger sister Lucy. Frank was killed in action in September 1914, while serving with the 16th Lancers in France.

Henry remarried, aged forty-nine, to the much younger Sarah Blowers, eldest child of his neighbour David, a bricklayer and Parish Clerk. At twenty-five Sarah was facing the possibility of becoming an 'old maid'. Emma's early death offered an unexpected opportunity. Within a year Sarah had produced a son, Henry Cyril, eventually producing three more children. Lucy was a great help to her stepmother. She had never been afraid of hard work.

By the start of the Great War both Ernest Skitmore and Lucy Leach were working at Attleborough Hall, the ancient seat of the Mortimer family, just outside the Norfolk market town. Ernest tended the gardens and worked on the vegetable plot, while Lucy was a member of the kitchen staff. Ernest stood only five feet, two and a half inches tall with a girth disproportionately wide. He was also illiterate, barely able to write his name, then not unusual in agricultural areas. When joining the domestic staff for his meals, Ernest was attracted to Lucy with her mop of black curls. She was three years younger and an inch or two shorter. Ernest was a lifelong member of the Plymouth Brethren, a Nonconformist pacifist religion. With no conscription at the beginning of the Great War, Ernest was under no obligation to join the military. Instead the couple were married on 8 May 1915 at the Chapel of the Primitive Methodists in the nearby village of Rockland St Peter. As a married man he was now safe from the front line.

However, in June 1916, with wholesale slaughter in the trenches decimating the troops, the Government revised the existing call-up regulations to include all men aged between eighteen and fifty-one, whatever their marital status. On 30 June, Ernest was conscripted into the 10th (Reserve) Battalion of the Norfolk Regiment and sent to Dovercourt near Harwich for basic training, later spending some time in France. It was a difficult time for his wife. On 14 December 1916, with her first daughter Joan just seven days old, Lucy wrote to the Regimental Paymaster from her home in Fern Cottage, Hargham Road, Attleborough. 'The wife of Private Skitmore begs to make a claim for separation allowance for wife and child. Birth certificate enclosed.'

In September 1917, Ernest's weight and height precluded him from front-line service. He was transferred to the Agricultural Company of the Eastern Command Labour Corps, based in Norwich, growing vegetables and crops. It was an ideal posting. Ernest was discharged from the Army in November 1919. With two young girls to feed and a third to follow in exactly nine months time, Ernest returned to work as a jobbing gardener and set about finding more space to house his growing brood.

Following the Great War, housing was in short supply. Families had to be resourceful and adapting old railway rolling stock into dwellings proved an innovative and popular method of creating a home. Ernest and Lucy bought a plot of land of just under one acre on Leys Lane in Attleborough, just half a mile from the main railway station. They then bought three railway carriages, painted in green with seats stripped out, which were delivered to their plot. It was here that their three girls, Joan, Marjorie and Jean along with their son Gordon, born in 1928, were brought up. It was a simple outdoor life of playing in ditches, feeding the livestock and digging up vegetables, all within the loving, if restrictive framework of the Open Brethren Assembly.

The train pulled into Attleborough. Joe felt oddly nervous.

Railway Carriages

'Down at the stables I said hello to a cow, a few pigs, a small friendly horse and lots of chickens; much like the little farms of my childhood.'

As the couple walked through the double entrance gate with its sign announcing 'The Oaks', then up the short gravelled drive Joe hesitated. What would this Christian couple think of him? He was from a Jewish family and yet did not practice a religion. He was a German. Britain was at war with his home nation. He was a soldier. He was trained to kill. What was he thinking of? But if the Skitmores did hold reservations or doubts, they certainly hid them well. Following warm handshakes, Ernest took his daughter's 'young man' on a stroll down the track to view his two small fields, dug over to create an orchard and pastureland.

Turning back towards the carriages Joe was given the tour of the smallholding; a substantial vegetable plot with cabbages, carrots, onions and peas; timber store sheds; corrugated iron piggeries and a stable. Here a small wooden hut adjacent to the stable, housed a basic toilet arrangement. The human waste was emptied daily onto the growing heap of used straw from the animal pens. A deep well was located nearby. To fetch fresh spring water for drinking, cooking or bathing, a bucket was let down into the well on a rope, hauled back up, before carrying it over 200 yards back to the kitchen. Joe greeted the pigs and the chickens, immediately more comfortable in the familiar pastoral setting.

The two railway carriages stood close together with a cobbled yard between them. The first held a kitchen area, a living room and a bedroom where Ernest and Lucy slept. After the expansive Army camp, the rooms felt cramped. The other carriage had two bedrooms with a wooden door between them and a further small area for storage. They were lit with candles and oil lamps, needing vigorous pumping to raise the pressure. In the winter months, freestanding oil fires warmed the bitterly cold carriages. Joe had been correct; Jean's parents were lovely people, not once raising the delicate subject of religion. Joe was intrigued to find that Lucy, like her daughter, did not speak with a pronounced Norfolk accent. She wrote in a beautiful hand, unusual for country people. He assumed she must have worked hard to better herself and he respected that. Most telling of all was when she served tea in her best Royal Vale bone-china tea set, the one with the thatched cottage design.

Joe had been accepted.

Brethren

'I went to a service once or twice. Jean pleaded with me to go because her parents were saying, "Wouldn't it be nice if Joe came along"'.

Tucked away in Hargham Road, just off Leys Lane in Attleborough stood the Gospel Hall of the Open Brethren, a simple timber framed hut with corrugated iron roof and central wood burning stove, once the property of the Ministry of Defence. In the late 1820s, in protest against extravagance and excess inside the Church of England, a group of Protestant Evangelicals broke away, setting up the Plymouth Brethren. The founders of this new Nonconformist church were determined to celebrate their faith in a more modest manner, focussing on following the Ten Commandments and adopting the teachings of Jesus Christ as a model for life. In 1848, following some internal disagreements on matters of doctrine and practice, the Plymouth Brethren divided into Exclusive and Open Brethren. It was to this latter group that, having made the move to Leys Lane, Ernest made his commitment, regularly walking to worship at the nearby Gospel Hall, accompanied by his wife and young family.

The services were an informal mix of prayer, singing, sharing testimonies, communion and feet-washing. The focus was on the faithful study of the King James Version of the Bible, memorising passages of scripture and confidently quoting the references. There were no vestments, incense, ornamental crucifixes or silver communion cups to distract from the central message. Male elders and lay preachers replaced professional clergy. Women and girls covered their heads inside the Gospel Hall, headscarves available on request, forbidden to preach or even to pray out loud. Just as in the Jewish tradition, often the womenfolk would meet together separately from the men. Infant baptism was not allowed. Membership of the church was only complete having maturely and publicly professed Jesus Christ as Lord and Saviour through a full-immersion ceremony. Brethren were pacifists, embracing a life of non-violence and non-confrontation. Life was about integrity of speech, family values and service to neighbours. Sundays were work free where at all possible; the day dominated by three services; Breaking of Bread in the morning, Sunday school in the early afternoon and a Gospel service in the evening. This regular 'coming together' of the forty or so Open Brethren in Attleborough and surrounding villages during these post-war decades, fostered a strong sense of warm fellowship and support, a refuge from the sinful world outside.

However, it was the teachings forbidding certain 'worldly' activities that increasingly impacted on the everyday lives of the Skitmore children. There was no place in the Brethren community for dances, popular music, alcohol, cigarettes, make-up, jewellery or inappropriate clothing. Relations with the opposite sex were forbidden until after marriage. Even listening to the radio or visiting the cinema were considered 'temptations' and a diversion away from Bible study. The children began to feel disconnected from their non-Brethren schoolfriends, maybe envying them their relative freedom to explore and embrace the world outside of the church. Until they were fourteen, the Skitmore children attended the 'all-age' council school in the town receiving a very basic education. Grammar Schools were fee paying and out of the question for agricultural families. When her time came, eldest sister Joan trained as a nurse and married Leslie Bidewell, a young man from a strict Brethren family from Norwich. Marjorie entered domestic service in Attleborough, continuing faithfully to follow the Brethren doctrine, not marrying until much later in life.

However, in 1934 when Jean, the youngest Skitmore girl, left school she deliberately steered her life in a different direction. Jean was bright and capable, a quick learner. But there was no question of any further education. Her first job was behind a shop counter. That was boring. She then applied for a job on the factory floor at the Briton Brush Company in Lady's Lane in the thriving town of Wymondham, a six-mile cycle or short bus journey from home. The factory, opened in 1933, was considered the most up-to-date brush factory in the country, with railway sidings, sawmills and engineering workshops. More significantly for Jean, the company demonstrated a benevolent attitude towards the workers, providing a canteen, playing fields and occasional works outings on special excursion trains. Jean worked alongside 500 women. Jean felt valued in her work, confident, capable. But the strict religious views of her parents set her apart. She was forbidden to join her colleagues in the town after work, or to enjoy away-days to the coast or Yarmouth Races.

Partly out of frustration and by way of protest, Jean removed herself from the Brethren, joining the Salvation Army at their citadel in Chapel Road. She felt good in her distinctive uniform, still able to worship Jesus but also engage with the community, collecting money in pubs, sing hymns on street corners, visit the sick and witness a world of which she hitherto knew nothing. In 1942 at twenty-one, legally beyond the control of her parents, Jean committed the ultimate transgression and volunteered for the British Army, training as an Ammunition Examiner. Fortunately for Jean her parents were followers of the Open Brethren, rather than the more extreme Exclusive sect.

Although Ernest and Lucy were hurt and disappointed at their youngest daughter's decision, they would never disown her.

A New Era

'I was told I would not be posted to Germany. It was policy, with a few exceptions, not to return ex-refugees in case anyone took revenge on the local population.'

As early as the summer of 1944, whilst advancing through occupied Poland, Soviet troops came across dismantled and abandoned Nazi death camps, including Belzec, Sobibor and Treblinka. In January 1945 Auschwitz was liberated. Every camp had evidence of mass murder on a colossal scale. On 11 April four soldiers from the 6th Armoured Division of the US Third Army stumbled upon Buchenwald Concentration Camp in East Central Germany. As they cautiously climbed through a hole in the barbed wire fence, they were greeted to an ecstatic welcome from 21,000 emaciated men. Joe read the witness accounts in the newspapers. He saw the photographs. He thought about his parents.

On 1 May 1945 the BBC announced Hitler's suicide. The finish-line was in sight. The following evening radio programmes were interrupted with the news that the German Army had surrendered in Italy. Two days later troops capitulated in Denmark. For two days no one knew what was happening. By Monday 7 May expectant crowds were gathering outside Buckingham Palace but still the news did not come. In fact, the British were waiting for Russian and American confirmation of the Nazi defeat. At 7 p.m. Winston Churchill broadcast on the BBC, declaring that the following day would be 'Victory in Europe Day'. The Nation could allow itself a 'brief period of rejoicing', but should remember that Britain was still at war with Japan. After five years people were ready to party. The morning papers led with photographs of vast crowds, many dressed in red, white and blue, celebrating in London the previous evening. That morning the same crowds cheered and sang as King George, Queen Elizabeth and the two princesses Elizabeth and Margaret alongside Churchill, waved enthusiastically from the balcony of Buckingham Palace.

Bramley barracks held a celebration parade. The Commanding Officer made a speech, thanking everyone for his or her valuable contribution to the victory, even if they hadn't been involved at the front line. That afternoon

Joe joined a group of comrades on the train to nearby Basingstoke where they danced in the street and invaded the public houses, the overjoyed landlords honouring the servicemen with a free first drink. It took some time to walk the six miles back to base late that evening, the men having either missed the last bus or more likely having spent every last penny on best beer. Jean and her friends stayed on base holding their own celebration. Young ladies didn't frequent pubs.

The mass demobilisation of servicemen following the First World War had resulted in devastating social, employment and economic problems. Learning from this mistake, the Ministry of Defence decreed that personnel could only be discharged once they had served a minimum of four years. As Joe had not signed up until 1943, he still had two more years to go. In Bramley the numbers of personnel began to dwindle. With workload greatly reduced, Joe turned his attention to his German classes, spending much of late May and June introducing sessions in politics, current affairs and classical music. Each of his fragile 78s could only hold one symphonic movement. Consequently it was necessary to change discs throughout the sessions, as well as winding up the gramophone. Having studied the lives and works of Beethoven and Mozart, he was able to incorporate a little historical context. Support for the sessions grew, some evenings attracting thirty or forty service personnel.

On 23 May 1945 Winston Churchill resigned as Prime Minister, the Coalition War Cabinet stood down and a General Election was called. The British people were looking for change and wanted a brighter future. The Socialists were promising a welfare state. But Winston Churchill was a national hero. Surely the country would support him. On the evening of 25 July Churchill was in Berlin at a meeting of world leaders seeking the unconditional surrender of all Japanese armed forces. If not then Japan would face the prospect of 'prompt and utter destruction'. Having signed the ultimatum alongside US President Harry Truman and General Chiang Kai-Shek of China, Churchill flew home to face the election results. Despite the newspapers being convinced that he would be returned to power, in fact the people returned the first Labour majority government, the first time that Labour had gained more votes than the Conservatives. During his acceptance speech, Prime Minister Clement Atlee said, 'We are facing a new era and I believe that the voting in this election has shown that the people of Britain are facing the new era with the same courage as they faced the long years of war.' Joe was convinced. He was already a strong supporter of socialism and the ideals of the Labour Party appeared to be in accordance with his views. With no chance of a transfer to Germany, Joe needed a challenge.

He was, after all, facing his own 'new era'.

Chapter 3

Parent and Politician, 1945–1955

Education and Making Plans

'I was conscious of the irony when first giving a lecture. Here was I, a refugee from Germany, talking as the "expert" on "British Way and Purpose" to mature military personnel, even though I had not even experienced a single Parliamentary election or been a local government ratepayer.'

Word got around that recruits were needed for the Army Education Corps. But the regulations stated that volunteers should be university graduates or qualified teachers. Despite this Joe sought advice from the recruiting officer.

'We need a minimum of one, preferably two passes at Higher School Certificate.'

'Sir. I've got three. Can I apply?'

'What's your rank?'

'Private, Sir.'

'Then, no. It's for non-commissioned officers and officers only.'

'But Sir, I have three passes, two of them with credits.'

'Well Stirling, I'll put you down as interested, but I don't expect you to be accepted.'

Much to Joe's surprise a letter arrived in Bramley Camp, instructing him to report to the Army Education College in Preston, Lancashire. He was to be assessed for suitability over a three-week period. Earlier in the year Joe had taken a one-month course in Modern European Affairs. That must have improved his chances. More excitingly, if successful he would stay on for a further three-month teacher-training course, involving two weeks in July as a real student, studying politics and economics at Southampton University College.

Everything went well and having completed his studies, Joe was sent to the Education Corps Headquarters in Aldershot to familiarise himself with administrative procedures. He met his new commanding officer, Lieutenant Colonel Green, a County Chief Education Officer in his past life. Although this man was probably the most senior Army officer Joe had ever spoken with,

Colonel Green was informal and friendly in his approach. Instead of expecting the young soldier to stand to attention, or even at ease, this officer invited Joe to address him as Mr Green, to take a seat and would he like a coffee? Joe found himself being briefed on the Garrison in Portsmouth on the south coast. It was badly in need of a new education centre.

'It will be a challenge Stirling. Would you be prepared to go down to Portsmouth and assess the immediate staffing needs?'

Joe nodded, hardly believing his ears.

'Until I can find an officer to join you, you'll be in charge. And I'll need a report.'

'Yes Sir . . ., Mr Green. Thank you for the opportunity but don't you think it might be too big a task for me?'

'I've seen the reports from Preston and your Commanding Officer in Bramley. You're obviously the sort of chap who doesn't flinch when you have to start from scratch. Anyway, I don't have anyone else.'

The rank of Sergeant was a minimum requirement for those in the Education Corps. Sergeant Stirling returned to camp triumphant with a promotion and a welcome pay rise. A hike from Private to Sergeant was rare and Joe was just a little overawed by his three stripes. His instructions were to remain at Bramley for the time being, continue his education programme and await further orders. Jean was ecstatic to have her clever soldier-teacher back.

Encouraged by his success and improved prospects, Joe seized his chance and proposed marriage. Much to his joy and relief, Jean accepted. Not only could they now be together forever, but also Jean could leave the Army as soon as she produced a marriage certificate. Expected to care for their husbands and produce the next generation, married women were banned from service in the Forces. The couple couldn't wait to break the happy news to Ernest and Lucy and applied for weekend leave passes. Congratulations over, the family sat down to discuss wedding arrangements. The date was set for Tuesday, 21 May 1946.

With Joe being a lapsed Jew and Jean losing touch with her childhood religion, everyone assumed it would be a civil ceremony. But the nearest Registry Office to Attleborough was in the market town of Watton, about 10 miles away. Ten miles may as well have been 100 for the many aunts, uncles, nieces, nephews, cousins and friends of the Skitmores. They would be travelling from Thetford, Norwich, Eccles, Great Ellingham and Little Ellingham. None owned cars and there was no direct cross-country bus or train service to Watton. But trains did come into Attleborough. Following much debate and many pots of tea, Jean eventually volunteered, 'There is only one thing we can do. We will have to have our wedding at St Mary's Church in Attleborough.'

Before returning to Bramley, the couple arranged a meeting with the Rector, despite very little hope that he would agree. The Reverend Stephen Dennett proved to be fair and open-minded. The couples' lack of religious commitment did not appear to bother him. Crucially, the Reverend had not officiated at many weddings during the war, and shrewdly recognised an opportunity to raise funds for his church. Joe was legally obliged to sign all official papers as Günter. It was when the Rector asked them both to sign the application forms for the special licence, that the bride-to-be discovered her fiancé's birth name.

It was a special moment.

In The Glasshouse

'It was to be my first job and I was worried over facing all those criminals. I don't know why they chose me. Maybe they thought, "He's new and nobody else wants it!"'

At about 5 p.m. on 23 February 1946, a major riot broke out in Britain's main military prison in Aldershot. Known as 'The Glasshouse' due to its expansive glass lantern roof, the name has since become synonymous with military imprisonment. Built in 1870 it was designed to hold 150 prisoners but by 1946 it housed over 400 in intolerable conditions. The violence lasted nearly twenty-four hours. There were many casualties and considerable damage. It was decided to move the prisoners to alternative penal institutions.

The Ministry of Defence commandeered the civilian gaol in Reading. The existing prisoners were transferred elsewhere and the building handed over to the Army. Someone from the Army Education Corps would be needed to resume the obligatory lectures in public affairs, in order to ease the transition of servicemen into Civvie Street. Bramley Camp was only 16 miles from Reading. The need was urgent. Fortunately Sergeant Stirling was available.

It was Joe's first posting as an Education Officer and it was to be inside a prison. With a certain amount of trepidation he packed his bags. Jean was in Attleborough finalising wedding plans when Joe received his orders. The railway carriages didn't have a telephone. In a rush to catch the post, he quickly scribbled a short message on a postcard. 'Just to let you know I am now at Reading Prison. Will send details later.' Jean and her parents had quite a shock! Joe felt an irrational 'terror' on entering the enormous wooden gates. The atmosphere inside the prison was very tense. Prisoners and guards still had visible bruising with many wearing bandages, trophies from the riot in

Aldershot. He was shown to his accommodation, a single damp cell with the thinnest mattress he had ever seen. All British soldiers, incarcerated or not, were entitled to an education for three hours a week. Prepared in 1942, the early volumes of *The British Way and Purpose* focussed on responsible citizenship, surviving in the workplace, health, education, financial and family issues. The following morning, with a pile of instructive handbooks tucked under his arm, Joe entered a prison classroom for the first time.

He was faced with sixty prisoners all wearing drab utility uniforms. At the back of the dimly lit room stood a number of prison guards, all at the rank of sergeant or above. The hostility between prisoners and guards was palpable. Joe attempted to take control. 'I should explain straight away that I have not been transferred from Aldershot so I have no involvement with what happened there. It is the Army's decision that you should all have the opportunity to attend some classes I have been asked to run.'

The atmosphere relaxed just a little. It was Joe's intention to run the sessions as a controlled conversation, prisoners encouraged to stand up and air their views during the debate. Here was his opportunity to share his knowledge of politics and economics. However, no one had briefed the guards about the format. Every time a prisoner stood, or even merely spoke up, one of them approached the perpetrator, aggressively forcing him back into his seat. Joe was stubborn; he refused to give in to pressure. 'I'm sorry, but it appears that these officers have not been given the correct instructions. While I am speaking, everyone is allowed to stand up and ask a question or make a comment. I hope the officers will check with their superiors should they have any doubts about that.'

Unfortunately for Joe, this approach did not endear him to the prison staff. When eating his meals in the Sergeant's Mess he was either ignored or picked upon. Whilst Joe was distracted, others dropped cigarette ends into his food, laughing loudly when he unwittingly put it into his mouth. The conversations in the canteen were boorish and coarse with much raucous laughter and bad language. A popular pastime was the invention of vile ideas for further degrading the convicts. Joe thought the majority of inmates less thuggish than some of these guards, speculating that certain individuals would have made natural Nazi 'Brownshirts'. In Nickenich and Koblenz he had witnessed professional bullies at work. On reflection, Joe admitted that in comparison, these prison guards were actually amateurs.

On speaking privately with a number of the youngest prisoners, Joe empathised with their fear and vulnerability, many guilty of nothing more than being Absent Without Leave. The men reminded Joe of the thousands of men thrown into Dachau alongside his father. He did his very best to build up their confidence and give some hope for the future. After four weeks, Joe was pleased to receive fresh orders from Aldershot. Portsmouth was ready for him, he would leave Reading Prison the following Monday. Having briefed his successor, he packed his small suitcase. He didn't look back.

On 8 April 1946 Joe officially received his appointment as Squadron Instructor in the Army Education Corps, based at the Portsmouth Garrison, still reporting directly to Colonel Green in Aldershot. With Jean permanently home in Attleborough using her leave allowance before the wedding, Joe set off to the South Coast alone. He had passed through Portsmouth only once on his way to the Isle of Wight ferry, one of his few away-days with Jean during their courtship. Joe was technically to be attached to the Royal Engineers on the outskirts of town. The welcome at the barracks was less than auspicious. Sergeant Stirling was not even under their command. Unable to see why they owed this soldier a billet, they recommended he try his luck at the Young Men's Christian Association (YMCA) in Alexandra Road. He was lucky. One of the dormitories had a spare bunk. The following morning, while putting on his shoes, one foot felt instantly wet. Had some joker filled it with water? One quick sniff told a different story. Reluctant to change into heavy Army boots for office work, Joe rinsed the offensive shoe and wore them down to the reception desk. It seemed this was quite common and the manager was extremely apologetic, suggesting that the soldier transfer into one of his single rooms while he sought more permanent accommodation. But house hunting would have to wait. Less than a fortnight after arriving in Portsmouth, he claimed two weeks' leave and took a train north.

Someone needed his very personal attention.

A Wedding

'We kept it fairly simple. I think we had just one hymn.'

Every bride hopes the sun will shine for her wedding and on Tuesday 21 May 1946, Jean Skitmore was not disappointed. The only sadness was the empty pews on the 'groom's side'. Joe had remained respectful of Freda's appeal for privacy as she endured her illness. Unbeknown to Joe, her daughter Margaret had died just two months earlier. As for the Allsopps, it was simply too far and too expensive for them to be there. Joe thought often about his absent parents during that special day, knowing how happy and proud they would be to see their son married, even if it was in a Christian church. The Skitmores, Leaches and Bidewells turned out in force, delighted to be involved in the first family wedding since the war, looking forward to the home-baked buffet back at Leys

Lane. On entering the Norman church they were almost overwhelmed by the enormous vaulted ceiling, slender pillars, fifteenth-century rood screen and ancient stained glass windows; a stark contrast to the Brethren Gospel Halls they were used to.

Proudly dressed in freshly-laundered Army uniforms complete with caps and polished buttons, the young couple made their vows, deeply moved by the solemn pledges to one another. The witnesses that day were Jean's younger brother Gordon and her father. Taking his responsibilities seriously, Ernest practiced and practiced his signature as the great day approached. Joe looked forward to a future surrounded by people who lived their lives as his parents and neighbours had done, simple country souls who welcomed him unconditionally into their close-knit fold. They knew that this young man would take care of their Jean and in turn they would take care of him.

Günter Stern had found his new family.

Hard Graft

'Attendances at the Education Centre grew at an amazing rate, soon filling our main hall on a regular basis. England had always seemed to suffer from an elitist attitude, yet here were soldiers and sailors from all ranks attending cultural events in their own time.'

The evening of their wedding the couple broke the journey to North Wales by treating themselves to their first night together in a modest London hotel. Joe was whisking Jean away for a six-day honeymoon in the Aran mountains, the area he had grown to love during his first five months in Great Britain. A sheep farmer had recently started taking paying guests. It was early in the season, so there was no problem finding a room. Despite a week of persistent rain, they relished the freedom to walk together hand-in-hand through lush springy meadows on the gentler mountain slopes.

All too soon it was time for Joe to return to Portsmouth. His priority was to find a home for them both. In London the newlyweds parted company, taking trains in different directions. At work his first responsibility was to find a suitable venue for the new Forces Education Centre, somewhere convenient, central and within budget. The manager of the YMCA suggested an empty property right next door. It had once belonged to the Royal Navy but had been disused for many years. Joe informed Colonel Green and arranged a viewing. The central hall would seat at least eighty people, with the bonus of four or five much smaller rooms leading off it. The Navy agreed, on the condition that the talks and cultural programmes were extended to Navy personnel. Before long the interior was repainted in combat creams and browns. Joe's new domain looked smart and fresh, with ample classroom and office equipment. He even had his own office, fitted with two desks and a typewriter, albeit rather ancient.

Joe held meetings with representatives of various army units, some of which were already providing education for the troops. The Royal Electrical and Mechanical Engineers (REME) had a continuing programme, including well-established electrical training schemes. They were stubbornly resistant to the possibility of a rival setup. However, illiteracy amongst the troops was widespread. Two or three people in virtually every unit could barely read or write. Whilst training in Preston, Joe had heard a well-kept secret; during the war men known to have literacy problems had nevertheless been recruited, very much against official policy. Part of his training had been how best to handle small classes of people who needed this most basic help. With additional educational officers, this controversial issue could now be made a priority.

Joe found a modest flat in Southsea, within reasonable walking distance of 'his centre' as he now thought of it. The Jewish lady owner had fitted it out with simple and tasteful furniture, curtains and linen. She and her adult daughter lived together in one section of the house, all three occupants sharing a common front door, landing and staircase. In conversation mother and daughter showed a natural interest in their tenant's Jewish origins, sad to hear of Joe's early and tragic separation from his parents. He detected a certain reticence from them when he explained he was now married to a Gentile. They even whispered the term 'outsider'. In Attleborough Jean packed her few belongings, thanked her father and mother for their kindness and made the journey to Portsmouth to start her new life, content to spend her days keeping house and caring for her husband.

For Joe it was a busy and satisfying period. In addition to his core students, there were six young band boys to educate. Nearby Gosport had a military school for lads from the age of fourteen who were given musical training before joining military bands. The Army was obliged to offer these youngsters a general education. With both the full-time teachers now demobbed, the boys would attend the new Education Centre for classes in reading and maths. Whilst commandeering furniture for the Centre, Joe came across a dozen wooden school desks with corner ink pots; ideal for his youngest charges. On two mornings each week Joe taught the boy in small groups, enabling him to offer individual attention.

More and more servicemen with literacy problems arrived to be assessed; Joe discovering that many of them had been 'bargees' in their youth, from families living on river barges and forever on the move. The children had simply turned up at the nearest school to the moorings, sometimes for just a few hours, at most for two or three days at a time. It was a relief to find that most were keen to learn. Students brought letters from their wives and girlfriends, asking for Joe's help to read them. Joe obliged, sometimes writing a reply, the soldier signing his name at the bottom, a necessary skill practiced to perfection. Within a few weeks Joe shared in the men's elation when, without help, they read their mail out loud. It did, however, take a little longer for some to pen their replies unaided.

Army and Naval personnel began asking for more diverse voluntary evening classes. Two additional sergeants were brought in to work alongside Joe, enabling the programme to expand. One led literature evenings, reading aloud selected passages from well-known classics, deliberately choosing a 'cliff-hanger' moment to end on. It was hoped that students would be tempted to read the rest of the story in their own time. Joe installed a gramophone and revived his classical music evenings. These events proved extremely popular. Many had never been interested in classical music before, some simply unable to afford to go to concerts, others afraid to be classed as 'cultural snobs' by their friends.

An inspection was due and Colonel Green and his team travelled from Aldershot. They sat in on classes in basic reading, foreign languages and *British Way and Purpose* lectures before staying on for the evening sessions. The following morning the Colonel requested to see Joe. He was impressed, adding that Portsmouth was now the largest and most active Education Centre in Southern Command. It had been planning to replace Joe with a commissioned office in due course. Instead he was now able to offer a promotion to Warrant Officer with effect from 4 September 1946. The posting was his.

Joe did not hesitate to accept. He was anticipating some additional expenses, as three months after the wedding Jean had told her husband she might be pregnant. They had not planned to start a family quite so soon and Jean had been concerned about Joe's reaction. She need not have worried. He had lived for many years without a family to call his own. The wonderful news promised to complete his happiness. Not even a nasty spell of morning sickness could dampen their enthusiasm. An increase in salary to over £17 a week would come in very handy indeed.

There was a baby on the way.

A New Generation

'I jumped on my bicycle and went into Attleborough to phone the doctor. There were only two telephone boxes for the whole town.'

As Christmas approached Joe and Jean made decisions about the birth of their baby. The due date was second week of March and Jean wanted to give birth in Norfolk. Everyone agreed the maternity home in Thetford, 15 miles from Attleborough, would be the best place. There was concern that the Leys Lane railway carriages, with the outside toilet and with no running water or electricity, would not be suitable for a newborn. Older sister Joan offered to accommodate Jean and the baby for two or three weeks at her house in Norwich, after which she should feel strong enough to return to Portsmouth. Joe approached his senior officer in Aldershot with a request for one week's leave before and one week after the birth. That was no problem. But the flat in Southsea would be too small. Joe found a comfortable house for rent at 11 East Cosham Road in the well-to-do northern suburb of Cosham, close to Portsea Island. Perfect for raising a new baby.

Early in January, taking advantage of an unseasonable mild spell, Jean travelled to Attleborough to prepare for the birth. On Thursday 23 January it started to snow. It never seemed to want to stop. That winter, conditions in Britain were exceptionally harsh. Southern England was smothered by severe blizzards with drifting of over 20 feet high in some parts of the countryside. The artic conditions continued throughout February and into March, the country suffering transport closure and disruption as well as intermittent power cuts.

On Monday 10 March, with a week to go before Jean's expected date, Joe left Portsmouth early wearing an extra jumper under his dress uniform. Although the fields were covered in a thin layer of snow, there were no hold-ups and his train pulled into Victoria without incident. The London Underground was running as normal. But at Liverpool Street, passengers were advised that the lines north were completely blocked with drifting snow. No trains would be running to Norfolk that day. The advice was to go to King's Cross, head for Cambridge and change at Ely. With the crowded train stopping at every single station, it was a tedious journey. One consolation was the sun streaming through the windows. That same sun was melting the snow at a rapid rate. By Cambridge an announcement warned of flooding on the line. The Isle of Ely was impassable. Joe had no choice but to stay the night in a small Cambridge hotel.

The following morning he continued his journey on a series of buses, through water often too deep for smaller vehicles. Eventually, after nearly two days of travelling, Joe arrived in Attleborough. All they could now was to sit it out during the wettest March since 1869. On 16 March Jean was a day late. That evening a severe gale pummelled the south-east of England. The railway carriages felt horribly vulnerable. The following days passed slowly, Joe watching Jean carefully for any telltale signs. His leave would finish on

22 March. With only three days before he was expected back at work, Joe felt compelled to get in touch with Colonel Green in Aldershot. Once again his senior officer was supportive, telling Joe to stay where he was most needed. He could return to work once the baby was a week old.

At around 11 p.m. on the night of Tuesday 19 March the couple were in bed. Jean complained of stomach pains and was sure the baby was on its way. It was late, dark and cold. Not an ideal time. Joe asked if she were sure. Jean was in no doubt. Joe knew the drill; he was to phone the doctor and ask his advice. But there was no telephone at the Skitmore residence. It meant riding his bicycle through the unlit area of the town in a howling gale, to find one of the only two telephone boxes. Making sure he had enough pennies, he laid out his supply on the ledge over the directories. First call to the doctor, press button A. The doctor, warm, safe and secure in his own bed, responded, 'There's no point in me coming out. I'll give you the number of the Thetford nursing home.' Joe rang and spoke to the Matron on duty who suggested he bring 'the mother' in right away. The third call was to the taxi company. By the time he had cycled back to Leys Lane the taxi was already there, Jean being helped into the back seat. The slow 15 mile drive after midnight was frustrating. Joe asked the taxi driver to wait. The midwife was adamant.

'This baby won't arrive until at least mid-morning tomorrow. We don't have room for you to stay. Is that your taxi outside? Mr Stirling, go home now and come back first thing.'

Joe got back into the taxi. Baby Jane arrived at 6 a.m. on 20 March 1947. Joe returned around 7 a.m. surprised to find he was already a father and delighted to find mother and baby doing well, despite their long difficult night. For five days Joe commuted between Attleborough and Thetford, getting to know his daughter as his wife regained her strength. Once discharged from the nursing home, Joe accompanied his little family to Norwich, placing them into the capable hands of his sister-in-law and headed back to Portsmouth. Four weeks later Jean and baby Jane joined him in their new house in Cosham.

Cosham, a suburb three miles north of the centre of Portsmouth appeared far less damaged than Southsea, having been spared much of the bombing inflicted on the dockside areas. It had a drab but well-served High Street, offering Jean welcome distraction while her husband was at work. An early task was to register with the butcher and grocer. Having a child less than five years old entitled Jean to claim extra milk and eggs. Weather permitting, Jean pushed little Jane in her large wheeled pram, coupons for meat, margarine, lard, sugar, tea, soap and sweets safe inside her ration books, to explore the shops. Woodward's Gripe Water, soap and nappy pins were available at Bakers of Cosham chemist shop. Rationed basic provisions such as gravy powder,

Ernest Skitmore in his First
World War uniform.

Lucy Skitmore (née
Leach).

The King's Head, Worstead, Norfolk. Lucy Leach, aged thirteen, is second from the left. Her father Henry Leach is the publican, standing in the doorway with the jug.

The Skitmore daughters, Joan, Jean and Marjorie.

Gordon Skitmore aged about twelve.

Gordon and Beryl on their wedding day, 5 November 1947.

Paul Skitmore.

Gail Skitmore.

Ernest and Beryl in Attleborough.

Joe as Labour Party Secretary-Agent for Norwich.

Family man. Jean, Joe, Jane and Ian.

He deserves the best—and he's got it

GARDEN STREET
CROMER
Tel. Cromer 2651,

Tom Watts

KING STREET
NORWICH
Tel. 29175-6-7,

Advertisement for Tom Watts Furniture Store in Norwich, 1950s.

Advertisement for Stirling Holidays in the *Evening News*, January 1960.

Stirling Holidays' shop at 71 Magdalen Street, 1960.

Councillor Stirling, 1958.

Stirling Holidays in Great Yarmouth, 1970.

Joe presents Marion Barron with the keys to her prize Fiat car.

Lucy Skitmore with her four grandchildren, Gail, Ian, Martin and Jane.

Joe and Jean enjoy a Lions Club function in the 1970s.

sugar and flour came from Threadinghams Grocery, where everything was weighed into blue sugar paper. Bread was baked at Campions and coal would be delivered from Curtis's Coal and Corn Merchants. Once a week, Jean joined the orderly queue at Pinks Butcher, at the bottom of the High Street, waiting patiently for her meat ration of two ounces of bacon and ham each person, but only once a fortnight, a couple of sausages, probably containing more cereal than pork, and even some corned beef, if it was available. Jean chose her meat at the counter before approaching the little glass-fronted office where Miss Rickman took her money and tore the relevant coupons from her ration books. On the way home she passed Chapmans' Laundry and two pubs, the 'Swan Inn' and the 'Ship Inn', where Joe might occasionally indulge in a half-pint of bitter after work.

During April Joe made a momentous decision. He had been in Britain for eight years. He had no intention of returning to live in Germany. He felt ready to file his application to become a British citizen. Joe was confident that he fulfilled the conditions. He had served in His Majesty's Forces since the requisite date of 3 September 1939. He had lived in the United Kingdom for more than five years and was a resident before enlistment. This initial form required him to state his plans for the future. Joe considered that carefully, writing, 'If I fail to get a job in adult or youth education I would sign on for two years, study for a Social Science degree and seek education employment. Alternatively I can apply for Civil Service entrance (Junior Executive Officer) if naturalised.' He posted the documents with a mixture of trepidation and certainty. He so wanted to be British.

After the misery of an appalling winter, the summer months were exceptionally hot. An early visitor to Joe and Jean's house was Hazel Allsopp, now fourteen years old, slim and bonny, standing about six inches taller than when Joe last saw her. It was Hazel's first independent trip away from her home in Lydney, excited to see her parents' old lodger again, meet his wife and welcome the baby. Joe slept on the sofa while Hazel shared with Jean and Jane. The couple were more than happy to entertain Hazel, talk about old times, hear the latest on 'the Great Man', take a ferry trip to the Isle of Wight, explore Portsmouth and promenade in the bracing sea air. Hazel couldn't help but address Joe as Günter.

He really didn't mind.

Demobilisation

'As my demobilisation date approached, I was asked if I would like to "sign on" for a three-year extension. Colonel Green made it clear that it would almost

certainly involve an overseas posting. The Army was desperate for staff in our West African colonies to work on literacy projects, and there would be substantial overseas allowances above my present pay.'

As Jean and Joe played happy families, the Army was drawing up demobilisation papers for Warrant Officer Stirling. He had been offered the chance to continue his Army career overseas. The financial rewards were tempting but it seemed unlikely that his family could travel with him. A further option was to take up his deferred place at Birmingham University to read Chemistry. He chose not to. That moment had passed. He was now a husband and father. Towards the end of July Joe received a letter from the Home Office containing a five-page naturalisation form for completion, a brief declaration document for signature and an invoice for the £10 fee.

With his demobilisation pending, Joe declared his permanent address as Leys Lane in Attleborough and signed 'G. Stirling'. He was thankfully unaware of how close his application came to being denied. At the end of June the Home Office had sent a request to the Security Service (MI5), asking whether anything was known or recorded about Günter Stirling. On 7 July a brief reply marked as 'secret' stated:

> Apart from a report that this alien, in 1945, was friendly with another Non-Commissioned Officer who had been connected with the Communist Party in this country for many years, and that Stern himself at the date of the report, showed an inclination towards a Communist point of view, we have nothing recorded against him.

Early in 1945 during his time in Bramley, Joe had befriended two soldiers, both committed socialists, one of whom had connections with the Communist Party. They introduced Joe to the works of Karl Marx, the nineteenth-century economist and philosopher. He had read *Das Kapital*, essentially a critical assessment of capitalism, in the original German, finding the economic logic interesting and persuasive. However, the communist arguments for 'the dictatorship of the proletariat' offended him. He had witnessed at first hand a far-right dictatorship in Germany; a dictatorship from the far left would be just as unacceptable. From the reaction of MI5, it seems that the soldier was further to the left than he had admitted to Joe. On 10 September 1947 he visited a solicitor in Norwich, swore an Oath of Allegiance to the King and became a British Naturalised Subject. His certificate bore the Home Office number AZ30418. He was no longer German.

Less than a month later, on 1 October Joe and his family left Portsmouth at the start of his two-month release leave. They returned to Attleborough to live once again with Jean's parents. Joe was finally out of uniform and entitled to a demob suit. If he were lucky, he would have received a superior three-piece suit including a waistcoat and spare pair of trousers, affectionately known as 'The Full Monty', named after the manufacturer, the Jewish tailor Sir Montague Burton.

He would need a decent suit to wear at job interviews.

Civvie Street

'The pay was atrocious, £4.10s a week, compared with £17.15s that I had been getting as a Warrant Officer in the Education Corps. It would be increased to £5 after six months satisfactory service!'

Jobs were hard to come by in Norfolk in the August of 1947. Jean suggested that Joe try her old employer, the Briton Brush Company in Wymondham. He could either cycle or take a bus to work. There was a vacancy in the accounts office and after a brief interview he got the job. He would be calculating the wages for all the workers and deducting tax. At first he used his school slide rule, spending a lot of time showing others how to use it. After six months the Company Secretary announced that a delivery of electric calculators was imminent. These were comptometers, bulky and heavy, requiring extreme pressure to punch the keys, yet considered very advanced, able to multiply and add up. Unimpressed, Joe continued to use his slide rule finding it ten times as fast as the machines. But before long he had to admit that when it came to fine accuracy, using the slide rule generally meant guessing the final portion of decimal fractions. He would get used to the machine.

But the work was uninspiring. It was much more interesting to visit the factory floor, talk with the foreman, observing how the workers shaped brush heads and inserted the bristles. Never frightened of asking probing questions, he was increasingly involved in discussions about how many scrubbing brush backs could be made from a tree trunk of a given size, able to use his knowledge of algebra to offer suggestions of how to reduce costs. The Company Secretary, a qualified accountant, was dubious about how Joe was coming up with his figures. Both men would start with the same basic information, the manager working with long division and multiplication, Joe applying an algebraic formula. Consistently they both came up with the same answer, only Joe about ten minutes ahead of his superior.

Finally it was agreed that Joe could use his method, providing each new formula had been first tested in the traditional way. At the end of his first year Joe was due an annual pay rise. Pleased with progress, his manager recommended an increase of £1 a week, double what Joe had been expecting. The Managing Director agreed. Although it was gratifying to be rewarded, the tasks were not intellectually demanding.

The days passed slowly.

Local Politics

'I found it interesting to be in personal touch not only with an MP but a member of the Government.'

Joe had learnt much about politics during his time in England. Mr Allsopp had taken him to union meetings, he had read the Army Education Handbook from cover to cover and he felt a deep connection with socialism and democracy. A by-election had taken place near Basingstoke shortly after the War. Joe had volunteered to help the local Labour candidate, delivering campaign literature and canvassing door to door. Army regulations forbade the wearing of uniform when representing a political party, so he borrowed a friend's demob suit. Despite Labour losing the election, Joe was hooked.

Once resettled in Attleborough he joined the South Norfolk Labour Party, attending meetings of the local branch in the evenings and at weekends. Although small, the branch unusually had a Women's Section. In time Joe persuaded Jean to join, although she was reluctant. She believed her father probably voted Labour and womenfolk tended to vote the same way as their fathers or husbands. Politics had never featured in Jean's life before Joe came along. But she was uncomfortable at meetings and soon stopped going, leaving her husband to his new hobby.

It proved a struggle to recruit members. Management at Gaymers Cider held unfounded fears of possible nationalisation, discouraging their 300 workers from joining the Labour Party. At first, Joe found the meetings dull, focussing on fundraising and social activities. Nonetheless there were occasions when he could express his opinions, many of them in line with the left of the Party. Most political debate took place at the Executive meetings of South Norfolk Constituency Labour Party, to which the Attleborough branch could appoint two members. When a vacancy next occurred Joe was nominated and elected.

Joe was familiar with speaking to an audience. It held no fear for him. He continued to attend branch meetings, proposing the formation of a local Labour League of Youth. He was given approval, surprised at the encouraging response. Joe was able to report success not only to the local branch but also at constituency level. He was charged with exploring the possibility of setting up other youth branches. At a national level the League of Youth was seen to have Marxist tendencies, suspected of taking a critical stance towards Labour Party leadership. It was replaced by the Young Socialists in 1960.

Joe was next nominated for the Constituency Executive Committee, dealing with financial matters, followed by the General Committee and subsequently the Management Committee. It was here where the real decisions were made. This elevated position found him working closely with the first Labour Member of Parliament for South Norfolk, Christopher Mayhew. Mayhew, from a wealthy Norfolk family with large estates in Felthorp, was also a distinguished ex-soldier who had served in the Special Operations Executive. His politics were too far to the right for Joe's taste, possibly explaining Mayhew's appeal to the so-called 'soft Tory' voters in the mainly rural constituency. As the preparation for the 1950 General Election began, Joe became a central figure in the organisation, called upon to chair public meetings, including one with Jim Callaghan, a future Prime Minister, as the main speaker. Along with many other Labour candidates Mayhew lost his seat.

During that 1950 campaign Joe worked alongside Secretary-Agent Jock Watson. Originally from Scotland, Jock was in his early fifties and a great character, grateful for Joe's help as he attempted to keep in contact with activists scattered throughout the rural area. Very few members had a car, including Joe, resulting in Jock having to offer lifts to everyone. Joe valued his advice and found himself inspired by this Scotsman, perhaps reminding him of the many he met while training with the Army in Glasgow. At work when it became known that Joe was a card-carrying member of the Labour Party, the bosses became nervous. Office workers, despite earning no more than those on the factory floor, were expected to side with management.

It was time to move on.

New Horizons

'In 1950 a vacancy occurred for a full-time Labour Party Secretary-Agent in the neighbouring constituency of Central Norfolk which totally encircled Norwich, including the suburbs, small towns, villages and hamlets.'

The job sounded perfect. The current agent in Central Norfolk was moving to Australia with her husband, clearing the way for someone new to take up the challenge. Joe approached a contact or two in Norwich to learn exactly which areas would be on 'his patch'. The office was based in the city, necessitating a house move for him, his heavily-pregnant wife and three-year-old Jane. Jean was quite keen to move; her parents had been wonderful but she wanted a place of their own again. Joe researched the salary, impressed by the £600 a year on offer, half as much again as he earned in Wymondham. Jock encouraged him to apply, decrying Joe's insecurity that the task would be too big for him to handle.

Joe ensured he was in good time for his interview, fervently believing that good timekeeping went hand-in-hand with good manners. He confidently answered all the questions concerning fund-raising, campaigning and office procedures. The panel chairman then delicately put a potential problem to the candidate. 'How do you think the farm workers in the villages, the base of our support, will react to someone who has a bit of a foreign accent?'

Joe calmly replied that the panel were probably in a better position than he to answer that one, adding that whilst at school, in the Army, at work or whilst visiting the branches for meetings or social events, he had never been conscious of any ill-feeling. Satisfied, the chairman offered Joe the job, subject, however, to him learning to drive and finding a house in the city. For Joe it was like a dream come true. Here was a full-time paid job where he could indulge his passion for politics. No matter that it was a safe Tory seat, he could work on that. He would have lots of support from the active branches in the villages of Sprowston, Thorpe St Andrew and Hellesdon.

It had been suggested at the interview that Joe might wish to apply to join the council waiting list for a house on the expanding estates in Tuckswood or West Earlham. There was concern, however, that the list was very long and they needed him as soon as he had worked out his notice at the Briton Brush Company. Fortunately the Constituency Chairman was in a position to offer Joe a small terraced house on Rose Lane in Norwich, suggesting that instead of paying the rent monthly in advance, Joe could settle at the end of each month. The property was a 'tied house', meaning that if and when Joe left the employment of Central Norfolk, he would have to vacate. Joe accepted, thinking it ironic that the issue of 'tied cottages' was, at that time a major concern in rural politics. The National Union of Agricultural Workers (NUAW), the mainstay of Labour support in the countryside, was leading the campaign for their abolition. Farmers were in the powerful position of being able not only to deprive workers of their jobs, but also to make their families homeless. Joe was now in the same situation.

It was the early spring of 1951 when the Stirling family moved into 44 Rose Lane, conveniently situated in the very centre of Norwich. It was exciting to live in a city with a Norman castle, red Routemaster buses, policemen wearing long white leather gloves while on point duty, 'Fifty Shilling Tailors', a permanent marketplace and six cinemas. There were reminders everywhere of the war; visible scars from over forty German bombing missions during 1942 known as the 'Baedeker Raids'. Whilst out walking Joe and Jean often had to negotiate potholes, cracked and uneven pavements, and mounds of bricks and boulders. Despite this the city was bustling, heavily reliant on manufacturing. Thousands of workers on their bicycles clogged the city roads on their way to and from shoe factories such as Southall's, Norvic, Bally and Van Dal, breweries including Bullard's and Steward & Patterson and the extensive Colman's Mustard factory down by the river. This blend of products meant that the city air was continually awash with a pungent cocktail of leather, spices and yeast. Jean felt sure they would get used to the smell in time.

Joe's priority was to refurbish their new home but his budget was tight. He laid linoleum throughout, bought second-hand furniture and designated the back parlour as 'Joe's Office'. There was very little storage space and the tiny kitchen was equipped only with the basics of kitchen utensils, crockery and glass. Just like both Joe and Jean's childhood homes, Rose Lane had no indoor bathroom, just a lean-to shed on the outside wall with an overhead-cistern toilet. But it was home and they made it their own.

A short stroll up the steep Rose Lane led them to the Norwich livestock market, stood beneath the walls of the eleventh-century castle. Opened in 1738, it was the largest cattle market in the country. Every Saturday Joe and Jean watched as over 3,000 cattle and sheep arrived on lorries or on railway trucks, driven across the bridge over the River Wensum and up Rose Lane, passing Joe's house, into the metal pens ready for viewing before the auction. An apocryphal tale claimed that in the past certain pub landlords would steal sheep by opening their beer cellar trapdoors to let one fall in as it passed by. The smells and sounds on market days reminded Joe of strolling around Koblenz cattle market hand-in-hand with *Opa*. As well as causing chaos to the traffic, the animals invariably left a dreadful mess on the roads, the stench lingering for days, blending with the already 'scented' air, particularly in high summer. It was the duty of the people who lived there to clean his or her half of the street. With no houses on the opposite side, Joe cleaned both sides, creating an ever-growing muckheap in his cobbled backyard.

There remained the issue of learning to drive and buying a car. With the Party's branches spread over a large rural area it was impractical for the Agent to rely on public transport. The Labour Party offered Joe a small loan enabling him to buy a pre-war car. During the conflict petrol had been severely rationed, only those in essential occupations allowed to use it. Comparatively few people owned a car before the war, and those who did simply left their vehicles in the backyard or in a garage for the duration. Joe was able to pick up a 1935 Austin

Eight with sweeping running boards, iconic grill and bug-eyed headlamps. He could not afford driving lessons but he had friends willing to teach him.

Anxious to obtain his licence Joe applied for his test too soon and was disappointed to fail. It was back to driving around a disused Royal Air Force airfield, north of the city, performing manoeuvre after manoeuvre, accelerating as fast as he dare down the wide runways. Test number two held its own challenges for the little car and an unsatisfactory emergency stop resulted in further failure. His examiner suggested he take some professional lessons, recommending he use a driving-school car for the next test. Two lessons later Joe passed, much to Jean's delight. The family could now drive to Attleborough, visit her parents, enjoy Lucy's Sunday lunch and relax while the proud grandparents entertained lively four-year-old Jane.

Well, that was the theory.

New Baby, New Job

'It was my job to design posters, write leaflets, organise helpers and issue press releases where meetings had not attracted a reporter.'

On Monday 23 April 1951, barely settled in to her new home, Jean gave birth to their son Ian. Jean adored the tiny baby stage and while she busied herself with the little chap, Joe spent more time with his daughter, helping her with letters and numbers. He was determined that Jane should be reading before joining Thorpe Hamlet Infant School the following September. Now that he was mobile, Joe could throw himself into the work, raising money for the forthcoming General Election campaign in October, called by the Labour Government needing to increase its slim five-seat majority. The Labour candidate for Central Norfolk was Jack Lambley, the District Organiser of the National Union of Agricultural and Allied Workers (NUAW). Most people were quietly convinced that Labour could not possibly win the seat, but Jack was an optimist, counting on the loyal support of the agricultural workers, ignoring the fact that the 40 per cent suburban population in the constituency were predominantly Conservative voters. On polling day, Labour lost both in Central Norfolk and nationally. The Tories took the country, winning with a majority of sixteen seats. Winston Churchill was once again Prime Minister of Great Britain.

Joe's fundraising scheme, from which he had to fund his own salary, was going well with every branch working hard to sell as many sealed draw tickets as possible. The activists and members were occasionally treated to a family double act, Joe and four-year-old Jane amusing the audience with a mind-reading act. Blindfolded, Jane stood on the stage facing away from the audience. Her father went up to a member of the audience and ask something like, 'Jane, what colour are this lady's shoes?' Jane would then miraculously give the correct answer. Joe had of course, taught his very bright daughter a number of code words, each denoting particular colours or numbers. With her father out at work for much of the time, the little girl loved these special afternoons together; relishing the opportunities to rattle, bump and shake around the Norfolk villages, snug in the deep leather front seat, alongside her hero, cocooned in their very own black box chariot.

Joe quickly joined the Trades Union for Labour Party Agents. With only 300 agents throughout the country, the Union was relatively small. But Joe was well aware that agents' salaries, terms and conditions would all be negotiated at national level and it was important to be involved. The Party welcomed the Union, finding the members' newsletter the most efficient method of communicating national policy and issues down to the agents. Joe spent three further years working for Central Norfolk, putting in long hours, increasing his knowledge and building both contacts and his reputation.

He was starting to feel at home.

Letter from the Past

'I had no death certificates for my parents and matters relating to the loss their business or income were beyond my knowledge.'

The Norfolk weather in January 1953 wreaked havoc throughout the region. On the afternoon of Saturday 31 January Norwich City players struggled to control the ball in high winds. By six that evening the North Sea was breaching the defences of Hunstanton, King's Lynn, Heacham, Sea Palling and Great Yarmouth. Over eighty people died. Although the city fared better than coastal towns and villages, Rose Lane faced a cascade of water mixed with mud and dung flooding down the hill from the Cattle Market, racing into Joe's backyard. Joe and Jean were two of the more fortunate residents, making sure the water failed to seep into the house.

During February an overseas letter fell onto the mat at Number 44. It was both a shock and a pleasure to be reconnected with his past so unexpectedly. His mother's eldest sister, Aunt Martha, by means that will remain a mystery, had finally succeeded in finding her nephew, having been trying to trace him since the end of the war. She and her family had been forced to flee their Alsace home in 1940 when the Nazis reclaimed the territory from the French. They settled in Vichy France, surviving both the war and the Holocaust. Once it was deemed safe, Aunt Martha and her husband returned to Germany to track down property and possessions left behind when they fled. They also searched for Alfred and Ida. There was no evidence of them or of their belongings, neither in Nickenich nor Koblenz.

In March 1952 formal negotiations had began in The Hague between the government of Israel and the Federal Republic of Germany. By September an agreement was signed leading to German legislation agreeing compensation payments to Holocaust survivors, albeit on a strict and limited basis. Martha was determined to advise her nephew of his right to compensation. Her letter enclosed two application forms. Joe simply refused to consider it. He wanted nothing to do with Germany. Without death certificates and with no idea of the worth, if any, of his father's business, how could he possibly answer the questions? He had been only a boy when he left Germany. Despite Jean's efforts to make her stubborn husband see sense, he wrote back to his aunt explaining why he would not be making a claim.

Martha was adamant; Joe was a family man now. Surely he could use the money? She went back to the authorities and obtained an official statement that Joe's parents had been deported to Poland. As there was no sign that they had survived, it could be presumed they were dead. A few weeks later a further letter arrived, urging Joe to put aside his principles and to be pragmatic. The envelope contained two replacement claim forms for the loss of two lives, helpfully completed by Aunt Martha, along with one for loss of educational opportunities due to expulsion from school following *Kristallnacht*. Aunt Martha knew nothing of Joe's education in England and so left him to fill in that one. To the question, 'What further education did you have in England?' Joe detailed his four years at Grammar School. He reluctantly signed the forms, enclosed proof of his change of name and returned the pre-paid envelope to the claims office in Bonn, the capital of post-war West Germany.

He wasted no time dwelling on it. Not only did he have a job to do, but also the country was ready to party. King George VI had died at Sandringham early in February 1952, having been unwell for some time. It had taken over a year for the government to make arrangements for the Coronation of Queen Elizabeth II, but now it was about to take place on 2 June. The day arrived with the weather sadly not in celebratory mood. Driving rain and cold winds throughout the day and evening endeavoured to dampen the British spirit. But it would take more than a few black clouds to spoil the country's optimism. Tea and sweets were now off ration and Britain had a delightful young couple on the throne. With Prince Charles born in November 1948, the future of the monarchy seemed assured.

Along with all children in Norwich, Jane and Ian received a souvenir round tin of toffees from local firm Mackintoshes, presented with a purple-coloured 'Coronation Book'. Family members, friends and neighbours, keen to watch the ceremony live from London on the BBC, inundated those households wealthy enough to own one of the early black and white television sets. Joe didn't yet own such a contraption and knew no one who did. The family listened on the radio, as the BBC commentary team of John Snagg, Frank Gillard and Audrey Russell brought to life the golden coach, 7,000-strong congregation, extravagant robes, sashes, sparkling jewellery and the charming figure of the young Queen herself. As they slurped Heinz tomato soup from Coronation mugs, the citizens of Norwich listened enraptured to the haunting choral chant of 'Vivat Regina' as it set the tone for an unprecedented display of tradition and splendour. Others chose to leave work early and watch the repeat at local cinemas, benefiting from the colour images, especially poignant as Elizabeth donned the shimmering golden cape in preparation for the Archbishop to hold St Edward's Crown aloft before creating the monarch.

Despite the pouring rain, during the afternoon Joe and his family joined the crowds to witness the procession of servicemen and women from all over the region marching with rifles, burnished buttons and whitened belts through Norwich city centre, the scene awash with union flags, the salute taken outside City Hall by the Lord Mayor, Ralph Hale Mottram.

Undeterred by the never-ending deluge, the people of Norfolk spent the rest of Coronation Day at tea parties, street festivals, family gatherings, fancy-dress parades (Quality Street sweet wrappers made authentic-looking jewels in cardboard tiaras) and carnival processions. Nothing was cancelled because of the weather, apart from in Great Yarmouth, where the extremely choppy waters on the river meant a planned procession of decorated boats was abandoned, organisers being unable to guarantee the safety of the children. Instead every child was given a free ice-cream cone to enjoy as they cheered the carnival procession through the town, albeit a wet and bedraggled one. Even the firework display went ahead that evening, although many of the rockets were lost from sight inside the low black clouds. It had been a great day. Dr Geoffrey Fisher, Archbishop of Canterbury later remarked that 'the Country and the Commonwealth had been on Coronation Day not far from the Kingdom of Heaven'.

Joe had almost forgotten his aunt's efforts when during the winter of 1954 he received a response from Germany. The notification stated that on the basis of the presumed murder of his parents by the State, he was entitled to a payment of £120 each for the lives of his father and mother. His claim for compensation for loss of education had been rejected, arguing that he had received a better education in Britain than he would have had in Germany. Joe did not disagree.

The money was welcome but receiving it was profoundly unsettling.

Harwich By-election

'I was asked if I would go down and help with the Harwich by-election. The candidate was a young woman called Shirley Catlin. I thought I knew her mum.'

In January 1954 Joe received a missive from Labour Headquarters in London. His experience working in rural villages and small towns would be beneficial in fighting the by-election scheduled for 11 February. The Member of Parliament for Harwich, John Stanley Holmes, having held the seat for the National Liberals since 1935 was about to be elevated to the peerage. A by-election would need to be called.

The previous autumn Shirley Catlin, at only twenty-two, had been proposed by constituency chairman Joe Watson, to be the prospective Labour candidate for the safe National Liberal and Conservative constituency of Harwich. In her 2009 autobiography *Climbing the Bookshelves*, Shirley Williams describes her selection as 'something of a fiddle'. In those difficult days for the Labour Party, with no hope of winning the seat, the selection committee found themselves with a straight choice between the constituency chairman Joe Watson, who had previously made it clear he did not wish to stand, or an enthusiastic female postgraduate with no experience of standing for Parliament. However, Miss Catlin came with good credentials. Not only had she been the first female elected president of the Oxford University Labour Club in 1950, but she was also the daughter of the pacifist and successful writer Vera Brittain, whose autobiographical study of the First World War, *Testament of Youth*, published in 1933, was a bestseller on both sides of the Atlantic.

Joe left Norwich for Harwich in January 1954 in bitterly cold conditions with threatening snowfalls. He was one of three professional party agents sent to help, all working in different areas. Joe's colleagues concentrated on the urban voters including those in Harwich and its Port, the holiday destination of Clacton-on-Sea and the more elitist Frinton-on-Sea. With his experience of rural areas, Joe's brief was to organise the campaign throughout the villages in the Parish of Tendring. Potential Labour voters resided in small communities such as Manningtree, Elmstead and Dovercourt, the latter where so many of the *Kindertransport* refugees had stayed in a summer holiday camp awaiting sponsors, following their arrival at Harwich during 1938–9. However, the lack of trades union activity in the mainly agricultural area meant that finding support for local meetings proved difficult.

On being introduced to the 'schoolgirl candidate', as the national press described her, Joe was impressed by this eloquent and ardent young woman. Joe arranged public meetings, often two or three in the same evening and Shirley would join him, searching in the blackness of the Essex countryside for village halls and back rooms in pubs. The audiences were invariably small but Joe had the knack of encouraging support from nearby settlements. His candidate deserved a decent turnout. In conversation, on breaks from knocking on doors, Joe told her of how his guardian in Birmingham, Freda Free, had often spoken of her friendship with Vera Brittain, her friend at Somerville College in Oxford during the 1920s. Mrs Free was so proud of Vera's success with her book and subsequent lecture tour of America. Günter had also heard all about Vera's little girl Shirley, three years older than Margaret. Mrs Free had included news of her friend in letters to Lydney. Anxious to reassure the refugee that others too were sent overseas by loving parents to ensure their safety, she told him of young Shirley and her older brother John being sent by ship to Canada in June 1940, to escape the bombing in London.

But that was nearly fifteen years earlier. Shirley had proved an ambitious and intelligent young woman, studying from 1948 at Somerville College in Oxford, as her mother and Freda Free had before her. Vera Brittain was unconditionally proud of her daughter, whom she addressed as 'Poppy', telling friends that Shirley would make her way by 'charm, vitality and sheer goodness'. Vera was determined to help Shirley with her first by-election, and despite hating the cold, spent two days canvassing in Harwich, addressing an eve-of-poll meeting. Vera took the precaution of arriving with warm 'woollen vests and pants of the kind neither of us ever normally wore'. Unfortunately for Joe, that evening he was kept busy in the outlying areas, pushing election literature through letterboxes, not coming into Harwich. His devotion to the cause meant he missed his only opportunity to shake the hand of Mrs Free's celebrated college friend. Labour lost the by-election to the only other candidate, the Conservative Julian Errington Risdale, a glass manufacturer. Regretfully for Joe and his fellow activists, the Labour share of the vote decreased slightly. The challenge had proved insurmountable and the Tory majority stood at 6,000.

Nevertheless, both Shirley and Joe had learnt important lessons about campaigning against the odds.

Promotion

'I knew that the pay in Norwich Party office was £1,000, a big jump. I wouldn't even need a car; I could walk or go by bus. My good friend in Rose Lane applied for the job and he encouraged me to do the same. I thought he would get it as he was experienced and a really nice chap.'

In March 1954 Bill Butcher, the secretary-agent for the Norwich Labour Party, resigned, returning to his previous life as a full time official of one of the print Unions. This left a tempting vacancy. Since boundary changes in 1950 Norwich was split into two parliamentary seats. In 1954, Norwich South was represented by Conservative MP Henry Strauss, with the more industrialised Norwich North represented by Labour MP John Paton.

In local government terms, Norwich was a county borough, responsible for controlling all the powers within its boundaries as granted by Parliament to local authorities. In the mid-1950s, the borough council was predominantly Labour and affiliated to the Norwich Trades Council, a miniature replica of the national Trades Union Congress. Consequently, the Norwich secretary-agent role was deemed to be far more responsible than that for the rural constituencies, justifying a greater remuneration of £1,000 per annum.

The benefits of the role were apparent and after four and a half years with Central Norfolk, Joe was interested, although dubious about his chances. Jean and Joe talked it over, Jean always willing to trust her husband and support his ambition. There were nine other candidates, with one agent travelling up from London for the interviews on a Saturday morning in May. Much to his surprise, Joe was offered the job. He commiserated with the runner-up, a good friend and neighbour. The two men agreed there were no ill feelings and their friendship continued unabated.

An immediate problem was the family home. The Rose Lane house was tied to the job for Central Norfolk. The Stirling family would have to move out. It was now that Aunt Martha's persistence really paid off. The compensation from the German government was safely in the bank and could now be used as a deposit on a house. The pay rise would enable Joe to support a mortgage. He applied to Norwich Council and was offered the favourable rate of a fifteen-year fixed-term loan at 3.5 per cent per annum. Joe considered himself very fortunate when, within six months, the interest rates started to increase steadily, rising within two years to 6.5 per cent.

Following Joe's resignation, his colleagues donated towards a parting gift. At the reunion event, the Labour Prospective Parliamentary Candidate for

Central Norfolk, Elisabeth Littlejohn, paid tribute to Joe's past work. She presented him with a substantial cheque adding, 'If Mr Stirling's record in Central Norfolk is anything to go by, he will succeed in Norwich at the next General Election by returning a Labour member to Parliament.' The applause echoed around the hall.

During the autumn of 1954, the Stirling family moved into a three-bedroomed mid-terrace town house, at 62 St Clements Hill, ironically in the middle of a Tory stronghold. Joe, Jean, and Jane unpacked boxes, finding homes for everything, while three-year-old Ian set about undoing much of their hard work. From the third floor, they could see over Sewell Park and into the grounds of the Blyth School, a girls' grammar school, directly opposite the house. Seven-year-old Jane was transferred from Thorpe Hamlet to George White Junior School in Silver Road, settling in and progressing well. The house had cost him a little more than Joe would have liked, but Jean loved the property, delighted at last to be buying instead of renting. A back boiler heated the water and the living room had a coal fire. Jean felt at last she could fully demonstrate her talents as mother and homemaker. It wasn't too long before she made close friends, particularly neighbours Peggy Williamson and Olive Tichurst. Peggy's children, Betty and Robert, befriended Jane and Ian, the four occasionally joined by Olive's daughter June as they played games of rounders outside the prefabricated houses in nearby Millers Lane.

The boys played Cowboys and Indians while Jane and the girls took turns to ride her scooter down the gentle slopes of St Clements. Ian built a trolley with a wooden platform on top of four old pram wheels. This contraption was confiscated following an incident when Ian failed to stop at the junction and shot across the main road almost in front of a bus. He was unhurt but Joe and Jean took no further chances. Ian may have been a reckless child but at least he slept at night. The house had a cellar with a door from the hall opening onto a flight of stone steps, leading down to the coal store. There was a hatch in the front wall of the house, through which the coalmen would empty their sacks, the coal tumbling down, coating everything with a thick layer of black soot. A nervous child and scared of the dark, Jane worried most nights that someone might be lurking down there. The children were discouraged from playing in the cellar.

Jane didn't need telling twice.

Trades Council

'I had more involvement with Joe at Trades Council meetings. Joe was a very good speaker and always spoke a lot of common sense. He used to wait until the very end before he made his comments and I would wait to hear what Joe had to say before making up my mind. He had such sensible ideas.' (Joyce Morgan, Lord Mayor of Norwich 1975–6, speaking in 2012)

Joe took his new role as Secretary-Agent for the Norwich Labour Party very seriously. He set about developing a working relationship with the sitting Labour MP for Norwich North, 68-year-old John Paton. On his occasional visits from London, his distinctive high-pitched voice and 'Queen's English' pronunciation contrasted sharply with the local broad Norfolk dialect. Joe embraced his new role, finding it both challenging and stimulating. Based at the Norwich Labour Club in Bethel Street, he shared an office with an assistant, who managed the Club, the bar and the social functions, allowing Joe to concentrate on the politics. His new patch was split into sixteen wards each with its own Labour Party branch. The strongest and most active ward organisations were in the marginal council seats, the very safe wards barely bothering to muster a quorum; whilst 'hopeless' wards limped along with very small membership figures. Fundraising was of prime importance, even more so than in his previous position. The Norwich raffle ticket scheme worked on a much larger scale than that in Central Norfolk, with proportionately higher value prizes. Tickets were sold in most factories and even in some city pubs.

Although councillors were elected for a four-year term, Norwich organised the local council elections 'by thirds'. A third of the elected members stood in three of the four years, with the fourth year being the county council election. This called for crippling annual campaign budgets. Joe spent much of his time preparing agendas and reports for monthly meetings of the Executive Committee, before taking, transcribing and distributing the minutes. He particularly relished the quarterly General Meetings, more widely representative of wards and unions. Members were encouraged to debate political issues, both local and national. The arguments and discussion was invariably excellent, Joe totally absorbed.

His job description included acting as Secretary to the local Trades Council. Despite being a member of the Labour Party Agents Union for some years, he still had limited knowledge of the structure and organisation of trade unions. He was relieved when Bill Butcher offered to assist with the preparatory work for his first meeting. Union members, representing very different jobs, industries and professions, populated these meetings. Representing the Labour Party itself was Joyce Morgan, petite and blonde, just two years older than Joe and one of the very few women involved at that level. The group discussed a variety of issues including working conditions, employment levels, specifically in relation to the City of Norwich. It wasn't long before Joe made his mark, speaking his mind with confidence, shrewdly ensuring he was the last to speak in a debate, his views fresh in the minds of his colleagues before any vote. Joyce was impressed.

Neither she nor Joe knew how close they were to become twenty years later.

Return to Germany

'Jean and I had talked for a year or two about visiting Germany and felt that with the children now seven and three we could go, as long my old banger was judged to be capable of getting us there.'

Until the mid-1950s very few people in Great Britain could afford to travel abroad. But as employment and the economy improved, the 'New Elizabethans' began to benefit from the fledgling welfare state. Luxuries, including overseas holidays, seemed finally to be within reach of the masses. It was in this spirit of adventure and widening horizons that Joe took on his new role in the Norwich Labour Club and before long his background became a topic of interest. A colleague approached Joe in the office.

'Joe, you come from the Rhineland. I hear it's a nice place. Why don't you organise a trip for the Labour Club?'

It was an intriguing idea. But Joe was not about to arrange anything in a hurry. It had been fifteen years since he was last in Germany, would it still be recognisable after the fighting? He would need to investigate; an ideal excuse to take a much-needed family holiday. During the late summer of 1954, suitcases packed and loaded, the Austin Eight rumbled into Dover, to be unceremoniously hoisted by crane into the hold of the Channel ferry, Jane and Ian gazing up in awe.

The journey took them through southern Belgium into Luxembourg, where as a boy Joe had waded across the River Sauer to escape Nazi Germany. His memories returned in sharp relief as he stared down into the water. After a night stop in an inexpensive hotel, their route followed the Mosel and on towards Koblenz. Joe had learnt of a small farm in the hills on the far side of the Rhine, towards his grandfather's town of Montabaur. The farmer had recently converted his stables into guest bedrooms, shrewdly taking advantage of the burgeoning interest in touring the Continent. The sights and smells of the farmyard fascinated the children and after tea the two of them followed their parents through the landscape of their ancestors, until little Ian complained of tired legs. But this trip was intended to be more than merely rest and relaxation. The final few days were spent in Koblenz and Andernach, researching small hotels and inns suitable for a touring group from England. Work done, Joe could now face the most significant visit of all for Nickenich was just a short drive away.

The children ran through chest high meadow grass, picking wild flowers on the banks of the *Laacher See*, just as their father had done nearly two decades earlier. Joe drove into the centre of the village, parking on the roadside at the foot of the quiet *Hintergasse*. As they strolled the length of the lane, Joe felt a little anxious as he pointed out the homes of friends and neighbours. It was all so familiar and yet as if from a dream. Joe's childhood home was exactly as he remembered it. His school appeared to still be a school. But the Egeners' house was no longer a shop. There was no sign of the Marx family. From nowhere, an elderly lady asked if they were looking for the lake. Joe felt the bile of hostility suddenly rise up in his throat. It hadn't occurred to him that he might be harbouring any bitterness. But it had been in these very homes, on that dreadful November night in 1938, that the villagers of Nickenich had turned their backs on his family, too afraid to help as his father was dragged into the street, his mother left to fend for herself and her son. Joe found himself uncharacteristically edgy and unhelpful, muttering something to the woman whilst ushering his family back to the car.

It was time to go home.

Tour Leader

'I discovered that with a group I would be entitled to a free travel ticket and the hotel would give me a room and meals free, provided there were at least thirty paying guests.'

Quite undeterred by his limited experience of arranging travel itineraries, Joe continued with his research into train and ferry tickets, Koblenz bus companies and possible destinations for day excursions. Throughout many complex overseas telephone enquiries, his German language skills proved invaluable and despite constantly being cut off, he was able to spend evenings during the winter and spring of 1954–5, designing a 'package holiday' for Labour Club members. Gradually the plan took shape. Taking into account the train from Norwich to Harwich, ferry crossing, Lorelei Express to Koblenz via Cologne, fourteen nights' accommodation, full board and excursions by coach and river steamer, he was able to establish a cost price of £25 each, about two weeks wages for an average worker.

With a young family and mortgage to support, Joe would have struggled to afford a place on his own trip. However, with his acute business sense, quite possibly acquired from Uncle Alex, he discovered that by booking thirty travellers or more on a group rate, the tour organiser benefitted from not only a free rail ticket but also a hotel room and all meals. Joe distributed some simple duplicated leaflets to members of the Labour Club; placing a classified advert in the *Eastern Evening News*, explaining that membership of the Labour Club was a requisite for joining the trip. Joe waited for responses, unconvinced he would have any takers.

Allied bombs had destroyed 85 per cent of the Rhineland city of Koblenz in 1944. Ten years later, here was a rare opportunity for the citizens of Norwich to witness how the old enemy was reinventing itself from the rubble. Joe was agreeably surprised. People were quick to respond. Joe's ambition to fill an excursion coach was fulfilled within a couple of weeks. Every one of the forty seats was taken. He had received enough enquiries to open a waiting list for a similar trip sometime in the future. Joe made no promises; he would wait and see how this first one worked out. Amongst those booking early were leading members of local society, Sheriff of Norwich George Carver and Councillor Alfred Nichols (a future Lord Mayor from 1960–1), accompanied by their wives, Elsie and Olive. Also packing his suitcase was Fred Watts, the Managing Director of Tom Watts Furniture Store in King Street, one of the largest in East Anglia and a senior figure in the local Labour Party.

The youngest travellers on this new venture were two colleagues from the accounts and the press office at Norwich Union. Brenda Buck and Josie Mitchell, both in their early twenties, had visited mainland Europe the summer before, visiting Bruges together. But Brenda had always wanted to visit Germany, ever since, as a fourteen-year-old, she had fallen for Heinz, a German prisoner of war. Heinz, from Kiel in northern Germany, had been in the Luftwaffe. At eighteen he and his best friend were shot out of the sky over Norfolk. His friend didn't make it. Heinz found himself in a prison camp on Mousehold Heath overlooking Norwich, a vast area filled with Nissen huts and tents.

To pass the time Heinz joined other prisoners to form a choir. Brenda's father invited them to his Methodist chapel in the city, as entertainment for a group of blind people. Brenda was taken with the young man, persuading her father to invite Heinz home for tea, more than once. Disturbed by this blossoming relationship, Brenda's parents 'had a word' with the authorities and Heinz was quickly transferred to Bedford. After the war, Brenda harboured a belief that if she were to visit Germany, she might just bump into Heinz. Joe's advert in the evening paper was too tempting to ignore. Brenda and Josie paid the five shillings' subscription each to join the Labour Party, turning up every Friday evening to pay the next instalment. Once there, they treated themselves to a Babycham and giggled their way through a German conversation lesson led by a bemused Joe. In August, the evening before the trip, Joe held a 'bonding' party at the Labour Club for his group. The councillors displayed their medals; Brenda and Josie demonstrated their jive moves.

The following morning Joe kissed Jean, Jane, Ian and their most recent baby Martin, born the previous January. Daddy would be gone for two weeks. The steam locomotive pulled out of Norwich Thorpe Road Station, the concourse thick with smoke. There was one change at Manningtree where they joined the Harwich train, heading for the night ferry to adventure. It was almost dusk when the train pulled into Parkeston Quay, the exuberant travellers catching their first glimpse of the ship. As the ferry steamed sedately from her berth, heading out through Harwich Harbour to the North Sea and the Hook of Holland, tour guide Joe was distracted by a personal Magic Lantern show, pictures from his past filling his head. He had sailed these waters before.

The group travelled by train through northern Europe to Cologne. Here they were astonished at the devastation. Only the famous cathedral was left standing, the remainder of the city a lake of stones and twisted metal. Cologne heralded a transfer to the Lorelei Express for Koblenz. Joe had booked modest accommodation in the city, convenient for exploring. It seemed that every building was pitted with bullet holes, roof tops blown away, sludge-filled craters at every turn and cracked windows held together with tape. Koblenz was in a far worse state than Norwich. The hotel was compact but comfortable enough, with shared facilities excluding running water. Every morning the hotelier carried jugs of hot water to the bedrooms. The locals were delighted to see valuable overseas visitors, making every effort to entertain them in return for their Deutschmarks. Severe post-war hardship and shortages meant that food was still fairly basic; mainly wild boar and sauerkraut, a German delicacy amounting to bowls of acidic stringy white cabbage. The English were not impressed. After several nights of this, somebody complained. 'Could we have some fish and chips?' Anxious to please, the chef tried his best. A whole pike, teeth bared, was served up on a plate. Joe, sympathetic, refunded everyone's five shillings they had pre-paid for the meal.

Coaches had been arranged to take the visitors out, including half a day at the *Laacher See* and Abbey. Everyone was thrilled to have a spectacular drive around the famous Nürburg Ring, complete with a waving chequered flag as the coach crossed the finish line. Afternoons were spent shopping in the towns of Altenahr and Andernach and then the highlight; a cruise up the majestic Rhine to the town of St Goarshausen, where *Die Lorelei* rock towers 120 metres over the river. Legend tells of a lovelorn blonde-haired beauty, looking remarkably like a mermaid, sitting high on the rock, luring innocent sailors to their deaths in the swirling waters with her sad songs. As tradition dictates, the German day-trippers enthusiastically sang the well-known song about the mythical temptress. Joe knew all the words.

Die schönste Jungfrau sitzet
Dort oben wunderbar,
Ihr gold'nes Geschmeide blitzet,
Sie kämmt ihr goldenes Haar,
Sie kämmt es mit goldenem Kamme,
Und singt ein Lied dabei;
Das hat eine wundersame,
Gewalt'ge Melodei.

(The loveliest maiden is sitting
Up there, so wondrously fair;
Her golden jewelry is glist'ning;
She combs her golden hair.
She combs with a gilded comb, preening,
And sings a song, passing time.
It has a most wondrous, appealing
And pow'rful melodic rhyme.)

Evenings were spent exploring the alleyways of the *Altstadt* close to where Joe had lived and relaxing in the *Weingarten* by the ruin of *Deutsches Eck* (German Corner), lit by magical lanterns, quaffing frothy German beer or sipping a glass of Riesling. With Joe in charge there was never any language problem, they simply let him speak for them. He had thought of everything. As a token of their appreciation, the group clubbed together to buy a Dresden vase. Much to the amusement of the girls, Joe was the only traveller to be stopped at German customs on their way home.

Sitting up on deck, the English coastline looming ahead of them, Joe was distracted by echoes from his past. Without warning, he felt a weight on his shoulder. He caught his breath, for a brief moment uncertain of quite where he was. Becoming aware of the bracing wind, Joe turned to find his friend Fred Watts gently shaking his arm. Fred glanced briefly towards his companions; George and Elsie huddled together on a wooden bench deep in discussion with Alfred and Olive. On the seaward side, over by the rail, he could make out Brenda and Josie, both tugging on their rayon silk circle skirts, preserving their modesty in the strong sea breezes. No one was within earshot. Fred leaned conspiratorially towards Joe.

'Joe, don't tell anyone I said so, but you're wasting your time working for us at the Labour Party. What you really should be doing is organising more trips like this. I'm sure you could build up a good little business.'

This was not the time to consider the implications. Once the ferry was securely moored, Joe led his weary party from the boat and onto the platform at Parkeston Quay to await the Norwich train. He was looking forward to getting home.

There was a pressing conversation to be had.

Chapter 4

Businessman and Lion, 1955–1970

Open for Business

'Bookings started coming in during January 1957. By the end of February all twelve tours to five different places were booked apart from one in mid-May. That also booked up, but it took a little longer.'

It was risky. They had no capital and any decision to give up a steady, reasonably well-paid job in order to become self-employed was not to be taken lightly. Without Jean's blessing Joe would not have taken that step. But Jean said yes. He was instantly energised to transform Fred Watts' suggestion into a reality. Fred continued to encourage his friend, offering him a small stand every Saturday on the shop floor of his furniture store in King Street. This way Joe could introduce his travel business to the public and gauge the response. It was too good an offer to turn down.

In 1955 there were no digital shortcuts to researching holiday destinations. For many months, when not actually working for the Labour Party, Joe borrowed books from the library, often working well into the early hours, researching German-speaking holiday areas such as the Black Forest, mountain and lakeside resorts in Austria and Switzerland and even a corner of Northern Italy, formerly the Austrian South Tyrol, where German was still understood. None of those locations were served by existing coach tour companies picking up at Norwich. He looked into how to find the best exchange rates for the Deutschmark, Schilling and Swiss Franc. Encouraged by this gap in the market, Joe used his leave entitlement from the Labour Party to travel by train and ferry to Freiburg and Innsbruck, areas as yet unfamiliar to him, exploring the regions, identifying suitable accommodation and coach companies. He negotiated the best possible prices for local excursions, increasingly enamoured by the business concept.

In Norwich, Joe called at a small printing firm he had used for Labour Party material, commissioning them to print his simple leaflets offering escorted visits to five different locations including Koblenz. Classified adverts in the local press invited people either to collect a copy at Tom Watts furniture store, or by calling at Joe's home in St Clements Hill. Confident now that this was his future career, Joe gave the Labour Party a generous three months' notice, allowing them plenty of time to find a replacement.

Without fully realising it, Joe was in a perfect position to benefit from an emerging market. During the first half of 1950s, life in Britain resembled a relentless treadmill of rationing, poverty and unemployment. Much of the country still resembled a war zone. Very few people could afford a holiday. Travelling abroad was simply an impossible fantasy. Those families able to take a break, looked no further than the nearest coastal resort. But by 1955 unemployment was at a post-war low of 1 per cent, and salaries and annual leave allowances were improving. For those in work holidays abroad seemed a little closer. The mid-1950s television boom, following the Queen's Coronation broadcast, brought exotic locations into everyone's living room. The response to Joe's advertising was encouraging. Poor Jean despaired as she scurried about, keeping the downstairs clear of drying nappies, wooden soldiers, coloured crayons and cobwebs, in case a potential client should turn up on her doorstep.

Stirling Holidays was open for business.

Trains and Boats and Buses

'On one occasion, as we got out of our excursion bus, some local children gathered in the hope of being given some sweets. After we got back in, one of the ladies sitting behind me said to the other, "You know these Germans are really clever. Their language sounds so difficult but even the young children can speak it".'

During his first summer season of 1957, Joe rode trains and ferries back and forth from Norwich to mainland Europe, introducing early clients to scenic towns and cities, previously just shadowy images on a Pathé newsreel. Joe assisted young and old lift their luggage onto unfamiliar Continental trains, counting them on and off coaches and checking them into hotels and guesthouses. For the fledgling travellers it was reassuring to be escorted door-to-door to a strange new land. They benefitted from a native German speaker acting both as interpreter and tour guide with informed commentaries in English. Meals were taken in the hotel restaurants, clients struggling with incomprehensible menus and waiters who only spoke German. Joe passed from table to table, helping them choose meals with confidence. But of course, Continental food was unfamiliar and Joe's tourists were invariably conventional in their tastes.

During one tour that first summer, two couples bravely decided to eat out on their own in a local restaurant. They fancied roast chicken, a real treat at that time, but could not make the waiters understand. One of the diners stood up, raised both elbows and flapped them up and down, clucking for all he was worth. 'Ah, ein moment', said the waiter, disappearing into the kitchen. Eventually four plates arrived, each covered with a lid. With much ceremony the lids were lifted and there was their dinner – four fat omelettes!

One young couple looking for a summer break were decorator Tom Wooldridge and his wife Margaret, a comptometer operator with Boulton and Paul, the well-known Norwich engineering factory. In a newsagent's window opposite Timber Hill, a typed notice advertised holidays in the Rhineland during August. Tom and Margaret had never been abroad. This could be the time before babies robbed them of Margaret's wage. The couple collected a leaflet from St Clements Hill and took it to show Margaret's parents, Geoffrey and Edith Grigglestone in Ketts Hill. Edith made tea and the family discussed the possibility of taking a holiday together. Geoffrey encouraged the idea. As a wounded veteran of the First World War, he harboured an ambition to see the homeland of his former adversaries. Most industry and commerce in Norwich closed down during August for the annual fortnight break. That was the time to visit Koblenz. The cost of the two-week holiday was £26, just £1 more than the Labour Party trip in 1955 with a £3 deposit requested from each client. Joe's confirmation letters, each typed individually, included a fully-detailed itinerary for a specific trip. Additionally he added invaluable advice, particularly pertinent for the first time traveller.

a. Don't wear your best clothes on the journey, that is our advice from much experience.

b. Take it easy. The best thing about a personally conducted STIRLING HOLIDAYS Tour is that you can completely relax and enjoy to the full the pleasures in store for you.

c. FOOD AND DRINK. Expect (in fact look forward) to finding things different. It is part of the fun of a Continental holiday. Be a little daring!

d. Rhine wines (if good) are NOT sweet, but if you want to you can soon acquire the taste. Tea is available but much weaker than at home.

e. Time on the Continent is the same as in Great Britain, so you will not have to change your watch. Punctual departures are important factors in keeping party holidays happy. You will soon be unpopular with the party if you keep them all waiting. Remember that if thirty people are waiting in a coach for five minutes, you have wasted 150 minutes of other people's holiday time.

The holidaymakers congregated on the evening of 1 August, exactly as instructed, outside the stationmaster's office on Thorpe Station concourse. Mr Stirling was already there, moustache trimmed, shoes polished, tie straight and raincoat brushed and buckled. He always looked his best for his people. Clutching a clipboard, ticking off the names, Joe was aware that this was their moment, saved for over many months. Stirling Holidays would allow nothing to spoil it. The steam from the train's engine hissed and spat as the time for departure approached. For Joe the journey was now comfortably familiar. For the clients it was a step into the unknown. Everyone was allocated cabins on the SS *Duke of York*, previously a troopship, the vessel that would convey them from Harwich to the Continent.

Tom and Margaret were by far the youngest on the trip. Margaret was intrigued to discover they were sharing their holiday, not only with Philip Hepworth the City Librarian, but also 'Old' Mr Howard and his wife, the senior partner from the family fish merchants in Fye Bridge Street. Mr Howard was suffering with rheumatism and he wasn't keeping quiet about it. Margaret's mum was concerned about seasickness but took comfort in Joe's instructive letter which stated categorically, 'You will not be seasick on this holiday, that is if past experience is any guide. Of the hundreds of people we have conducted, no-one has ever been sea-sick on the Harwich night boat.'

Koblenz remained in a parlous state of disrepair following intensive wartime bombing. Once the party got over this unexpected shock, they began to relax and enjoy the benefits of a full-time escort. Joe could not allow these overzealous tourists to wander far alone. They could be injured by falling debris on demolition sites, or stray into sensitive military zones. Joe kept them out of trouble. He organised visits to the winemaking village of Rüdesheim, on the Rhine Gorge near to the Lorelei rock. Cruising down the River Mosel, the boat passed the Koblenz headland known as *Deutsches Eck*. Sadly for Joe, the statue of Emperor Wilhelm I on his enormous horse was no longer there, badly damaged in 1945 by an American artillery shell, not to be replaced until 1993. He held such fond memories of visiting his *Opa*'s house in Koblenz-Lützel, taking time to visit the horse with his father, clambering up the stairs for the wonderful view of the two mighty rivers. The Norwich group took a ferryboat across to the east bank, visiting the Prussian Ehrenbreitstein Fortress, high on the rock face opposite Koblenz. Joe informed his spellbound audience that Hitler had held a rally on that very spot in August 1934, thousands of Germans gathered to salute and cheer their Führer.

The highlight for Tom and Margaret was the after-dark 'Rhine in Flames' festival. Abandoned during the war, this traditional event resumed in 1948 and still features on the summer tourist calendar, with an even more spectacular format. While Joe's group tucked into the customary *Wildschweinbraten* (roast wild boar) at a hillside restaurant overlooking the Rhine, hundreds of beacons were lit in turn, starting some miles away and culminating at Koblenz. From their vantage point, the Norwich travellers watched, transfixed as the glowing reflections tricked their eyes into believing the water must be alight.

Throughout the ten days away, Joe remained the consummate professional, dealing patiently with needy guests who insisted on following him everywhere. Margaret felt sorry for him, observing as he dealt diplomatically yet firmly with issues about poor food, lost belongings or language misunderstandings. Tom and Margaret were happy to be independent, exploring the waterfront, cobbled lanes and shopping of Koblenz.

The family agreed. Booking with Stirling Holidays had been an inspired decision.

Magdalen Street

'I could imagine people saying, "It's a funny old travel agents in Magdalen Street, I went in to get a Horizon brochure, but they didn't have one!" I had never worked in the travel industry before, and I hadn't a clue really.'

Anticipating an increase in business for his second summer season, it was not reasonable to prevail upon Jean's goodwill any further. He began looking for premises, settling on a small ground floor shop at 71 Magdalen Street, directly opposite his landlord, Frank Price, the owner of the popular drapery and soft furnishing store. At that time Magdalen Street was reasonably busy but still very much a secondary shopping street, 'over the river' from the city centre. Run-down and tired looking, Number 71 had stood empty for some time and needed help. Joe negotiated a seven-year lease with the option to buy the premises at any time during that period for a fixed price of £2,000. Having scraped together three months' rent as the first quarterly payment, he booked a sign writer to paint 'Stirling Holidays' on the fascia board, laid his holiday leaflets on the counter, set up his trusty typewriter in the small back office and turned the sign on the door to 'Open'.

His leaflets proved very popular. Shoppers began asking for rail or bus tickets. Joe found himself repeating, 'I'm sorry, but we don't sell tickets'. While he was working from St Clement's Hill, British Rail, Eastern Counties Bus Company and ferry companies had all refused to appoint him as an agent. Once in Magdalen Street, Joe completed the application documents, delighted to be supplied with tickets and timetables. An impressive British Railways sign was secured on the outside wall, attracting people wishing to travel by public transport to popular destinations such as Devon, Cornwall, North Wales, the Lakes and Scotland. The nominal commissions began to add up.

A basic rule of business is to listen to the needs of your customers. People stood in his shop gossiping about the high prices of organised coach tours, complaining of the inconvenience of changing hotels. Joe talked his ideas over with Jean. He could create packages using existing train and bus services, reserving accommodation in advance in centrally-placed guesthouses. Local coach companies could provide optional daily excursions to beauty spots and other attractions. This way, Stirling Holiday travellers would have a base for the week and above all, Joe need not accompany them.

This called for further research. During that first year when not overseas, Joe travelled to the northwest coast of England, visiting Blackpool and Morecambe. Meeting with landladies and hotel managers, he persuaded some to hold a number of rooms exclusively for Stirling Holidays over a limited summer period, with him giving final confirmation six weeks in advance. Joe spoke with coach operators about the viability of day trips to the nearby Lake District. He considered offering evening entertainment in the package, reserving seats at the pier variety shows on a sale or return basis. Back in Norwich he produced more simple black-and-white leaflets detailing the new offer, making it clear that travel by scheduled services would mean bus or train changes along the way. Word soon spread and this unique holiday format met with enthusiastic approval.

Joe's Continental tours also continued to sell well. In 1959 Tom and Margaret dropped into Magdalen Street to book with Joe again, this time choosing the Swiss Panorama Tour. Once the overseas summer season was over, Joe spent autumns and winters planning programmes for the following season, both abroad and at home, discovering new destinations such as Edinburgh, the Yorkshire coast and Essex seaside towns. Twenty years earlier Joe had been a German refugee, barely able to speak English, he had now travelled to more places in Great Britain than the average Englishman.

Staff and Expansion

'I have never run the business on the basis that if this doesn't work out I will be in trouble. Lots of people who have built up successful businesses far larger than mine are risk takers and proud of it. I was always much more on the cautious side. I was never in business to make it big, the business drove me at every stage.'

Joe was feeling swamped and exhausted. He was working day and night to make this business work. Jean helped when she could, hand addressing mountains of envelopes for mail-shots, occasionally manning the counter in Magdalen Street, but since 1956, virtually single-handed, she had been caring for four children, Jane, Ian, baby Martin and her niece Gail. It was time for Stirling Holidays take on its first paid member of staff. The best option was to employ a qualified shorthand typist who could type letters, keep the mounting ticket receipts in order and run the shop while the boss was away. Offering the job to the best candidate, Stirling Holidays had its first paid employee.

To help pay her wages, he considered different ways of increasing his turnover. Armed with a vague idea about stocking travel accessories, Joe went to the Norwich Free Library on the corner of Exchange Street looking for inspiration. He asked for magazines featuring travel goods. The assistant couldn't help, instead directing the earnest young man to a periodical called *Travel Trade Gazette*. Launched in 1953, it is now the world's oldest travel trade newspaper. Joe had never heard of it but he scribbled down the details, later writing to request a sample copy. He was tempted by the annual subscription, reasonable at £3 including postage. He took a chance.

Articles and news on the rapidly expanding travel industry proved inspirational. National travel firms outlined their latest generation of overseas package holidays, inviting travel agents to stock their brochures. Horizon had recently gained permission to offer charter flights into Spain, a country still governed by a fascist regime under Franco. Although tempted, Joe stuck to his principals, refusing to travel to Spain. There were many alternative destinations and he applied to stock brochures including those from Horizon, Cosmos and Sky Tours. Some replies informed him they already had an agent in Norwich, adding there was no room for two in such a small city. Others gave him a three-month trial. Joe's main objective was to promote his own tours, but he had to admit the glossy brochures with their tempting photographs looked impressive piled high on his shelves.

Joe was increasingly aware of the consequences of how cash flow operated in the travel business. It very much favoured him. Customers paid for tickets on collection. After taking his commission, Joe was not required to pay the rail and bus companies until the end of each month. Hotels requested only a modest deposit, normally 10 per cent, with the remainder payable after the guests had left. With so few people holding bank accounts, Stirling Holidays offered a weekly payment scheme. By the month of May most people had paid in full, not actually travelling until July or August. None of his capital was tied up in stock. By managing the cash flow positively and investing well, the acquired healthy interest became a significant part of his income.

Early in 1958, two years after the start of his lease the shop required minor structural alterations. His original landlord Frank Price had since died, his family selling the properties to a city firm of estate agents, who were not inclined to invest money in 71 Magdalen Street. Joe made a personal visit to the agency, met with Frank's son and, refusing to extend the lease for a further ten years, instead offered to buy the property. However, Joe considered the asking price of £2,000 as too high.

Leaving the agency, Joe went to his bank, Barclays in Magdalen Street, conveniently opposite his shop, with an appointment to talk to the manager, Stanley Cross. Passing through the columned portico, Joe felt a rush of anticipation. Mr Cross, a close professional friend, offered Joe an overdraft, aware from experience that following the quiet period in the autumn, incoming funds from Stirling Holidays would pick up well during the winter. Returning to negotiations on the shop, Joe offered £1,700. On being forced up to £1,750 Joe agreed, shaking on the deal. The following day the father, now retired, telephoned Joe, furious at his son accepting a deal at less than the original £2,000. Not wishing to come between father and son, Joe offered to pull out. The response was unexpected. 'No, we can't do that. My boy tells me you shook hands on it. I can't make him break his promise. It will have to go ahead.'

On Tuesday, 15 March 1960 Joe and Jean met with their solicitor. Mr Solomon was instructed to convert Stirling Holidays from a sole trader to a limited company. This momentous step was relatively straightforward, achieved with a nominal share capital of £100. Both Joe and Jean were appointed directors, Joe as Managing Director with Jean as Secretary. Initially two shares were issued at £1 each. A brass plate for the registered office at 71 Magdalen Street would be obtained forthwith.

In August the business in the next-door unit, Central Electrics Limited, moved out. As soon as the 'For Sale' sign appeared, Joe again approached his bank manager. The asking price was £9,000. The benefits of buying Number 73 entailed a far more impressive shop area, a larger rear office and top floor space running right the way across both premises. Joe's financial situation was secure; he could buy the shop for cash. Furthermore, he would rent out the ground floor section of Number 71. The registered office was transferred to 73 Magdalen Street. It would now be possible to engage additional staff, leaving him more time to research new destinations. Turnover grew steadily, due largely to repeat business from satisfied customers. Joe's competitors, Thomas Cook, Co-op Travel and George Wortley in Charing Cross, were all coming to a disturbing conclusion.

For the people of Norwich, booking with Stirling Holidays was becoming quite a habit.

'If in Doubt Throw it Out'

'In this city of Norwich is an ordinary English street. Nothing special about it. It is called Magdalen Street, but in a sense it stretches for mile upon mile through all our towns and villages. I want to tell you about what happened to this street, an experiment never attempted before but is already being copied in many different places.' (Colonel K. G. Post, Director of the Civic Trust, speaking in the introduction to *The Story of Magdalen Street,* promotional film produced by the Civic Trust, 1960)

In 1958 Magdalen Street, an important thoroughfare since medieval times, was targeted by the recently established Civic Trust for an experimental makeover scheme. Officers from London met with Norwich city councillors and eighty shopkeepers and tenants, outlining plans for a co-ordinated approach to improving the look of the street. Russian-born designer Misha Black was drafted in as co-ordinating architect. His work on the Festival of Britain in London had established him as one of the foremost exhibition designers in the country. Later, his iconic 1968 designs for the Borough of Westminster street signs in London secured his reputation and a knighthood in 1972.

There was no denying that Magdalen Street was run down and tired, historical features hidden beneath decades of paint. Unimaginative shop signs, worn-out awnings, countless traffic signs, broken fencing, bent railings and street lampposts obstructing the flow of pedestrians. Traders with premises between Fye Bridge and Stump Cross were asked to redecorate simultaneously to a combined plan drawn up by Civic Trust experts. Stirling Holidays sat just outside the designated area meaning Joe was not obliged to donate the required £80 contribution towards expenses. But Joe was supportive of the project, appreciating the potential benefits for the city and to his own business. In the true spirit of the scheme, Joe decided to upgrade his shopfront and consulted the design team in order to ensure a match with his near neighbours.

Early in May 1959 the street was ready for unveiling to the public and the large number of MPs, architects, engineers and representatives from local amenity societies from all over the country, curious to see exactly what had been achieved. The film cameras were rolling to record the Grand Opening. The co-ordinated approach had been based on eighteen pastel colours and a range of thirteen different styles of lettering, creating a harmonised, far brighter street scene highlighted by gallons of whitewash. Barclays Bank was rejuvenated with decorative original plasterwork exposed, bricks cleaned of grime, roman pillars freshly painted. Shop fronts were resized and designed to complement the one next-door, iron street lamps replaced with modern lantern lights, attached directly to the buildings. New blinds, awnings, bus-shelters and smart railings added the finishing touches.

There was an air of self-congratulation in St Andrew's Hall that afternoon. Every seat filled with businessmen in dark suits and black felt Derby hats. Cigarette smoke swirled into the high rafters, order sheets studied and stained-glass windows admired as the audience, including Joe, awaited the parade of dignitaries to take their places on the stage behind enormous tubs of mixed flowers. First to endorse the project was international architect, Basil Spence, best known for his modernist Coventry Cathedral, still under construction at that time. Designer Misha Black explained the ethos behind the refurbishment. 'We had a very simple formula, if in doubt throw it out.'

John Paton, MP for Norwich North, with whom Joe had worked a few years earlier, summed up the view of many in the city: 'I have passed through Magdalen Street over the years, hundreds, if not possibly thousands of times. I realised this morning that I have never seen it before.' Over the following weeks traders noted a rise in the numbers of shoppers, resulting in the previously defunct Magdalen Street Traders Association reconvening. Joe was invited to join the committee. It would be his pleasure.

No sooner had the paint dried, than rumours spread, hinting at further plans for change. Nowhere seemed exempt. During the opening three years of the 1960s the Norfolk livestock market was moved from its home since 1738, underneath the Castle mound, to a purpose-built facility in Hall Road two miles to the south. The farmers' wives were now obliged take a bus to the city centre for their Saturday shopping ritual. The last scheduled steam train left Norwich station. Joe's customers could no longer start their holidays in carriages pulled by iconic 'Iron Horses' such as the *Oliver Cromwell*. Earlham Golf Course, on the western edge of the city, was selected as the site for the new University of East Anglia, opening its doors to students in 1963. Work began on widening St Stephen's Street and the Corn Hall, operating for exactly a century, closed its doors for the final time, much to the dismay of those who had auctioned their wares in that building every Wednesday for decades.

Just as improvements in Magdalen Street were paying dividends for traders, planners at Norwich City Council responded to the Government's 'Buchanan Report on Traffic in Towns', commissioned by the Minister of Transport Ernest Marples. The Government wanted to know how cities and towns would cope should every household own a car. City planners reviewed key sections of the defunct 1945 Norwich City Plan, eventually announcing a new scheme in the form a four-lane inner link highway. An integral part of the plan was the construction of a major flyover, sweeping above Magdalen Street. Public and traders alike were not impressed. Protest, anger and debate were to preoccupy

Joe and the Magdalen Street Traders' Association throughout the decade and beyond.

Councillor Stirling

'The resignation is announced of Cllr. F. S. Mickleburgh from Hellesdon. Only one nomination has been received: Mr Gunter Stirling (commonly called Joe), a travel agent. He is deemed to be elected on October 2 1958.' (*Eastern Daily Press*, 18 September 1958)

At the same time as architects, carpenters and painters were over-hauling Magdalen Street a vacancy arose on Norwich City Council. Joe was a very busy person. Despite his immediate protestations, his colleagues at the Labour Party, using flattery and coercion, persuaded him to stand for the safe Labour seat of Hellesdon, a suburb three miles northwest of the city centre. Joe was the only nominee.

The retiring Councillor Mickleburgh had sat on the prestigious Education Committee. Joe would take his place. On the morning of 10 November 1958, Councillor Stirling strode confidently in between the two heraldic lions, up the wide flight of stone steps and through the grand entrance of City Hall for his first meeting. If he felt any nerves, he did not show it. As a past Agent-Secretary for two constituencies, Joe was no stranger to the procedures, conflicts and complexities of local government. Chairman of the Education Committee, Councillor Arthur South, welcomed Joe onto his nineteen-strong committee.

South was first elected as Labour councillor for Catton in 1935, at twenty-one the youngest councillor in the country. By 1954 he had served as Sheriff of Norwich and three years later was the city's youngest Lord Mayor. Possibly his greatest achievement during his year was to champion a successful public appeal on behalf of Norwich City Football Club, raising £250,000 to save the Third Division side from certain bankruptcy. Portly and florid with a thinning comb-over, the whiff of tobacco clinging to his suits from habitual pipe-smoking, his peers considered him forthright with a ruthless streak but 'straight as a die'. A furrier by trade with a successful workshop and showroom trading in St Stephens Street as the Norwich Fur Company, Arthur and Joe would become good friends, Joe occasionally relating stories of preparing animal pelts with his father back in the Rhineland.

In the same month as Joe joined the Education Committee, a select committee of the House of Lords was set up under the chairmanship of Lady Albemarle, former Chair of the National Federation of Women's Institutes.

Her brief was to lead a review into the problems faced by youth growing up in a rapidly changing society. The war had robbed a generation of their fathers; the number of anti-social and gang crimes committed by young people was on the increase. In May 1959, local council elections were held in Norwich with one third of the sitting councillors up for re-election. At the first meeting of the Education Committee, following council elections in May 1959, councillors were allotted to sub-committees. Joe was to join fourteen colleagues on the Further Education (Youth Service) sub-committee. Through teaching young soldiers in Portsmouth, Joe had experience of dealing with teenagers. However, when reviewing his extensive time-timetable of meetings for this and other committees, he seriously considered whether he might have just made a big mistake.

Within three months Joe was appointed as Chairman of the Youth Sub-committee. Plans were already under discussion for a youth facility provided by the local authority in line with recommendations in the government report. It was important that the new club, unlike so many existing ones, be independent of schools. A worrying number of youngsters were refusing to remain on school premises a moment longer than they had to. These so called 'Unclubables' were the very youngsters who could benefit from something new. Joe's committee began drawing up a list of local voluntary organisations to be approached to provide expertise and resources.

By 1960 Joe's political career was escalating. A firm supporter of democracy, he chaired a number of sub-committees at City Council, at the same time holding positions within the Norwich Labour Party. These included Chair of the Finance Committee, Political Education Officer and Youth Officer. It was through this latter post in 1958 that Joe first met Roy Blower, a fifteen-year-old schoolboy from Lakenham Secondary School. Roy was an energetic member of the Young Socialists, but not yet old enough to become a card-carrying member of the national Party. He approached Mr Stirling to ask whether the Party might permit him to join early, his sixteenth birthday seeming such a long way off.

Although this breach of the rules was clearly out of the question, Joe admired the boy's enthusiasm, putting him to work delivering bundles of campaign leaflets as well as offering additional responsibilities during social evenings held at the Herbert Fraser Hall twice a week. Curious, Roy asked others about Mr Stirling's long involvement with the Labour Movement. He was struck by the man's genuine interest in him and the respect he commanded from all who met him. On 6 April 1959 Roy was finally sixteen. His membership card was already prepared. It was the start of a lifelong association with local politics; Chairman of the Young Socialists by twenty, two years later sitting on the

Regional Executive. This was just the start. The coming years would see Roy fulfilling many of his early political ambitions.

At the Labour Party Autumn Conference in October 1960, Hugh Gaitskell, Leader of the Opposition for the previous five years, delivered what was to prove an historic speech. His topic was multi-lateral nuclear disarmament, the concept of every world power giving up all their nuclear weapons simultaneously. Although Gaitskell believed in the ideal, he was unwilling for Great Britain to lead the way, in his view, risking the security of the country. Some members, including Joe, considered Gaitskell to be too right wing, particularly those in the pacifist wing of the party. Despite an impassioned plea he lost the vote, sparking a leadership challenge from the younger and more left-wing Harold Wilson a few weeks later. However, Gaitskell triumphed, winning the ballot of Labour MPs on 3 November with a comfortable majority of eighty-five. Incensed, Joe resigned from the Labour Party.

A week later a letter signed by Joe was read to executive members at the Labour Club, shocking many of his long-standing political colleagues. His fundamental socialist views, combined with high moral principles were well documented, but his high-handed and arguably pompous self-sacrificing language in his letter suggested an ill-advised knee-jerk reaction. The fall-out was instantaneous. Noel Armstrong, a leading Independent City councillor wrote, 'Mr Stirling's resignation is a loss to the Labour Party. But he will only be welcome to the ranks of the Independents if he is willing to eschew national party politics altogether. From his last paragraph it looks as though he is not going to be independent, but wishes to put his great talent to a left-wing movement.'

This veiled suggestion that Joe might join the Communist Party was strongly denied. Although admitting that as a young man he had been attracted by Communist literature, having spent his childhood in Nazi Germany any notion of dictatorship was abhorrent, whether from the Right or the Left. Joe continued to represent Hellesdon, attending council meetings and forwarding the cause of the Youth Service, until spring 1961 when he announced he would not stand for election in the May, citing pressure of work. But he had also found the experience of being a councillor an uncomfortable one. He took pleasure in his committee work, but thought full council meetings to be 'a bit of a sham', taking issue with parties agreeing an 'official line' in advance of full meetings.

Despite re-joining the Labour Party a few weeks after his hasty resignation, his colleagues could not persuade him to again stand for the Council.

The New Arrival

'My only worry was that Gail would be a heavy addition to Jean's work, what with Jane and Ian and a new baby. Jean's only worry was how this little girl would react to being taken from her mother and transplanted into a strange family.'

After becoming very lost in the unfamiliar Staffordshire countryside, necessitating a U-turn in a muddy farmyard, the two men arrived at the house. They were expected but not invited in. The woman passively placed the toddler into the arms of the younger man, as she might a parcel. No ceremony, no fuss, no tears. Throughout the long journey to Norwich the child slept or sat without fidgeting, apparently undisturbed by being in an unknown car with two strangers. With no conception of their destination, the girl never once asked, 'Are we there yet?' Gordon was dropped at his home in the city. Joe drove on to St Clements Hill. As the little girl was carried over the threshold, a woman's hands reached out, her smile offering the warmest of welcomes. 'Hello Gail. This is your new home.'

Gordon was the youngest child of Lucy Skitmore. Born on 15 August 1928, eight years after her previous baby, he became a plaything to be fussed over and 'mothered' by three big sisters, Joan, Marjory and Jean. Ernest delighted in having a son, finally another man in the family. As the baby grew into a boy Ernest lost no time in teaching him about crop rotation, maintaining the wagon, grooming the horse and delivering piglets. By twelve Gordon was already very much the young Norfolk gentleman, tweed jacket and matching shorts to the knee, quite comfortable with a shotgun under his arm. As his teenage years passed, he empathised with his sister Jean as she struggled with the restrictions of life in a Brethren family. Shortly after the end of the Second World War at seventeen he left home to enlist in the Royal Navy.

Gordon was assigned to Clayton Hall in Newcastle-under-Lyme in Staffordshire. The Italianate style building with its ionic columns, arcades of arched windows and a three-storey corner turret had been the home of wealthy landowners, the house and grounds were now established as the Royal Naval Training Establishment, HMS *Daedalus II*, with aircraft hangers and a gymnasium. After the war a 'stone frigate' was built in the grounds, a dummy ship to train naval personnel for battle conditions. The villagers became accustomed to the early-morning bugle, hordes of marching feet and daily band practice. During his training as a Stoker and Mechanic, Gordon met and fell for Beryl James, a young woman from nearby Stoke-on-Trent. Her chestnut curls, sparkling eyes and petite figure guaranteed a marriage proposal, their wedding held on 5 November 1947 at the Clyde Naval Base in

Faslane, Scotland. The groom was just nineteen, his bride two years his junior. The happy couple posed for photographs outside the church, Gordon in his naval uniform; characteristic sailor hat with navy blue trim set jauntily over his abundant yellow curls, tunic with decorative white ribbon and, of course, his bell bottom trousers. The bride chose a soft blue two-piece suit with gathered waist, feature buttons and a fur-trimmed hat, corsage of three pink carnations adding a touch of feminine elegance. Sadly, there were few family members to share their moment, even Joe and Jean deciding against such a long journey.

While briefly stationed in Scotland, Beryl gave birth to a boy, Paul Stephen, on 28 June 1951 at the Braeholm Nursing and Maternity home close to Loch Lomond. Fathers were not permitted to enter the building. Instead Gordon peered through the large bay windows as his wife held their infant son close to the glass. With Gordon at sea, his parents were happy to have Beryl and her baby live with them in the railway carriages in Attleborough, growing to love their daughter-in-law and grandson. Gordon visited them whenever he was on leave and two years later, their daughter Gail was born in Thetford on 14 April 1953.

Gordon was a hopeless romantic. Despite suffering from seasickness, he wrote to his young wife every day. The local Attleborough postman delivering these letters was Elias Williams, a Welshman far from home. He looked forward to trudging up the lane to the Skitmore residence, passing the time of day with the dainty daughter-in-law. Their growing relationship concerned Ernest and Lucy. During late 1955 on arriving home after months away, Gordon found Beryl in a distressed state. She admitted that her friendship with Elias had escalated; she was pregnant with his child. Gordon was a proud man. Although he loved his wife dearly, he had been raised in a patriarchal society within a strict religious framework, his view of life influenced further by Navy discipline. This was no time for discussion. There could be no forgiveness. The family would be split up, four-year-old Paul to remain in the care of his grandparents, Beryl returning to her parents in Stoke-on-Trent with two-year-old Gail. Gordon really wished to keep brother and sister together, but he acknowledged that the toddler needed her mother. Before she left, Gordon made it clear he would be suing for divorce on the grounds of her adultery.

Ever since Paul could walk, Ernest and his grandson had become quite a double act. Ernest loved having a boy around, reminding him of raising his own son. Paul adored his Granddad, enjoying many adventures with him on the smallholding, a vast and exciting place to live. Ernest lifted Paul onto his horse-drawn cart, so high that the boy could see the whole world around him. As they clip-clopped to the town the grumpy horse complained through the metal bit whilst his tail swished away the flies. Passers-by waved up at the curly-headed blond child, rewarded by his huge grin.

When Ernest's sow produced her latest litter Paul were always the first to visit the pigsty at the bottom of the garden. The boy loved to watch the mother pig lying on her side grunting with contentment as her fine fat piglets suckled and snorted. When noisy hooting outside his window disturbed Paul's sleep, leaving him anxious, Ernest eventually had no choice but to shoot the offending owl. Once, the boy's trike went missing, Elias telling Ernest that the local gipsies had stolen it. Paul stayed with Nana Lucy while his hero set off down the road, soon returning with the favourite toy tucked under his arm.

Shortly after Beryl and Gail had been sent packing back to Stoke, Ernest was taken ill. At sixty-nine the strain on his heart from long-term obesity, exacerbated by the recent family stress, proved too much. He was admitted to hospital following a heart attack, where Paul made just one visit before his beloved Granddad died on 14 November 1955. The funeral over, the family looked to the future. It was evident that Lucy was unable both to care for Paul and manage the smallholding. After much family discussion a decision was made. 'The Oaks' would have to go. Auctioneers W. S. Hall & Palmer of Market Place, Wymondham were hired to assess the value of the railway carriages, the pastureland in Leys Lane and Ernest's three rental properties, Numbers 1, 2 & 3 Market Terrace, Chapel Lane, Attleborough. These were to be sold with sitting tenants. The auction date was set for Thursday, 26 January 1956 at 3 p.m. in the Royal Hotel, Attleborough. The brochure described the property as a 'Railway Carriage Bungalow'. The previous year Ernest had connected both mains electricity and water into the carriages along with other small improvements, making the property a far more attractive proposition. The three lots sold for a total of £508. Ernest also left cash in the bank. Probate was agreed. Adding together death benefits and insurance policies, less legal expenses, Lucy was left with £789.5.11 to buy a new home for herself and her grandson.

The Skitmores and Joe urged Lucy to move into Norwich to be closer to both Jean and Joan. Joan's husband Leslie was a respected Brethren leader in the city and they had been blessed with three boys, John, Michael and Andrew. A modest three-bedroom terrace directly opposite their home in Stafford Street came up for sale just at the right time. The house was priced at £750, just within Lucy's budget. On 17 February 1956 removal company G. Jarrett of Devonshire Street, Norwich drove Lucy's furniture and personal belongings from Attleborough to 60 Stafford Street, on the western fringe of the city centre, close to Norwich cemetery. The bill was £12.

A few weeks after moving in, Paul was admitted to hospital for the routine removal of tonsils and adenoids. Lucy seized the opportunity to cover the walls of her grandson's new bedroom with coloured photos of flowers, cut from *Amateur Gardening*, her favourite weekly magazine. Having lost her husband and countryside home after thirty-five years the floral display, more economical than wallpapering, would be a welcome reminder for both Lucy and Paul.

After ten years' service Gordon was ready to leave the Royal Navy. He moved into his mother's new house and took on two jobs, postman during the early mornings, followed by afternoons spent learning the carpet-fitting trade at Tom Watts furniture store. This job was at the suggestion of Uncle Joe, still friends with the Watts brothers. While his son was in hospital, Gordon brought home samples of discontinued sofa fabric. Lucy lovingly sewed them into a cosy 'welcome home' eiderdown for Paul.

In Stoke-on-Trent, Beryl's father, an intolerant man at the best of times, had quickly become tired of the whinging child, endless nappies and disturbed nights. He felt disgraced by his daughter's growing belly and the solicitors' letters landing on his doormat. At about the same time as Paul was moving into Norwich with his Nana, in Stoke-on-Trent Beryl's father threatened his daughter with eviction. Desperate and unable to cope, she appealed to her husband for help. But Gordon was still dealing with a life outside the Navy, holding down two jobs. He was a provider, hands-on childcare not in his remit. The family was uncomfortable with Lucy, at nearly seventy, becoming a full-time mum to both youngsters. Jean persuaded Joe to offer their home to the youngster.

After all, Gail was family.

Settling In

'I called my Dad Uncle Gordon because Joe's children called him Uncle Gordon.'
(Gail Scott, née Skitmore, speaking in 2014)

Despite Jean's welcome that first evening, Gail would allow no one but Joe to touch her. He cradled the two-year-old throughout the night as she sobbed and sobbed for her mother. However within a few days, the little girl relaxed into the family routines, smiling and eating. One-year-old Martin fascinated Gail and the two of them became firm friends. She joined Jane and Ian in their make-believe games. Jane lent her dolls to cuddle and dress, happy to share with the vulnerable newcomer. Gail stopped asking for her mother. Growing in confidence, she began to call Jean 'Mummy' and Joe 'Daddy'. The adults found this endearing and chose not to discourage her. Gordon paid occasional visits to the Stirling home, habitually greeting his daughter by tossing her into the air and bellowing, 'Hello sugarplum, how are you?' In reply Gail addressed this tall fair man as 'Uncle Gordon', in line with her new siblings. It was less complicated if Gordon went along with it. Gail was aware that this man paid her more attention than he did the others. She had no idea why but knew she liked it.

Paul and Gail continued to live parallel but very different lives, unaware of each other, one on each side of the city. For many months Paul did not attend school at all, his presence in the city unknown to the authorities. However, Lucy soon realised that he was slipping behind with reading and writing, enrolling him into The Avenue School not far from Stafford Street. His new friends all had mums. He asked Lucy if he could call her 'Mum'. 'I'm not your Mum', replied his grandmother. It was a trying time.

Paul and Gail lived two and a half miles apart – a long walk for short legs. Buses were expensive and very few people owned cars. It is conceivable that the families deliberately resolved not to further confuse the siblings by bringing them together. In Stafford Street Lucy did her best to raise Paul, a wilful and boisterous boy, often forced to call on the goodwill of daughters Joan and Marjorie.

In St Clements Hill over the next three years, Gail became an integral part of Joe's young family, thriving alongside her 'brothers' and 'sister'. At five years old Gail joined Ian at the nearby Angel Road School, settling into her lessons and enjoying the freedom of the nine-minute unsupervised walk cutting through Millers Lane to and from school. One afternoon, Gail developed a sore neck and felt very poorly. She left the school, crying all the way home. Arriving at the back gate Gail was surprised to find Joe standing in the garden. He picked her up in his arms, wiping her tears. Gail held on to him, the pain and fear ebbing away. Joe explained that Jane had also been taken ill at her big school and he had been to collect her. Both girls had mumps. Another time, Gail was pushed in the playground, falling heavily and splitting her head on a drain cover. Joe arrived and once again his calm reaction made the child secure and safe as they took the bus to casualty. Gail adored her 'Daddy'.

Gordon's marriage to Beryl had been dissolved in February 1957. The court ordered that both children remain in the custody of the petitioner until they attain the age of eighteen. Beryl did not contest the ruling. She had given birth to her lover's baby during the previous summer and lost no time in legitimising him by becoming Mrs Williams on 23 March. Despite a tumultuous marriage, she bore Elias three children. Their parents told them nothing of Beryl's first husband nor of their half brother and sister. Gail never saw her mother again after she left Stoke in the car with Joe and Gordon. Her only memory is of herself as a toddler, her sandal slipping down a grate and becoming trapped. An adult female figure in soft focus, barely discernable, leans down, long hair sweeping over her face and head, gently manoeuvring the tiny foot to safety.

On 17 May 1958 Jean delivered a little 'afterthought'. It had been a difficult pregnancy, Jean struggling to deal with her own fragile health while caring for four youngsters. But everyone loved the baby, agreeing to call her Joanna. Joe went to register her birth. He was familiar with the name from his youth in Germany and naturally spelt the baby's name as the German version Johanna. Jean forgave her husband. For some time after Johanna's birth, Jean suffered with post-natal depression. Her mood was lifted temporarily when her sister Marjorie married her beau Alan Franklin in the summer of 1958. He was a caring man, a little younger than Marjorie. It was too late to hope for children. Joe thought about how best to help his fragile wife, employing Ada Worley, a local lady about the same age as Jean, happy to take on the more demanding domestic chores in the house. Ada was content that the children address her by her Christian name, but knowing that Father would not approve they continued to call her Mrs Worley. In years to come, baby Johanna took a shine to Ada, looking on her as a second mother. Ada worked for Joe and Jean for many years, remaining good friends until her death.

After his divorce, Gordon found new love with Norwich girl Pauline Barber, a work colleague at Tom Watts. A year later they announced their engagement. Gordon applied for a council house in Lakenham. He was now ready to be the head of a family again and wanted his children back. Pauline was twelve years younger than Gordon and would be just twenty-one when she became the second Mrs Skitmore. Joe and Jean were disturbed; surely Gordon could see that Gail was settled and content? They would be happy to have her stay with them permanently; she was part of their family. Pauline was so young and inexperienced; was it really fair to foist two growing youngsters onto her so soon? But Gordon was resolute. Joe made it clear that if at any time he and Pauline could not cope, Gail would be welcomed back as part of the Stirling family. The time came for Joe and Jean to break the news to Gail. She was six years old, sitting at the kitchen table along with the others, enjoying a family meal, as they did every evening. Jean had dreaded this moment all day. Once the others got down, Jean and Joe took Gail aside.

'Gail, We've something to tell you. You're not going to be living with us anymore.'

'But why?'

Jean and Joe, their hearts aching, patiently explained that Uncle Gordon was actually her Dad, she had an older brother and Auntie Pauline was going to be her new mummy. They would all be living together as a family.

'But I don't want to. Can't I stay here?'

It was the saddest day of Gail's young life.

On 5 December 1959, Gail and Paul arrived separately at the Gibraltar Gardens Pub in Heigham Street. Although both dressed in their Sunday best, the children were totally unaware that the cold buffet and fizzy drinks were to celebrate their father's wedding. That evening Paul and Gail were driven to a semi-detached house in Harwood Road, Lakenham. Gail was now aware of Paul but had no idea how best to approach him. Paul was not so informed. Upstairs on the landing Gordon, believing he was doing the right thing, took his son by the shoulders and gently pushed him towards the shy girl with the blonde curls.

'That's your sister, son. Why don't you go over and give her a kiss?'

Confused and disgusted at the very idea, Paul retaliated. 'But I don't have a sister. I'm not kissing her.'

Their father's instructions did not stop there. Both children should cease referring to his new wife as 'Auntie'. From now on they would address her as 'Mum'. That first night Gail lay in the strange bed telling herself over and over, 'I will not call her Mum, I will not call her Mum.' When Pauline came into say goodnight, Gail defiantly replied, 'Goodnight Auntie Pauline'.

There was a long road ahead.

Unthank

'The house needed a lot doing to it. The ceilings in the bedrooms were black because there was no central heating and they used oil fires, which had blackened the ceilings. It was in a terrible state. My wife loved the garden though.'

In 1959 Jane was in her final year at George White Junior School. It was naturally assumed that when she reached the age of twelve she would move to Blyth Grammar School for Girls, conveniently opposite their home in St Clements Hill. However, Joe and Jean were becoming aware of developing problems at Blyth. The Head appeared unpopular, teachers were resigning and the school's reputation was suffering. Sometime after Jane's eleventh birthday, Jean received a letter from Silver Road explaining that every year, the Educational Trust of Norwich High School, a private fee-paying school in the Newmarket Road, offered five scholarships based on ability to pupils from Junior Schools throughout Norwich. Silver Road had nominated Jane for a place, in competition with about twenty others. The school was now pleased to inform Mr and Mrs Stirling that the application for Jane had been successful.

Jean was delighted but Joe found himself with a moral dilemma. He was still an active member of the Labour Movement, opposed to the notion of buying privilege. Under normal circumstances he would stick to his principles and turn down the offer. But Jane had passed the eleven-plus with excellent grades, so thanks to the 1944 Education Act a free grammar school place was guaranteed. Jean and Joe talked it over. Jean was fully in favour of offering her clever daughter the best chance possible for her future. She gently explained, maybe over a slice or two of her signature coffee and walnut cake, that they were not actually choosing to buy an education. Someone other had chosen this path for her, a reward for Jane's hard work. Despite his reservations, Joe remembered the chance he had been given at Yardley Grammar School. He capitulated. Jane would take the place at Norwich High School, considered by many as the finest all-girls school in Norfolk.

In September Jane stood in front of the mirror admiring her new school uniform. She was nervous. The journey from St Clements Hill to Newmarket Road involved two buses, into the city and out again. It was a punishing schedule. Joe looked at his accounts. The business was making good money. The family lived modestly, well within their means. The sale of their present house, considering the small mortgage, should produce a profit. They were already aware that Gail would be moving out in early December. It seemed that change was inevitable. Joe began looking for a new house further to the south of the city. One estate agent was anxious to show Mr and Mrs Stirling a large detached late Victorian house in Unthank Road. The owner of the property had been a retired doctor, recently deceased. His wife and only daughter were residential patients at Hellesdon Mental Hospital. They were unlikely ever to come out.

As the Stirling family were led through the front gate, the adults were pleased to see how far back the house was from the road. A long path stretched down the left-hand boundary. To the right lay a large area of lawn beneath imposing square bay windows. A tall fir tree stretched upwards. The agent led the way through the front door. They felt the temperature drop the moment they crossed the threshold. Four doors led off a large entrance hall and an impressive curved staircase stretched upwards on the right. There was a distinct odour of dust and decay. The wallpaper was faded and the woodwork scratched and dirty. Next to the kitchen was a small breakfast room. The black-leaded stove with remains of its last coal fire fascinated Jane. Was that a slice of charred toast in the ashes? The sensitive girl felt as if she had discovered a remnant of life from the previous occupants, echoes that remained throughout her teenage years.

The agent led the way up the stairs to three good-sized bedrooms and one smaller one at the front of the house, adjacent to the master bedroom. The overuse of oil fires had caused unsightly smoke damage to the ceilings. Jean was pleased to find the bathroom equipped with adequate sanitary ware for a growing family, even if it could do with modernising. One of the doors from the generous landing led up to two attic rooms, once upon a time servants' quarters. Jean saw scope for plenty of storage or maybe a spacious playroom. Joe imagined a train set. Downstairs again to examine the two reception rooms. At the back there was a view over the rear garden through large wooden sash windows. The wooden fire surround was panelled both below and above the mantelpiece. Joe thought to look upwards, disappointed to find the decorative plaster ceiling painted an oppressive black. His earlier optimism was dented. That would need thinking about.

Jean and Jane were desperate to take a look at the garden. Jane had always hankered after a garden with trees, and here was a whole row of apples and pears running down one side – almost an orchard. Jean walked slowly down the path, cradling one-year-old Johanna in her arms, inwardly hugging herself as she surveyed the neglected flowerbeds and trellises, imagining instead climbing scented roses and lush herbaceous borders. By now the others had joined them, Ian running ahead to explore the very end of the plot, whooping with delight as he came across a greenhouse with traditional brick walls and decorated ridge, complete with ancient gnarled vine, straight out of a scary fairy tale. Jean considered which bulbs might be sleeping under the soil. It was now well into autumn and evidence of previous colour was scarce. In the following spring there could be swathes of snowdrops, daffodils and purple crocus opening their heads to greet the sun. She would plant a mixed pallet of foxgloves, irises and verbena. Here was the perfect spot for a rockery, to be stuffed with alpines, heathers and sedums. There should even be room for some vegetables. Jean was in her element as she made plans for the wonderful space. Oh and the children too would have lots of fun here.

Still concerned about the black ceiling and before making any rash decisions, Joe asked his friend Bernard Fielden to come and inspect it. Bernard was a partner in the architect firm Fielden and Mawson just off Magdalen Street. Joe had first become aware of him when he joined the Magdalen Street Traders Association following the Civic Trust make-over six months earlier. Bernard was also secretary of the Norwich Society. He knew about old buildings. Reassuring his friend that the problem was purely cosmetic and that the ceiling could be transformed with a few coats of white paint, he encouraged Joe to buy.

The location was just perfect, only a five-minute walk from both Norwich High School and a new Junior School for Ian. The easy, flat walk to the city centre was only thirty minutes. Joe negotiated the price down to £3,000 about double what he expected to get for St Clements Hill. They sold that house quickly and all seemed to be progressing well. But before the purchase could be completed, solicitors acting as trustees for the doctor's widow informed the Stirlings of a higher offer. Under the terms of the trust, they were obliged to accept it, unless Mr Stirling was willing to match the sum. Joe needed to find a further £250. This was potentially heartbreaking. Neither he nor Jean wanted to lose this extraordinary house. Once again, Joe paid a visit to Barclay's Bank. The manager agreed to make a loan to Stirling Holidays, confident that for at least six months of the year the cash flow would cover the amount several times over.

Shortly before Christmas 1959 the family moved in. The house was freezing cold. Despite this the children were exuberant. The boys were to share a room, excitedly filling the wooden shelves with Dinky Toys, Monopoly, Mr Potato Head, *Eagle* comics, teddy bears and tin soldiers. Jane took her time, folding her school uniform into her dresser, displaying her favourite books and allocating a home for her project folders, all the while wondering if Father would allow her to pin posters on the walls.

A closer inspection of the attic was long overdue. The door from the landing was eased open and three pairs of assorted feet clattered up the narrow staircase. The spidery expanses in the roof would give both Jane and Johanna some nervous nights over the following years, as the old house creaked and sighed. Joe unpacked boxes while Jean patiently placed her cooking utensils into the many cupboards and drawers. She was already thinking up ideas for baking, steaming and roasting delicious meals in her new kitchen. Sitting on the kitchen floor, Johanna provided the musical accompaniment, beating a wooden spoon on Jean's copper pan.

Jean mused. If only Gail were here to share the fun.

Lion Joe

'They had about 25 or 30 members attending and Fred said, "Mr Chairman, do you mind if we invite Joe to stay for the rest of the meeting?" I think now, and we have often laughed about it since, that I was always seen as a possible prospective new member.'

Fred Watts had been keeping a careful watch on his 38-year-old protégé, quietly impressed with how the new travel business was expanding. On 8 April 1960, as a founder member of the new Norwich Lions Club, he invited Joe to be his guest at their first Charter Dinner. Joe felt slightly out of his depth.

The Flixton Room at Samson and Hercules House was awash with ladies in long, sequinned evening gowns, costume jewellery and hairspray. Black tie was *de rigueur,* evening jackets cleaned for the occasion. The dignitaries, including Lord Mayor Michael Waldo Boone Bulman, a senior consultant in Gynaecology and Obstetrics, were seated at a top table, barely visible through the cloud of cigar smoke. The hall was filled with city society, the after dinner entertainment by Scottish baritone singer, Niven Miller much appreciated. The menu, for the early 1960s, was contemporary and sophisticated, including Plaice Mornay, Roast Norfolk Duckling and Ice Gateaux, designed for a special occasion at the start of a modern decade.

Prior to their charter being granted, the Norwich Lions had spent months publicly wearing large badges with a prominently displayed 'L' for Lions. They arranged for underprivileged children to enjoy a local pantomime and sold homemade biscuits and cups of tea at the annual Norwich Trades Fair in St Andrew's Hall. But that April evening was all about Charles Allison, District Governor of 105 District (Great Britain and Ireland), handing the new Club's Charter to President Bill Stannard. Before the coffee was even cleared away, Norwich Lions Club was officially a member of The Association of Lions Clubs International.

Fred chose not to press Joe about membership of the Lions for nearly two years. Then early in 1962, sensing the time was now right, he approached Joe, requesting he speak to the Club about his travel business, at a meeting to be held in the King's Head Public House in Thorpe St Andrew. In the 1960s Lions Clubs were populated with professional men or those in business. Raising money for good causes ran alongside mutually-beneficial networking. The group listened attentively. As Joe stood to leave, Fred requested that Mr Stirling might remain for the remainder of the meeting. As he sat listening to updates on projects, budgets and innovative ideas, Joe was lured in, engrossed by the stimulating discussion and decision-making. It was not long before he was officially invited to join their ranks and attend meetings held on the second and last Monday of each month.

Joe read every word of his welcome pack, inspired by the simple motto 'We Serve'. He learnt that Lions Clubs International had been the dream of Chicago insurance man Melvin Jones. Twelve businessmen had met in a hotel lounge on 7 June 1917, voting to approve the inauguration of the 'Association of Lions Clubs'. Just three years later, membership stood at 60,000 in a total of 1,183 Clubs throughout the United States, Canada, Mexico, Cuba and China. Joe was intrigued to hear that it was during the Second World War that the first Lions Club in the UK, known as 'The Host Club' was established in London.

Although the Lions were primarily thought of as a fundraising organisation, it was their community work, visiting old people, helping with shopping, driving, gardening and decorating, that made them most proud. Joe was struck by the extent of their activities. There were no social services in the early 1960s. The flat-rate state pensions were barely adequate, daily essentials expensive. There was much deprivation amongst the old in Norwich. Each member of Norwich Lions Club was allocated eight elderly people to visit regularly, identifying their needs and reporting back to meetings. In 1962 spring came late to parts of the UK and firewood was in short supply. Charter member and wealthy businessman Joe Hackett owned a small estate of woodland opposite Sprowston Manor. He invited fellow members to cut down surplus trees and chop them into kindling for bundling and distribution to the most needy. Joe spent many hours working in a team, sawing and stockpiling the wood. The Club continued this service for many years, until the onset of central heating and social benefits reduced the demand.

At the Club's fifth anniversary Charter Dinner in March 1965 a new mini-van was driven onto the dance floor at the Norwood Rooms, the keys handed over by the President Eric Gould, to Walter Cutbush, Chairman of the Committee for the Welfare of Old People. Eric was proud to report that Norwich Lions Club was the first club in the country to have donated two Meals-On-Wheels vehicles to Norwich organisations. Formalities over, Joe and Jean took to the dance floor. As midnight approached and the candles burned low, the final toast was the Norwich Lions Club.

It had been a wonderful fifth birthday party.

President Joe

'It is not given to a great many men in the ordinary conduct of their lives to exercise leadership within a group, yet every member of a Lions Club has this opportunity.'
(Melvin Jones, Founder of Lions Clubs International)

Joe found it relatively straightforward to adapt his organisational skills to the planning and implementation of Lions fundraising projects. Over the following months and years, the hierarchy noted his enthusiasm and willing nature. Despite all the other things he did, he never missed a meeting. By 1966 he had worked his way through the structure and on 1 July became President of Norwich Lions Club. To achieve this honour within only four years was exceptional. When the role was first suggested, Joe's reaction was 'Don't you think it might be a bit soon?' He had never sought a leadership role, satisfied just being a member of the team. Nevertheless, it was a proud moment for the boy from Nickenich when he first wore the badge of office.

On the evening of 14 September Joe hosted his first major function as President, celebrating the Golden Jubilee of Lions International. A dinner was held at the Royal Hotel on Agricultural Hall Plain in Norwich. This magnificent Victorian building opened in 1897, featuring majestic turrets, pinnacles and gables. The hotel, with its marble halls, was undergoing something of a revival during the 1960s, popular with actors filming dramas for nearby Anglia Television. Of more personal interest to Joe, local MPs used the Royal for election campaign meetings. As a result of the many eclectic fundraising activities and the public's generosity, the Norwich Club had built up healthy reserves. At the end of February 1967 the *Eastern Evening News* published the astounding story that Norwich Lions Club was planning to buy and then give away a house. The recipient would be Norwich and Norfolk Association for Mental Health. The 1959 Mental Health Act had abolished the distinction between psychiatric and general hospitals. Until the 1960s, most people diagnosed with mental illness were accommodated in asylums, often for life. Advances in drug and therapy treatment, along with a greater awareness of human rights, led to a government initiative seeking alternatives. As an interim measure between residential care in a secure institution and living independent lives, patients were moved into 'half-way houses'. By 1967 Norwich and Norfolk Association for Mental Health already owned one property, but with increased demand and limited funds the Board approached the Norwich Lions Club for help.

Under Joe's leadership the officers ascertained how much the club could afford to spend on one major project. A large five-bedroomed terraced house in Churchill Road had been identified as a suitable property. The asking price was £17,000, representing many months of fundraising activities. In an interview for the newspaper Joe explained, 'We think this is wonderful scheme and want to do all we can to bring another five people back into the community. We have sufficient funds for the deposit on the house and hope to arrange an overdraft for the remainder, which we can pay off as we raise the money.' The deal was struck and the house decorated by volunteers and simply furnished with donated items. The Mental Health Association paid the Norwich Lions Club a peppercorn rent of £1 a year.

The project proceeded well, Norwich City Council offering council houses to the Mental Health Association at a nominal rent. Once again the Lions stepped in, paying the rents on behalf of the Association. Once sufficiently recovered patients moved out into the community. There were always plenty

Joe at Lions International Headquarters, Oak Brook, Chicago.

Joe leads British contingent in the Grand Parade at the Lions International Convention in Montreal, June 1979.

Past District Governor Joe speaks at a Lions Club event in the 1970s.

Joe enjoys his apartment in Maderia Beach, Florida.

Jean and Joe at black-tie event.

Joe in 1979 in his Lions jacket with badge for 100 percent attendance record over ten years.

Joe in 2013 in same Lions jacket with pin badge collection.

Joe became Sheriff of Norwich on 20 May 1975. Top row Ian, unknown, Jane.
Middle row Martin, Joan, Marjorie, Johanna. Front Jean and Joe.

Joe descending the City Hall steps to ride in the Civic Carriage to meet a High Court Judge on 24 April 1976.

Joe speaks at Norwich Civic Association, April 2014. Sheriff Graham Creelman (left) and Lord Mayor Keith Driver.

At his ninetieth birthday party, Joes receives a gift from the Mayor of Nickenich. Left to right, Johanna, Jutta Hansen, Joe, Jessica Hansen.

Meeting with old friends at his ninetieth birthday party. Doreen Hardy, Jane, Joe and Judith Marjoram (née Hardy).

Joe with Lord Mayor Judith Lubbock at his birthday party .

Joe reunited with Shirley Williams on 8 April 2015 after sixty-one years.

Joe is ninety on 18 October 2014.

of others to take their place, some from Hellesdon Hospital, but mostly from Little Plumstead, a home with 350 patients.

It was a project that would have long-term implications.

International Youth Camp

'To create and foster a spirit of understanding among the peoples of the world.'
(Lions Clubs Objectives)

During his summer as President, Joe was invited to visit the historic City of York and attend the first ever Lions International Youth Camp held in Great Britain. The aim was to bring together 30 young people from all over the world to learn about Britain and its people, experience different ways of life and develop friendships. Publicised through *The Lion* magazine, distributed worldwide, clubs were to nominate young people aged between fifteen and nineteen to travel to York, stay in University accommodation, and experience a full programme of visits, outdoor activities, speakers and social events with all expenses covered by Lions Clubs. An appeal went out for financial donations. Joe spent two days in York. For this first year, the delegates were from countries within Europe, the stipulation being that they had a reasonable command of English. It was an enjoyable week with York Lions Club volunteering to repeat the event the following year. Joe, inspired by his two days there, persuaded Norwich Club to host the International Youth Camp in 1968.

Having handed on the Presidency, Joe took over the role of Secretary and Organiser for the Camp. He was ideally qualified for the role, negotiating to hire the conference facilities at Keswick Hall College of Education, soon to be incorporated into the University of East Anglia. Seventy youngsters, all aged seventeen or eighteen, representing Holland, Norway, Sweden, West Germany, Austria, Eire, Northern Ireland, Iceland, Greece, Finland and Czechoslovakia converged on Norwich. There were also delegates from the United States, Canada and Australia. Joe called on clubs from Great Yarmouth, Lowestoft and Acle to offer accommodation in members' homes, offering a taste of English family life to the international visitors. The Norfolk Broads Club arranged a boat in which to explore the world-famous inland waterways. A coach brimming with excited anticipation drove the young people to London, destination Carnaby Street, Mecca of 1960s' style.

Senior officers from UK Lions Clubs Headquarters travelled to Norwich to see for themselves how the International Camp was operating. The 1960s had seen prodigious growth in the number of Lions Clubs established throughout the British Isles and Ireland. By 1968 Multiple District 105, as it was designated, was divided into six areas. District 105A covered a vast geographical area from Hampshire to London, Oxfordshire, Northampton and East Anglia. Joe and his team welcomed John Holdham, the recently-elected District Governor for 105A. He was impressed with Joe's vision, planning and implementation of the Youth Camp, writing to him afterwards with an intriguing proposal. Holdham explained that he was in the process of appointing his District cabinet. During his tenure he intended to focus on links with overseas clubs, proposing the creation of a new role on the cabinet, International Relations Officer. Would Lion Joe be interested in being the first to hold that office?

During the Lions year 1968–9 Joe attended briefings on his new position; how the funding worked at international level, the procedures dictating quarterly cabinet meetings in London, as well as speaking to seven or eight Lions Clubs who were interested to learn more about what exactly the role of an International Relations Officer entailed. His increased profile and aptitude for leadership meant that the following year, Joe was elevated to Region Chairman, a cabinet post responsible for East Anglia and London north of the Thames. Although not obligatory, Joe was encouraged to accept as many invitations as possible to attend Club meetings around the Region. He was pleased to have the opportunity to represent both the District cabinet and his own Club.

At the turn of a new decade, the future of Lion Joe Stirling was under discussion at the highest level.

The Three Cs and NOAH

'The Police heard about the club and thought there must be a lot of undesirables, as the Police called them, going there. They thought it would be a good place to catch people on drugs and so on and raided the club two or three times. They didn't know, just as the youngsters didn't know, that this was a Council-run youth club.'

After Joe stood down from the City Council in April 1961, the Education Committee continued to debate, consult and decide on matters relating to the establishment of a Youth Club in the city centre. In May 1963 Joyce Morgan, Joe's colleague on the Trades Council during the 1950s, was elected as councillor for Bowthorpe Ward, taking her place on the Education Committee. Arthur South was still in the Chair and appointed Joyce to sit on the Youth Sub-committee. At a meeting in early September it was noted that all previous potential venues for the 'General Mixed Club', including the ground floor of Central Library, were no longer available. A sum of £6,000 was ring-fenced for adaptations and improvements to any suitable building, once identified.

On 11 November, the Education Committee resolved that the project should receive priority and recommended the Town Planning Committee reserve a site for the erection of a new building in the Rose Lane Clearance Area, preferably one large enough to allow future extensions. In the meantime, members should continue to make enquiries about a suitable existing building. By the end of November it was agreed that Rose Lane would not be suitable 'in view of the commercial development envisaged in that area'. During April 1964 the councillors failed to reach agreement with Norwich City Football Club over a joint-venture proposal. Another summer went by with no sign of finding suitable premises.

In October 1964 the City Education Committee had a breakthrough. A large building, previously a furniture store was available at 17/19 St John Maddermarket. The Council could only afford to renovate the ground floor. With adaptation work budgeted at approximately £14,600, the extra money would be raised by a loan. Joyce Morgan was given the honour of signing the lease on the property. Sometime between the autumn and end of May 1965 the working title of the project, 'General Mixed Club' had been replaced with the name 'Charing Cross Club' with a projected opening date during September 1965. A revised Furniture and Equipment budget of £2,700 was agreed to include new carpets, stepladders, a milk-cooling machine and six table tennis bats.

The early summer was spent coercing distinguished and influential individuals to join the Governing Body and Committee of Trustees. Viscount Mackintosh of Halifax, heir to the successful confectionary business, was approached to be President of the Club. Local businessman Andrew Jarrold accepted the role of Honorary Secretary. Heading up the Trustees was the ubiquitous Alderman Arthur South, representing the City Council, alongside his colleague Alderman Sutton, Joe's business neighbour in Magdalen Street. A public appeal was launched with a target of £35,000.

The next objective was to set up a hands-on management committee. Norwich Lions Club pledged to lend their experience to this new venture, nominating Vice-President Joe as their representative. He was well qualified for the role and had many influential contacts. At the first meeting, the management team shared their reservations about the name 'Charing Cross Club'. It was agreed that the word 'Club' in the title might be offputting to some young people. Taking the first letter of each word from the name, the title 'Three Cs' was agreed as a good alternative. There were just a few months remaining for painting, cleaning and deliveries.

In September 1965 the Three Cs opened its doors on schedule. Joe and his colleague were astonished at an unexpectedly high turn out. Scooters and motorbikes were heaped outside, the coffee machine was on overtime, modern pop tunes blasted through the building. It was exactly the type of venue the youngsters craved. The professional Youth Organiser, a Mr Burnett, was overwhelmed by the response and in November the Education Committee agreed the need for an additional full-time leader. However, it wasn't long before it came to the notice of the local police that some of the clientele were on the 'wanted' list for under-age drinking, joy riding or even dealing in soft drugs. More than once, Joe witnessed uniformed officers rushing up the staircase and arresting an individual or two. Something had to be done. This activity would attract bad publicity and deter law-abiding youngsters from attending. The police claimed to have not been informed about the origins of this new group or the nature of the supervised activities available. Joe and a colleague met with the Chief Constable of Norwich, resulting in a middle-rank inspector joining the Three Cs committee. The unannounced visits from the 'boys in blue' abruptly stopped.

Joe spent much of his time at the Club circulating between groups of youngsters, discussing their interests, lives and aspirations. The venue also offered live music gigs, including one memorable evening when Screaming Lord Sutch, a rock-and-roll singer specialising in horror rock, filled the venue with excitable fans. Lord Sutch was notorious for challenging mainstream politics when creating the Monster Raving Loony Party early in the 1960s. Joe unfortunately didn't appreciate his music.

As Treasurer and later as Chairman of the Three Cs management committee, Joe occasionally worked alongside City Council representative Joyce Morgan, by this time promoted to Vice-Chair of the Education Committee. In 1967 Joyce was appointed as a Magistrate, an honour she accepted with a great deal of pride. However, she soon found herself passing judgement on youngsters she recognised from the Three Cs. Faced with this conflict of interests Joyce was forced to resign her place on the Education Committee as from 17 March that same year. Sadly, she also felt obliged to step down from the Three Cs management committee. Joyce brought humour, vitality and commitment to everything she did, qualities that were sorely missed.

During 1968, a group of sixth-formers from the four Norwich Grammar Schools joined with a number of young churchgoers to promote their vision of young people assisting the elderly and infirm with everyday tasks such as shopping, decorating and gardening. They didn't anticipate major financial outgoings, but nonetheless there would inevitably be minor expenses. The sixth-formers approached Joe for guidance and advice. Although applauding the concept, he urged them to accept experienced adult help. Norwich Lions Club provided some funding and in March 1969 the Norwich Organisation for Active Help (NOAH) was established. The young people worked from a single room in Duke Street, affectionately known as the ARK. At times the situations they encountered were humbling. Richard Webb, an early volunteer and later Chairman of the management committee, admitted, 'We tried to hang wallpaper in a room so damp the paper would not stick to the walls. One time I cut the grass for a severely disabled man who had previously just about managed on his own with a pair of scissors. We couldn't simply brush those experiences under the carpet when we'd finished.'

It was an idea that was to grow and grow.

Family Fun

'We used to go on holidays to Spain. That was quite interesting because it was before all the high rises. We went to Benidorm and Torremolinos, and it was just so exotic. The tourist industry was just starting. The hotels did not cope well with young families. I was at the age when I was always fussy about food.' (Johanna Stirling, speaking in 2013)

Despite continuing uncertainty around the future road layout around Magdalen Street and the possible effect on footfall, Stirling Holidays continued to grow, business benefiting from a national surge in consumer spending. In 1964, seven years after opening his first shop, Joe was employing a staff of six. Customer satisfaction, new enticing destinations and imaginative package deals ensured valuable repeat business.

That summer found Joe escorting four trips to the Continent. During September, as Secretary of the Norfolk and Norwich Ypres Association, he escorted a group of the old soldiers to Poperinghe in Belgium where the Mayor hosted a welcome reception. Instead of returning home with the veterans, he went on to the Black Forest, confirming arrangements for the next season's programme. From thence he travelled to Florence in Italy for a Lions International Europa Forum. Copenhagen and Norway were next, with business visits to Oslo, Bergen and the fjords, before attending an International Convention of Travel Agents in Stockholm. On the return trip, Joe stopped over in southern Sweden to do a little networking. It was a punishing schedule.

He appeared tireless, attending Lions meetings, supervising his children's homework and keeping an eye on Gail and Paul. He never missed a birthday or Christmas, turning up on Gordon's doorstep in Lakenham, laden with gifts. Gordon and Pauline now had three youngsters of their own. The stress of supporting five children was taking its toll on the couples' relationship. Despite this, Gordon retained his sense of fun. He saw life as an adventure. As an ex-Navy man he felt a deep affinity with the sea, taking his family to the coast as often as he could, even during the winter months, setting up a plastic shelter on the snow-covered beach. There they sat, snuggled together watching the waves of the North Sea crashing on to the shingle. Once she was old enough, Gail often took the bus after school to Unthank Road on the other side of the city. She still felt drawn to the Stirling family.

Business success led to a number of home improvements. Central heating was installed, the kitchen extended, attic rooms cleared to take a large model railway. Both front and back gardens were redesigned with a number of fruit trees cut down to accommodate extensive herbaceous borders. The coalbunker was demolished, the greenhouse cleared of its non-producing vines, space created for trays of seedlings and winter shelter for Jean's more delicate specimens. During long summer evenings the lawns were filled with children's laughter and the sound of croquet mallets tapping wooden balls through hoops.

True to form, Joe was anxious to see for himself how the developing Spanish resorts were shaping up. In 1965 instead of the annual sojourn to the Welsh mountains, Joe took his family to Benidorm on the western Mediterranean coast for a break under guaranteed sun. Following the tedious two-hour coach journey from Valencia Airport (the nearer Alicante would not open until 1967), they discovered a superb sandy bay, spectacular mountain views, palm-fringed boulevards, stylish hotels lined with balconies looking over the sea, swimming pools, bright sun umbrellas and bars offering jugs of Sangria complete with floating fruit, the measures of gin, whisky and vodka far more generous than at home. The food had unfamiliar names including paella, gazpacho and tortilla. Johanna was not at all sure.

In the mid-1950s the residents of Benidorm relied on fishing for their livelihood. When the stocks declined and the tuna industry failed, the Mayor of Benidorm approved a plan to throw all the town's resources into tourism. A massive building programme began, starting with the beachfront with the aim of accommodating a potential influx of overseas visitors. Joe could immediately see the potential for his business. The beaches were lined with tanned bodies, shockingly some women wearing revolutionary two-piece bikinis. Joe's children had barely completed the first sandcastle when four-year-old Johanna erupted in pinprick red spots. Chicken pox. Joe and Jean took turns to sit with her in the hotel room, while the other supervised the older children on the beach. Despite this, the holiday was a success, all agreeing to return the following year. With the economic growth experienced by much of Spain during the early 1960s, Spaniards and the rest of the world began to view Franco as more of an elder statesman than as a fascist dictator. It was time for Joe to let go of his previous high political principals.

Spain became a welcome addition to the Stirling Holidays portfolio.

Great Yarmouth and ABTA

'It took several months but we eventually gained ABTA membership. Our new headed paper and brochures proudly displayed the ABTA symbol.'

In September 1966, Stirling Holidays established a foothold in the East Anglian seaside town of Great Yarmouth. Fellow Lion, newsagent and part-time travel agent, Anthony Barker, suggested to Joe that he promote Stirling Holidays products and ticket sales in his modest shop at 19a King Street, trading as Vanity Fair Travel Agency. Anthony's core business was essentially news agencies, requiring exhausting early morning starts. Although initially happy to be Joe's East Coast agent, the sudden and unforeseen rise in the number of travel enquiries became unsustainable. The little shop was running out of space for the daily papers. He had signed a four-year lease on the property two years earlier and now wanted rid of the commitment. Would Stirling Holidays take it off his hands for a nominal sum? Joe called a special meeting of the directors, effectively just him and Jean. The purchase was agreed. Joe had bought a company, taken on a lease and was now responsible for four additional employees. That was worth celebrating.

Following a year studying at Warwick University, Jane concluded her choice of module had been a mistake. She dropped out in 1967, joining the family firm as a counter clerk in Magdalen Street working on the British coach tours. She found herself writing out hundreds and hundreds of coach tickets, one copy for the client, one for the file and one for the coach company. Her hands were relentlessly inky black from the carbon paper. She copied itineraries using a Gestetner duplicator, cutting the sheets into little booklets. During particularly busy periods Jane worked with the team until nine or ten at night. Her escape came when, aged twenty-three, she married Alan and moved to Kent. Jane had survived her time working for Father.

The boom in travel was not without casualties. In 1964 Fiesta Tours had collapsed, stranding 5,000 British tourists overseas without any possibility of redress. The following June a party of holidaymakers with the Omar Khayyam Travel Agency, bound for Cairo, were stranded in Paris when the United Arab Airline refused to accept the Agency's travel vouchers. The company closed the following month. It was clear that something had to be done. In

1950 twenty-two leading travel companies had founded a trades organisation known as the Association of British Travel Agencies (ABTA). In the wake of the Omar Khayyam debacle, it set about restoring confidence in the industry, creating a Common Fund based on 50 per cent of membership subscriptions. In the event of a member company failing to deliver, ABTA guaranteed to arrange repatriation, refund deposits or provide alternative holidays. For peace of mind, customers began buying only from bona fide ABTA members. It was essential that Stirling Holidays joined the club.

This was no easy task. Joe had to demonstrate his company's credibility by increasing the share capital to £30,000, a substantial amount of money. He provided ABTA with copies of past accounts, proving his company was trading successfully and that management members had at least five years' experience. The application was successful and Joe's notepaper was amended accordingly. He was immediately launched into yet another world of conferences, meetings, newsletters, small print and regulations. Very soon he was elected as Regional East Anglian representative for Retail Travel Agents on the Association National Council. Over the following twelve years Joe became one of very few people who served for eight years on the Travel Agents Council, followed by four on the Tour Operators Council.

Opening in Great Yarmouth proved a prudent decision. King Street was a central location and Joe was aware of the hundreds of family-run guesthouses and bed and breakfasts in the town. These people worked hard all summer, taking their own holidays out of season. National Tour operators placed special value on off-peak business. Stirling Holidays was now far better placed to provide it. Joe could look forward to a more balanced turnover all year round. Of even greater significance to both Great Yarmouth and to Stirling Holidays, was the invasion of the oilmen.

In 1965 the first offshore oil and gas wells were drilled off the coast of East Anglia. American giant Conoco built their first fixed platform just 50 miles off Great Yarmouth and by 1967 gas was being piped ashore from the Leman field. The Duke of Edinburgh opened the Bacton Gas terminal in 1968. Senior company directors from Texas and the Gulf of Mexico virtually took over Great Yarmouth, bringing the mighty dollar and prosperity in their wake.

Within two years, with the lease on Number 19a coming to a close, Joe looked for bigger premises in Great Yarmouth. An empty shop at 26 King Street was up for sale, close to the popular Market Tavern. The bank agreed the finances and Joe added a further retail property to his growing portfolio. While the shop fitters transformed the building, Joe recruited additional clerks. When curious customers stepped through the door, they were stunned by the impressive contemporary design, sleek low counter, vast selection of brochures and the smiling faces of Joe's new staff.

For those staff new to the travel trade, working for Stirling's was to prove a steep learning curve. Since the 1950s, technical innovation in civil air transport had advanced beyond imagination. By 1958 more transatlantic passengers travelled by air than by ship. Jets, with the shorter journey-times, more comfortable seats and increasing passenger numbers, swiftly followed the introduction of turbo-propeller aircraft. If Stirling Holidays were to be a part of this modern age and reap the potential rewards, it was crucial that Joe and his staff train in the complexities of issuing airline tickets. The International Air Transport Association (IATA) had been established in April 1945 in Havana, Cuba, to 'create, promote and control standards, practices and procedures' within the rapidly expanding airline industry. Learning from his experience with ABTA, Joe realised the importance of Stirling Holidays being officially recognised by IATA.

Leading by example, Joe invested in a correspondence course, learning the technical procedures of preparing tickets from blank pro formas, including calculating airport tax, checking passenger personal details, keeping a strict record of sales and how to claim commission. Following weeks of study, he attended a three-day course in London, culminating in a formal examination. Once IATA issued his license, Joe was qualified to train a number of his key staff. Towards the end of 1969 Joe applied to the IATA offices in Geneva, requesting they enter into a Passenger Sales Agency Agreement. The combination of ABTA membership and his agreement with IATA, led the way to the most significant advance for Stirling Holidays since the opening of Joe's first shop.

Access to the lucrative business travel market was within touching distance.

Chapter 5

Tour Guide and Sheriff, 1970–1980

'Chaos and Confusion'

'For Council members to say it is a ghastly planning mistake and still say it must go on is too silly for words.' (Harry Perry, former Lord Mayor of Norwich 1966, quoted in *The Eastern Daily Press*, 7 May 1970)

The public gallery of Norwich City Council Chamber was full. Joe and his colleagues from the Magdalen Street Traders Association sat together in a show of solidarity. It had been nearly ten years since the announcement of a controversial proposal to disfigure their street with a four-lane flyover. Since then Joe had attended scores of protest meetings, appealed to Members of Parliament, eminent architects and planning experts to help with the fight, and helped collect over 2,000 signatures. Despite every effort, following a public enquiry in 1965 the Transport Minister had given the go-ahead for the project. The people of Norwich had been living in a building site for the past five years. But it wasn't over just yet. There was still hope of the flyover plans being scrapped. Councillors and exasperated city planning officers were debating whether finally to reject the flyover, the money to be switched to another section of the proposed link road with the route of the northern section reconsidered. The newspaper reporters sharpened their pencils.

As early as March, members of the Planning Committee had voted almost unanimously to defer a final decision for at least four months. They would look again for alternative options for easing the disruptive traffic problems in the city. But what would that mean for the proposed flyover? The Leader of the Council, Tom Eaton, was concerned that the Ministry of Transport had only recently given loan sanction for the money to pay for it. The City Engineer Mr Binks was frustrated; he was ready to send out tenders inviting contractors to submit quotations. Had anyone considered how Sovereign Securities, the construction company scheduled to build the Anglia Square Shopping Centre, might react? The flyover was integral to their plans, providing access from the inner link road directly into the complex. This uncertainty could jeopardise their entire project. Any change of plan could risk serious financial penalties.

It was the evening of 6 May 1970. The Conservative-controlled City Council returned to the issue at the final full council meeting, crucially just two days before the local council elections. Joe and his colleagues were well aware of the importance of the evening's debate. The opening remarks established an agreement that the original plans had probably been 'a ghastly planning mistake'. However since the result of the Public Enquiry, work on the link road had already started. Journalists and protestors alike scribbled notes furiously as the early measured discussion escalated into uproar, erupting with passionate interjections from interested parties on both sides. Tom Eaton concluded his remarks in support of continuing with the flyover by saying, 'In my view, business and industry is entitled to feel that once the council has made a decision, it is a firm decision. If we suddenly decide to throw out something which has been planned for ten years we lose not only respect, but create chaos and confusion.'

Harry Perry fought back. 'I am adamant that the building of the flyover could and should be stopped. Every argument in its favour since it was conceived in 1959 has gone by the board in the light of changing circumstances.' If Joe had been hoping for support from his old friend and colleague Arthur South he was out of luck. As Leader of the Labour Group South confirmed his long-standing opposition to the scheme, but seriously doubted if the Council could reverse the decision at that late stage.

Two days later the public voted. Labour regained control of the City Council. Arthur, as Leader of the Council, outlined to the press his plans for Norwich including encouraging new industry and increasing the number of new homes. What was his view on the flyover? Arthur repeated that the plan would have to go ahead for practical reasons. Any radical reversals would involve putting everything back, maybe for years, with inevitable expensive and disruptive delays. It appeared that Joe and his fellow protesters were to lose this fight.

Plans for the flyover were now set in concrete.

Norfolk Oilmen

'*Dear Sirs, We acknowledge receipt of your account for £4.0.0. for interior and exterior photographs taken of our new premises at 26 King Street, Great Yarmouth. Frankly, we feel this is rather an excessive amount especially as two of the four exterior views had been taken in such a way (obviously not taking reflection into consideration) that although having been open for less than a week we were already declaring ourselves "bankrupt". We trust you will reconsider the charges.'* (Letter from L. G. Williams, Branch Manager, Stirling Holidays, Great Yarmouth, October 1970)

Leonard Williams had been managing Joe's new shop at 26 King Street in Great Yarmouth since the opening. It was now October 1970 and IATA, slow to issue his licence to sell airline tickets, had requested photographs of the Great Yarmouth showroom. The shop opposite was offering bankrupt stock but the professional photographer failed to notice the reflection in the plate-glass windows. Mr Williams, an ex-Coldstream Guardsman and later to retire as a Chelsea Pensioner, was not best pleased. And neither was his boss.

The year had begun with the first American Boeing 747 Jumbo Jet landing at Heathrow on 12 January amidst much excitement over new innovations such as automated 'lavatories occupied' signs and colour-coordinated 'saloons.' The jets could seat over 300 passengers. The world had just got smaller. Travel agents were busier. Early in 1972, Doreen Hardy walked the length of King Street on her way to the hospital on St. Peters' Plain. She was hoping to find a job, having recently moved down from the Midlands with her family to set up a bed-and-breakfast business in Great Yarmouth. Her husband and mother would cook and clean, Doreen would find a way of supplementing the household income. On passing Stirling Holidays, a notice in the window caught her eye. 'Clerk wanted'. Mr Williams interviewed her right away, explaining it was only a temporary position covering a maternity leave. Was Mrs Hardy trained in office work? Indeed, Doreen had experience of secretarial work with a local council before training as a nurse. Mr Williams was satisfied. When could she start?

It would be some time before Doreen met Mr Stirling. He usually worked from the Norwich office or was away on research trips or escorting a group. For the first few weeks she sat in the corner typing invoices and studying the mysteries of savings and credit schemes, designed to help clients pay for their holidays as painlessly as possible. All the while she listened to the smartly-uniformed counter staff dealing with the public, poring over the latest Stirling Holidays brochure. Had Madam considered Margate, Morecambe, Lake District, Torquay, Llandudno, Blackpool or perhaps the bright lights of London?

Most intriguing were the escorted Continental tours, many of them led by Mr Stirling himself, including romantic sounding places such as Ostend, Lake Lucerne in Switzerland, the Austrian Tyrol, Strasbourg and Alsace. Once the manager was confident that Doreen was a conscientious worker, it was suggested she might like more responsibility, perhaps contacting airlines and booking flights. But it would mean taking the IATA exams. She was reluctant but knew someone who would be ideal for the task, suggesting her seventeen-year-old school-leaver daughter Judith for the role. Joe took the risk and was satisfied to find her lively, personable, bright and willing. Judith fitted in well. It was the start of a mother-and-daughter working relationship that would endure for nearly thirty years.

Over the following months over 10,000 American families settled in the Great Yarmouth area. Although everyone struggled to understand each other's accents, the incomers brought with them many benefits but especially business. The region was booming. With money to spend and time on their hands, they were keen to discover the tourist hotspots of London, Cornwall, the Lakes and especially Shakespeare Country. There were only two travel agents in Great Yarmouth, Seaforth's and Stirling's. But with more than enough work for both companies, days were busy. Evenings too, with Doreen and Judith often staying late to keep up with administration. Quick to learn, Judith was soon made manager of the air travel section, reserving First Class flights to Houston or enquiring directly with airlines on the most cost-effective method of flying a group of oilmen to India or Nigeria. The discovery of 'black gold' was becoming a priority around the globe and Stirling Holidays was more than happy to play its part. Judith was always willing to open lucrative accounts for both major and smaller drilling companies, her personal service and attention to detail and rewarding the company with 7 per cent commission on each airline ticket.

One favoured client was the Senior Director of McDermott Marine Construction Limited, an Offshore Field Development Company, established in 1923 in Texas, USA. One morning Judith received a telephone enquiry. Could Stirling's arrange for some of the guys to fly from Norwich to Aberdeen for a golf tournament?

During the early 1970s Norwich Airport was still establishing itself as a commercial airport, dealing mainly in freight. Through a friend of a friend, Joe was able to contact the owner of East Anglian Airways, a tiny operation boasting just one Douglas DC-3 propeller-driven airliner, the plane that had played a significant part in popularising air travel in the United States. It sat twenty-six passengers, who were obliged to enter at the back of the plane and walk uphill, pulling themselves up the aisle using the backs of seats. Flights were invariably noisy and shaky but thankfully reliable. Stirling Holidays chartered a private flight for the American oilmen, the first company to do so out of Norwich Airport. Joe waved them off personally. At Aberdeen, the plane waited on the apron while the oilmen enjoyed their eighteen holes. Two days later on flying back into Norwich, they found Mr Stirling there to greet them.

McDermott Marine would not forget Mr Stirling's professionalism, ingenuity and good humour.

Everyone in Great Yarmouth hoped the oilmen and their deep pockets were there to stay.

A Pride of Lions in Sin City

'You have a name badge with a ribbon on which says "Elect". The new International President tells you all to pull the ribbon off and then you are a District Governor.'
(John Jones, President of Norwich Lions Club 2014–15)

On 13 November 1970 Joe's mother-in-law Lucy died. She was eighty-one, suffering with debilitating arthritis and had been fading over a period of time. Undeterred, this plucky lady had continued to cook Sunday lunches for her grandchildren, followed by tea and treats at her home in Stafford Street, until a major stroke proved fatal. The Skitmore clan rallied round. Jean would miss her mother. She did not believe in children attending funerals, warning Jane, now twenty-three, that it would be a long and tedious Brethren ceremony. None of Lucy's grandchildren were there when Lucy's body was buried in the same plot as her husband in Attleborough cemetery.

Some months later the family commissioned a figure of an angel to be carved into the stone, along with a verse from the Song of Solomon, 'Until the Day Break and the Shadow Flee Away'. Jean found it a comfort that her mother had lived long enough to see her eldest grandchild Jane married and settled in Kent with her husband Alan; her grandson Ian, at nineteen volunteering at Help the Aged and the two youngest, Martin fifteen and Johanna twelve, studying at the Hewett School in Cecil Road. Lucy had watched Paul and Gail grow into adults, Paul now in work and with his own home, Gail training as a hairdresser, still living with Gordon and Pauline. Nanny would always be remembered for her dark curls, caged budgie and yummy sponge cakes.

Regrettably, Lucy did not live long enough to see her son-in-law rise through the ranks of the Lions Club Hierarchy, invited in February 1971 to stand for the highest regional office of all, that of District Governor for District 105A (British Isles and Ireland), representing one of the seven districts in the United Kingdom.

For most Lions this elected position, held for just one year, is the pinnacle of their career in Lionism. Joe was competing against two other candidates from Great Yarmouth and London. Joe was convinced that with the East Anglian vote split London was bound to win. The result was announced in March. The winner was Lion Joe Stirling from Norwich. He felt both humble and honoured. This was a period of great expansion in the Lions Club of Great Britain, with unprecedented increases in membership and formation of new clubs. Joe's region was vast, comprising a number of counties in East Anglia and the South East, including Heathrow and Gatwick.

As part of his extensive duties, Joe was obliged over the course of the year to visit all forty-two clubs in his district, submitting a report on each to include details of membership, attendance and financial data. He would chair four cabinet meetings with specialist officers, preside at his own District Convention and attend both the incoming and outgoing International Conventions. In addition, he and Jean would be in demand for a number of celebratory charter dinners, preparing and delivering a speech, donning a white dinner jacket, traditional formal dress for District Governors, not forgetting the obligatory bow tie. He would officially take up this new office during the installation ceremony on the final day of the Annual International Convention at the end of June, that year to be held in the party city of Las Vegas in the heat of the Nevada Desert, USA.

Joe had never been to a Lions International Convention. He had never visited America. But then neither had the other six incoming District Governors (DGs). In the spring they met together to discuss strategic policies for the year ahead. When they reached agenda item 'International Conference', someone said, 'Look, we're lucky this year. We've got Joe here; he's a travel agent. Maybe he can organise the trip to Las Vegas for us?' Up until then all Lions attending the International Convention, including the DGs, had made their own travel arrangements. With so few individual travellers from the UK flying across the Atlantic there were no discounted fares. The best value for the Multiple District, responsible for paying fares and expenses, would be to arrange a group fare, the minimum requirement being fifteen people. Joe was the best man for the job. Seven incoming DGs, seven wives. Where to find the fifteenth member?

Joe recalled one of his regular clients at Stirling Holidays, a retired lady teacher in her late sixties, speaking at length of her ambition to visit America. While browsing the brochures in Magdalen Street she once said, 'If you ever hear of a group going to America let me know'. Joe contacted her, explaining she would be joining a party of Lions, but it wasn't all business; a variety of excursions would be available. She didn't hesitate. Joe had his minimum number.

He spent the next few weeks planning every aspect, leaving nothing to chance. The Convention opened on 22 June with Joe and his colleagues obliged to arrive four days earlier in time for District Governors' School. His planning was meticulous. This trip would involve far more than just a convention.

Flights into New York led to a couple of days riding yellow cabs, taking the elevator to the top of the Empire State Building and a ferry to the Statue of Liberty. It was just like being in a movie. An internal flight to San Francisco, almost as far again as London to New York, took them the Golden Gate Bridge, Fisherman's Wharf and views over the Pacific Ocean. Finally it was time to discover the playground city of Las Vegas.

As the party descended the aircraft steps, they hit a wall of air measuring 107° Fahrenheit. The transfer bus, thankfully fitted with air-conditioning, drove down The Strip and Fremont Street, the British delegates and the 'lady from Nor-wich', gawping through the windows. Had they landed on a different planet? Cocktail lounges, topless clubs, 'Coin Castle' amusement arcade with its 20-foot cowboy figure in neon-yellow shirt and ten-gallon hat, stood alongside the outrageous hotel-casinos; 'Silver Spur', 'Flamingo Hilton', 'Lady Luck', 'The Sands' and 'Bonanza'. There was great excitement amongst the ladies when passing the enormous billboards announcing Tom Jones playing Caesars Palace and Elvis himself appearing at the International Hotel. Lovingly polished Chryslers, Plymouths and Cadillacs cruised past the bus, ferrying long-legged showgirls to work. Strolling the streets were 15,000 Lions and their wives, recently arrived from all over the world.

While husbands attended District Governor classes, Jean, the other wives and the 'the lady from Nor-wich' experienced a breathtaking flight over the Grand Canyon in a light aircraft. What tales they brought back to the hotel! Every building with a roof was air-conditioned, kept at a manageable level of around 70°. Outdoor social activities were reserved for after sunset, when the temperature dropped to a 'cool' 82°. In keeping with tradition, the incoming DGs from every country led their contingent in the Grand Opening Parade through the city streets, national flags proudly held high. Setting off at 8 p.m., the parade was loud, brash, colourful and vibrant with decorated floats and flotillas of extravagant cars, accompanied by baton-twirling cheerleaders. By the time the final contingent crossed the 'saluting base', duly acknowledging the outgoing International President, the sky was black, city lights obscuring the cosmos above. Wives, officials, tourists and locals packed the streets, cheering, applauding and straining to catch as much as possible of this spectacular event, laughing aloud at 'Lord' Dawkins of Andover from the British contingent who strolled along the Strip in City of London attire of bowler hat, rolled umbrella and copy of *The Times*. Joe had never heard the Lions' inspirational song, 'Don't You Hear Those Lions Roar!' performed by quite so many people.

Inside the vast convention hall the opening speeches included news of the extended Lions Headquarters in downtown Chicago, now complete and doubling its space. Earlier in the year Lions had seen the formation of Club number 25,000. The honour went to the small wine-growing town of Fredericksburg in Texas. It was a hectic few days with Joe keen to hear every key speaker, attend fringe meetings, join in debates, vote on decisions and meet with like-minded Lions, never losing sight of his responsibilities as a tour leader. The final day of the convention arrived. Jean took her seat for the Installation Ceremony, the highlight of the entire event. She was weary of the non-stop fashion shows, coach tours into the desert, wives' tea parties and boozy sessions long into the night, having to keep that smile going all the while. But it was Joe's special moment. She was ready. With International Officers for the coming year introduced and welcomed, it was the turn of the incoming District Governors. Hundreds of men, tall, short, balding, bespectacled, thin, not so thin, hailing from all continents, marched into the hall under the flag of their nation. The welcome from the audience was deafening, close to pandemonium in the hall as loyal Lions cheered their friends and colleagues. The International President, industrial engineer Robert J. Uplinger from Syracuse, New York, gave the instruction to pull the ribbons, previously pinned to the lapels of the shiny new DGs, revealing the special metal badge confirming their new rank. Not since her wedding day had Jean Stirling felt so proud of her husband.

Before leaving Las Vegas, the delegates swapped pin badges, a popular ritual at Lions events. Many members were avid collectors of the unique metal badges; rare and unusual ones much sought after as collectors items, occasionally sold on as part of a fundraising drive. Originally known as 'Friendship Pins', they were designed and produced by Clubs, themes including flags, maps, transport, flora, fauna and predictably, the ubiquitous King of the Jungle. At the crowded hotel lobby, with the airport bus waiting impatiently outside, there were the inevitable tearful goodbyes to old and new friends. But for Joe's contingent the fun was far from over. His programme took them to Hollywood and the excitement of Mann's Chinese Theatre with the handprints of iconic movie stars. Washington D.C. was next on the itinerary. A quick look at the White House, Capitol Hill and Arlington Cemetery and they were homeward bound on an overnight flight. As they sipped celebratory gin and tonics at 30,000 feet, two of Joe's fellow DGs leaned over his seat.

'Joe, you must organise this again next year.'

'That will be up to the new DGs.'

'They'll be keen once we tell them of the experience we've just had and how you've saved us money.'

As Joe and Jean approached little old 'Nor-wich', the city felt very provincial compared to the wonders of the United States.

District Governor and that Flyover

'Reaction to the flyover seems to have mellowed since those early days when the Magdalen Street Traders' Association fought against it and a public enquiry was held. Traders have adopted a "wait and see" attitude, but cautiously admit that the flyover does have its good points.' (The Eastern Daily Press, 8 June 1972)

Six weeks after Joe's return home from Las Vegas, the Assistant City Engineer Frank Jones gave notice of the closure of Magdalen Street, with 5,000 leaflets distributed throughout the city. Ninety concrete beams, each weighing 30 tons and measuring 75 feet, would be laid along the street in preparation for the controversial flyover. It was business as usual at Stirling Holidays but the unrelenting racket and gritty grey dust clogging the air, covering all the brochures with a layer of fine power, made working conditions intolerable.

Conveniently for Joe, for the twelve months July 1971 to 1972, he had rather more to concern himself with than just road works. As District Governor his diary was packed. Colleagues at the Norwich Lions Club were proud to have one of their own take on this prestigious mantel. The official year began on 5 July with an Installation Dinner held in Norwich, followed by visits to Clubs in Horley, Harrow and Bedford. The Council of Governors met in Solihull in August at the beginning of a relatively quiet month. September and October saw Joe back in his car driving to Leighton Buzzard, Farnham and then Hemel Hempstead, where he made a speech at the Clubs' tenth anniversary Charter Dinner. The Lions Europa Forum was held in Palma de Majorca and he called in at no less than ten Clubs during November. Stirling Holidays had been granted the task of arranging travel for the International Convention in Mexico in June 1972. It proved a heavy workload. Jean wondered if she would ever share a dinner with her husband again.

A most prestigious guest from Montreal in Canada arrived in Norwich during April 1972. Tris Coffin, Second Vice-President of Lions International, was undertaking a tour of British Lions Clubs. He was renowned as the 'Fruit Cake King of Canada', for his sales of over 40,000 fruitcakes over many years, raising money for community projects. It had been five years since an International Officer had visited Norwich. Coffin first met with the Lord Mayor, followed by a whirlwind visit around the sights of Norwich proudly accompanied by District Governor Joe Stirling. The two men inspected the fleet of Meals-on-Wheels vans, donated by the Club, witnessed key social work projects associated with Lions and spent an extended time admiring the beauty of Norwich Cathedral.

On Monday, 12 June the city street pattern in Norwich officially changed when the flyover linking Barrack Street roundabout to Pitt Street opened to traffic. The project was completed ahead of schedule and civic dignitaries, council officers and honoured guests gathered to witness the ribbon cutting ceremony. Demonstrating typical Norfolk eccentricity, a restored Victorian Ladies' Phaeton, an open horse-drawn carriage with extravagantly large wheels, became the first vehicle to cross the bridge, driven by Norman Laidlow, a member of the British Driving Society.

The Civic Party followed in a fleet of limousines, gazing down from a great height onto the businesses and homes below in Magdalen Street. Years of wrangling and ill feeling seemed forgotten, as during a grand celebratory luncheon at City Hall, Mr J. Holmes, Director of the construction engineers May Gurney presented the council with a silver rose bowl to commemorate the successful completion. Joe did not attend the lunch. He was still smarting from the failure to overturn the planning decision. But this was not the time to dwell on the past.

He was due in Mexico City in less than two weeks.

Down Mexico Way

'One must not linger over happenings, such as the epic climb of a certain old lady locked in the loo at Acapulco Airport, of two lost dithering Lions and a taxi meter boiling over, or how Joe Stirling stood up to the strain as our Mother and Father in times of stress and Jean's remarkable patience.' (Burgess Hillienne, 'Woman's World', *The Lion*, September 1972.)

Mexico was new territory for Joe. Resolved to approach the Convention trips with the same professionalism as he did in every aspect of his business, he took a brief reconnaissance trip during the second half of 1971, exploring Mexico City and identifying attractive excursions. He was excited by the location finding it vibrant and exotic, so very different from anywhere he had visited before. By the late spring of 1972 his party was complete, the seven outgoing DGs and their wives but this year with sixteen additional Lions, who having read reports about the success of the previous year, were keen to experience a 'Stirling Holidays Convention' for themselves.

Their initial impressions of Mexico City through the glass of the airport bus were very different to those of Las Vegas. The air was oppressive, saturated with carbon monoxide from stationary queues of traffic clogging the streets. Angry horns, revving engines and screech of brakes denied the travellers any chance of relaxation after such a long flight. Twenty-five miles to the west, the snow-capped Popocatépetl volcano dominated the skyline. The most recent major eruption had been in 1947; everyone quietly prayed it would remain dormant for at least the next four days. A mix of squalor and grandeur was on open display with modern blocks and hotels mingled with overcrowded slums and the remnants of intricately carved stone buildings.

The arrival of 30,000 delegates was just as in Las Vegas, a heaving mass of humanity of all shapes, sizes and hues, laden with suitcases, cameras and wallets, each seeking a shower and a beer after standing in a seemingly never ending line to check in to their convention hotel. At the welcome tea party for the wives of District Governors, outgoing and incoming, the ladies were on their best behaviour. Jean once again found herself exchanging pleasantries and 'friendship pins', sitting in the lounge of the Hotel Marie Isabel amongst the other 'Dandelions', the affectionate term for Lions' womenfolk.

The following days passed quickly. The flag ceremony, excursions to pyramids and silver mines, business meetings, key speeches and tequila parties in hotel suites. On the final day, the new International President was sworn in, unusually a Frenchman, George Friedrichs. Then, as last year, the moment came when District Governors entered the convention hall. Joe felt a touch perturbed to be so abruptly dismissed from his coveted role. He was however, genuinely pleased for his successor Claude Timewell, the publican of the Royal Hotel, Great Yarmouth. Jean secretly felt relieved. She would like to have her Joe back please.

Joe was, once again, approached to organise the travel for the 1973 Lions International Convention to Miami in Florida. Feeling a little nervous about his ethical position, he responded, 'I have enjoyed doing this and am happy to do so as long as you want me, but I didn't join Lions to get business.' He requested an advertisement be placed every autumn in *The Lion* magazine, inviting other travel companies to tender quotations. Stirling Holidays' proposal proved competitive and was duly accepted.

Miami, Mickey Mouse and Gumbo

'I read that Walt Disney had recently opened a new attraction called Walt Disney World in a small town in the middle of Southern Florida called Orlando. I had never heard of it. I thought that might be interesting for some.'

Joe read in the *Travel Gazette* that in 1965 Walt Disney had announced his visionary 'Florida Project'. Tragically the entertainment tycoon did not live to see his project develop, dying from lung cancer in 1966. However, his company had already bought up thousands of acres of cheap swampland in Orange County. The outcome was a theme park five times the size of that in California, complete with linked resort hotels, opening to the public in October 1971. Joe knew that this could make an appealing addition to his 'side trips' and set about investigating the travel logistics. Within a month of Joe's advert appearing, every available place was taken, his party once again larger than the previous year. As he checked his British contingent into their convention hotel, Joe felt the pressure of being the tour leader, rather more than before. As his numbers increased so did the responsibilities. It was becoming difficult to remain 'one of the boys'.

It was in Miami that the Lions International Pin Trading Club was set up with thirty-six charter members, each agreeing to pay an annual membership fee of $10. The concept quickly spread throughout the 26,000 clubs in 149 countries. The Convention over, the British contingent divided into two groups, some looking forward to simply relaxing on Miami beach for a few days, others heading for Walt Disney World and New Orleans, accompanied by Joe and Jean. A short hop on a noisy DC-4 propeller plane took the party to Orlando. They felt a little strange to be a group of just adults as they explored the Magic Kingdom, Adventureland, Bear Country and Fantasyland. Everyone agreed it had been a bewitching experience.

An internal flight took the group to New Orleans. Some naively asked whether they would need to speak French to fully appreciate the French Quarter, surprised to find the architecture more closely resembling southern Spain. Jazz musicians played at every junction. The traditional creole gumbo and Sazarac brandy cocktails served in the low-lit nightclubs went down extremely well.

Joe's organisational skills were becoming indispensible.

Oil Crisis and San Francisco

'I started organising convention groups, nothing to do with Lions and of course some of these people became individual clients. If someone had a business trip to New York or Washington, here was someone who knew the quickest and most economical routes. Our sale of air tickets went up and up.'

Shortly after Joe's arrival home in July 1973 from New Orleans, the Three Cs closed its doors. Increasingly tight budgets and the resurgence of suburban youth clubs hastened its ultimate demise. Although recently reducing the time he spent there, Joe had invested much time and effort and was sorry to see it go. However, there was better news from NOAH, a youth project with which

Joe had been associated since 1969. Its application to the Charities Commission for charitable status had been accepted.

Joe could see business potential in Florida. The Walt Disney attraction had been inspirational. He lost no time in designing a new package to add to his Stirling Holidays brochure for the following year. During any free time during the Miami Convention, he had been making contacts in the travel trade, assessing attractions, checking hotels, costing up excursions, tasting speciality dishes in restaurants. A two-week holiday would cost £129 per person, staying at the Monte Carlo Hotel in Miami, with its swimming pool virtually on the beach. Doreen and Judith in the Great Yarmouth office were intrigued, unaware that they would be personally escorting this tour on more than one occasion over the following seasons.

In October 1973 continuing conflict between Arab and Israeli forces led to the Middle East oil-producing countries refusing to export to the United States, accusing the Superpower of supporting Israel. Global implications included immediate increases in the price of oil, fuel shortages and rationing, reduced speed limits, frequent power cuts and television broadcasters forced to close down the network by 10.30 p.m. With so much disruption, uncertainty and inevitable price increases in air travel, business at Stirling Holidays took a severe downturn. People simply did not dare commit large sums of money to travel.

In December Joe and his fellow Lions faced real difficulties collecting food donations from around the city, destined for onward distribution to the elderly. The club's publicity officer, Roy Woodhouse, promised in the local press that even if the club had to pay for all the food itself, about 100 old people would definitely receive Christmas food parcels. Three businesses volunteered as collection points, including Stirling Holidays. Joe's members of staff were happy to co-operate, even if the office did soon resemble a branch of the Co-op.

In the early spring of 1974, in response to the annual advertisements in *The Lion* for Convention tenders, Grays World Travel, an agency associated with the larger Hogg Robinson Travel Company, undercut that of Stirling Holidays. Joe was under pressure to reduce his quote, but on this occasion he was more than happy to allow someone else take the strain. With the fuel crisis gradually lessening, business was once again on the up and Joe was fully occupied dealing with a flood of bookings for the new Miami package. Joe assigned Doreen and Judith to escort the groups. Right from the start their Florida adventure was more stressful than imagined. The clients were demanding with questions, questions and more questions. Mr Stirling stubbornly refused to have one of the new business credit cards, which was a problem, as the Americans would deal with nothing else. Judith mistakenly booked two single men into a double-bedded room and had to face their wrath the following morning. Two elderly ladies requested a private day excursion to the Bahamas, Doreen undertaking to book them onto flights, only for them to change their minds and Judith struggled to get up at two in the morning to wave off three men on their Marlin fishing trip. Doreen and Judith returned to the office looking forward to a rest!

Joe's reputation was spreading well beyond Norfolk. Following a telephone call from the British Association of Electrical Engineers he was booked to personally escort a business convention trip to Chicago, his first not involving Lions Clubs. In response to new optimism and facing increasing competition, international hotel chains and airlines offered members of ABTA and IATA exciting opportunities to join all-expenses paid 'educational' trips. There was never any shortage of takers amongst Joe's staff, keen to enjoy first-class travel, hotel suites with breathtaking views, chilled champagne and complimentary four-course meals. In return, all the agencies had to do was recommend their products to potential clients.

During May 1974 Joe took an unexpected telephone call from the Convention Chairman in the UK. A misunderstanding between Grays World Travel and Lions International Headquarters in Chicago had resulted in a standoff. The Lions were insisting on normal upfront payments for accommodation, Grays claiming they had been misinformed and refusing to divert from their normal business practice of paying for accommodation after the clients had left the hotels. Could Stirling Holidays please take over the convention travel as before? Fortunately Joe already had a comprehensive list of contacts in San Francisco. He could make last-minute arrangements from his Norwich office. Most Lions immediately rebooked with him and by the end of June 160 Lions were on board.

The party flew on a Pan-Am 747 Jumbo into Los Angeles, but not before an unscheduled stop in Detroit. One of Joe's delegates, irate at the delay, complained forcibly to the airline, compensated with a first-class seat for the last leg of the journey. He was fascinated to find himself seated next to the infamous pornographic actress Linda Lovelace. His colleagues heard about little else for days. A convoy of coaches took three days to wend its way up the spectacular West Coast route to San Francisco. As so many of his delegation had already been to Las Vegas and Los Angeles, Joe offered a post-convention trip to Honolulu in Hawaii. This island state in the North Pacific promised beautiful mountain views, sandy beaches, six or seven different islands to explore and a traditional warm welcome from beautiful native women in grass skirts. Jean particularly enjoyed her time there, delighted when it was announced as the venue for the 1976 Convention. Not wishing to risk a further debacle, once back in the office, Joe began work right away on his quotation.

At home the family were looking forward to Gail's wedding. She was to marry her sweetheart, local boy Peter Scott, on 2 November 1974. Knowing how difficult Gail had found it sharing a home with her stepmother, Joe was pleased that at twenty-one she had found happiness. He was also on hand to congratulate his friend of fifteen years, Sir Arthur South, on his recent knighthood for services to the community. For Arthur, an inveterate self-publicist, it was an honour that trumped even his achievements as Magistrate, Leader of Norwich City Council, Chairman of the Area Health Authority and Chairman of Norwich City Football Club. For Joe too, the future looked positive. His in tray was heaped high, cash flow healthy, staff in both office locations seemed content. However, in the Great Yarmouth offices of McDermott Marine, optimism was in short supply. Despite the recent oil crisis cementing the worldview that the North Sea was a critical and valuable sector within the industry, the anticipated reserves off the Norfolk coast were proving disappointing.

Unknown to Joe, the American oil barons were reconsidering their position.

Sheriff of Norwich

'Though I have travelled the world extensively, there is no other place than Norwich I would rather live.' (Joe Stirling quoted in *The Eastern Evening News*, 21 May 1975)

It was an average February lunchtime in 1975. The office telephone rang. Joe answered. 'Joe, it's Arthur. How would you like to be the next Sheriff of the City?'

Joe laughed out loud. 'Arthur, are you sure you haven't been drinking?'

'Not at all old man, what do you think?'

'But I'm not even a councillor. Not for ten years.'

Sir Arthur reminded Joe of the Local Government Act of 1972 when the new regulations, much to the chagrin of many in the City, had effectively demoted Norwich City Council to the status of a District Council, with many previous responsibilities such as Education, Highways, Social Services and the Libraries transferred to Norfolk County Council. Before this change, the law had allowed the Lord Mayor to be chosen from outside the council, in practice about once every five years. Joe's friend, businessman John Jarrold, had held the honour from 1970–1. With this option now removed, the councillors were seeking a different method of honouring deserving citizens.

The position of Sheriff had a long history. During the Anglo-Saxon period, before the Normans invaded Engalnd in 1066, a Sheriff was appointed in every county, responsible for the military tax collection and the law, including arranging public executions. In 1402 the King granted that the City of Norwich be a county of itself, separate from the County of Norfolk and that each year the citizens should choose a Mayor and two Sheriffs. The Municipal Corporation Act of 1835 reduced the number of Norwich Sheriffs from two to one, the Sheriffs Acts of 1887 further reducing his legal powers. In modern times, the position of Sheriff had no involvement in council decision-making; he had no need to attend meetings apart from sitting in the public gallery, forbidden to speak. He would no longer hold legal powers apart from continuing to perform the ancient ceremony of welcoming the circuit High Court Judge two or three times a year. Accordingly, it had been agreed that the apolitical post of Sheriff would be an ideal honorary position. The first City Sheriff from outside the Council would be appointed in May 1975. After a short debate the councillors had chosen Joe Stirling for his tireless services to the voluntary sector in Norwich.

Joe sat at his desk calmly considering the offer. Before he left the office a civic officer called in with some details of the role. This information would help Joe when talking with the one person who was pivotal in making his decision. He left work early that afternoon. Jean asked all the right questions. How much time would it involve? How would it impact on the business? What about his Lions activities? Her experience as Joe's wife would undoubtedly help her carry out the role of Sheriff's Lady. She had lost count of the gala occasions, standing by her man as the 'dutiful wife', best frock, smiling widely, making small talk, applauding at the right times. But Jean was a private person. She was not enthusiastic about this latest prospect. Joe persevered. He had trustworthy people managing the business. His responsibilities would be close to home in Norwich, events held mainly in the evenings. He might have to make speeches now and again but Jean wouldn't have to speak. Jean relented. Joe called Arthur with the good news.

'You must have asked lots of people before you got to me.'

'Joe, I don't want to make you more boastful, but you were top of the list.'

The April edition of *The Lion* published its congratulations to Past District Governor Lion Joe Stirling for his forthcoming appointment as Sheriff of the City of Norwich. Now hundreds of thousands of Lions throughout the world knew of his honour.

Joe allowed himself a moment of satisfaction.

The Making of a Sheriff

'You have to go through this strange procedure at the special Annual Meeting of the City Council. The nominee for Lord Mayor and the nominee for Sheriff are

not allowed into the Chamber, you have to sit in the Lord Mayor's Parlour. In the
Council Chamber a speech is made to thank the outgoing Lord Mayor and Sheriff.
Then someone nominates the new Lord Mayor (it has all been agreed beforehand)
so it is purely ceremonial.'

The Stirling family rose early on Tuesday 20 May 1975. Jean made breakfast
for her brood as they fought over the bathroom to clean and preen for this
momentous family occasion. In the city the ceremonial civic carriage had been
washed and polished, the two dray horses groomed meticulously. Over 200
people gathered in the streets outside City Hall to see outgoing Lord Mayor
William Spear and his wife complete their journey from the Unthank Road
in the carriage, for what would be their final day as Norwich Civic leaders. It
was a momentous day too for Fred Peed, retiring as the Civic Sword Bearer
on the following Friday.

In a different part of the city, the new Lord Mayor fixed her make-up and
hair in readiness for her big day. Councillor Joyce Morgan had been doubly
delighted when the Council announced the names of the Lord Mayor and
Sheriff for 1975–6. She had fond memories of working with Joe Stirling on the
Trades Council and the Three Cs. They would make a great partnership. Joyce
and Joe greeted each other warmly before sitting together in the Lord Mayor's
Parlour, waiting for their moment. The Parlour was a delightful octagonal
room, panelled in sycamore with French walnut trim, a solid mantelpiece
bearing framed photographs of visiting royalty, sunlight pouring in through
the French windows leading to an iron balcony overlooking St Peter's Street
and the Market Place. They talked in nervous hushed tones or paced the floor
a little, privately wishing they could hear for themselves what was being said
inside the Chamber. Along the corridor in the Council Chamber, elected
members were indeed making celebratory speeches, explaining the reasons for
nominating Councillor Morgan and Mr Stirling. Donald Pratt Lord Mayor
in 1971–2 reported that Joyce Morgan would be only the fourth female Lord
Mayor in forty-five years adding, 'By her ability and record of public service
she is someone well qualified and deserving of this high office.' Arthur Clare,
successor to Joe as Secretary-Agent for Norwich Labour Party, proposed the
nomination for Sheriff. He said, 'This election symbolises the understanding
Norwich has for internationalism and in recognition of voluntary services
outside the city council. Joe Stirling came to England as a frightened boy with
a label on his coat. He will be proud to wear the chain of office of Sheriff.'

Joyce was the first to be ushered from the Parlour by Fred Peed, the
costumed Sword Bearer on his last ever day in office, to be escorted to the
Chamber down the mahogany lined corridor, portraits of former Lord Mayors

staring down reverently. Joe was left alone with his thoughts. Some twenty minutes later he once again heard a loud knock on the English walnut door and knew his moment had come. The decorated doors to the Chamber were opened wide and a voice boomed out, 'Ladies and Gentlemen, the Worshipful the Sheriff Elect.' Joe stepped across the threshold, seeing the art deco space as if for the first time. The far wall lined with horizontal wooden panels set in a brickwork pattern, the curved benches, the grand 'top table' with the central tall-backed chair framed by an oversized bed canopy of silk drapes in greys and gold. Alongside, silently watching proceedings as they had done for decades, were four enormous portraits of past civic leaders. Joyce stood at the front of the chamber looking resplendent, despite only standing 5ft 4in, in her civic Mayoral full-length robe of black cloth with embellished gold silk trim, decorative sleeves, white lace neck-ruff and cuffs, the gold chain and medal weighing heavy from her shoulders. Atop her head sat the distinctive tricorn hat with its enormous black ostrich feather. Joe was aware of familiar faces in the gallery, old council colleagues and close friends, each eager to catch his eye as he walked towards the splendid-canopied throne set behind the front bench, the Norwich civic regalia of maces and swords proudly displayed for the occasion. The previous Sheriff, Ronald Brooks, ceremoniously transferred the calf-length purple robe with its wide band of brown fur down to the hemline, and elaborate black hat, resembling an eighteenth century Admiral's dress hat, to the new incumbent.

There may have been some in the chamber that day mature enough to recall the debacle in June 1965 when the hat was declared too small for Sheriff Harry Perry. The City Treasurer suffered the same embarrassment, one officer describing the men as looking like 'absolute nincompoops', another stating that he had heard the Sheriff comment it reminded him of the children's cartoon character Captain Pugwash. The council voted to purchase two new hats, at the cost of £20 each, before the next civic church service in July. Happily for Joe, his hat fitted perfectly.

Then came the moment when Joe felt the 22-carat gold chain of office carefully lowered over his head. With 420 small links, joined by one large link and hung in three large loops, it was presented to the city in 1739 by Thomas Emerson, a Norwich sugar refiner. For this he was made an honorary freeman of the city, becoming Sheriff himself forty-six years later in 1785, the same year in which he died. Having been duly sworn in, Joe Stirling was now Sheriff of Norwich.

It was still pleasantly warm outside as the Civic Party took to the steps of the City Hall, the same steps occasionally trodden by royalty since its opening by King George VI in 1938. The group lined up for the photographers, both professional and family as the citizens of Norwich waved and cheered, welcoming the new dignitaries and enjoying the pageantry of traditional sword and mace bearers in smart dark jackets, bow ties and black-trimmed top hats, alongside the playful Norwich Whifflers, originally Norwich Morris Dancers, in their colourful medieval style costumes.

Joyce and Joe took centre stage, flanked by their spouses, joined by Deputy Mayor Ralph Row, his wife and Gordon Tilsley the Town Clerk, in his white legal wig. The official photo call over, there was just time before lunch to pose for family photographs. Joe gathered his children and Jean's two sisters Joan and Marjorie to the foot of the steps. Jane at twenty-eight, her chestnut hair neatly framing her elfin face; Johanna at just turned seventeen, wearing a hippy-style floral dress, platform sandals and knitted shawl; Ian and Martin, twenty-four and twenty respectively, very much the young men about town with matching 'Easy Rider' sunglasses and fashionably long wavy hair. Jean, demur and elegant as ever, chose to wear a crushed velvet two-piece over a white blouse, matching white brimmed felt hat and gloves.

Despite the increasing heat, Joe had absolutely no intention of removing his magnificent fur robe.

The Guildhall, Dallas and Royalty

'Having been involved both through the Lions and the Three Cs in various aspects of community life I thought I knew it all. How wrong I was. Invitations rolled in, some from organisations I knew by name and others I had never heard of. It was an educational experience that lasted the year through.'

It was the first time that most of those guests invited to Joe's private tea party during the afternoon of Mayor-Making had been inside Norwich Guildhall, let alone seeing inside the Sheriff's Parlour. As they approached the medieval building they noted how it much resembled a flint castle, complete with battlements, a clock tower and gated arches. They admired the chequerboard pattern on the wall beneath the clock and the gothic-style Victorian windows. Once inside the excitement mounted as the group was guided up two flights of stone stairs, the rises set irregularly many years earlier to prevent prisoners escaping; up to the Mezzanine floor and into the Sheriff's office. They had so many questions.

Dating from 1407, Norwich Guildhall, considered to be England's largest and most elaborate provincial medieval city hall, was built to house the Mayor's Court Chamber. It was the centre of city government from its completion in 1412 until its replacement by City Hall in 1938. As well as a courthouse, the building had in the past been used as a prison, chapel, tax collection office, storage for civic regalia and at different times as police and fire stations. For Joe, the idea of having his office in such an historical building meant far more than it being inside City Hall.

The guests mingled together, congratulating Joe and Jean on this wonderful achievement and envying them this little hide-away world. The vaulted wooden beam ceiling, diamond-leaded windows looking over Guildhall Street, where once trams ran on their way through the city. There in view was the corner of London Street with the grand entrance to Jarrold's Department Store. The room smelled of beeswax polish. Leather button-backed chairs, low sofas, farmhouse style wooden chairs, fresh flowers in cut glass vases, a keyhole desk with leather inset, small gilt framed paintings of Norfolk scenes and a Tudor-style fireplace. Amongst those gathered to enjoy the leaf tea served in civic china cups and the dainty cakes and scones, were Kathleen and Grace Bidewell, spinster sisters-in-law to Jean's older sister Joan. Kathleen spoke privately to Joe during the reception, 'Joe, this is so kind of you to invite us, we are not even related to you.' Joe replied, 'I always think of you as family.'

Throughout that year of office, Jean relished her time in the Parlour. Often, when shopping with Jane in the city centre, knowing that Joe was either at work or away, the two of them would pass the clerk's office, exchanging brief greetings, close the door, drop their bags to the floor, put the kettle on in the tiny kitchenette and put their feet up for a while. When Joe's year came to an end, it was this treat that Jean missed the most. It came as a revelation just how many invitations to local organisations the Sheriff received. Not quite as many as the Lord Mayor maybe, but enough to require the help of a legal professional in the guise of a Deputy Sheriff, essentially a legal officer of the Council, as well as sharing the Civic Office diary secretary. These requests included speech days, exhibitions, official openings, dinners and dances, plays, church services, ceremonial visits and parades. For some events the Sheriff was asked to make a speech, others to chair an Annual General Meeting. Neither of these held any fear for Joe, well versed in such matters, but he always made it his business to research thoroughly the purpose and objectives of the organisations prior to his visit. Joe was able to attend the Annual Civic Service at Norwich Cathedral in late May before once again jetting off with a group of Lions heading this year for Dallas Texas, home of the Great Yarmouth oil men.

The 58th Annual Lions Convention opened on 26 June. Joe had a pressing engagement as Sheriff on the first day of July so a fast turnaround was imperative. But for those few days he focussed on the job in hand. The bus from the Fort Worth Dallas airport, opened the previous year in 1974, drove along the dusty freeway past rows and rows of oil pumps, aptly nicknamed Nodding Donkeys, alongside 1950s-style diners offering 'Tex-Mex' cuisine, each claiming their menu included the fiercest throat-burning chilli sauce. On 28 June, as the incoming International President was announced, an independent fruit packer from Kingsburg, California, the more literary among the audience applauded enthusiastically. For his name was Harry J. Aslan. C. S. Lewis would have been proud that his 'Great Lion' was now President of all Lions.

The crowds lined the streets of Norwich early on the morning of Tuesday, 1 July. Joe had recovered from the worst of the jet lag and looked forward to wearing the Sheriff's chain again, this time in the presence of Prince Philip, Duke of Edinburgh. The Duke was visiting Norwich to inspect an award-winning conservation scheme dubbed 'Heritage-Over-The-Wensum'. At Thorpe Road Railway Station, Joyce in her Mayoral chain was part of the welcome committee, on this occasion obliged to defer to the Lord Lieutenant of Norfolk, Sir Edmund Bacon as first citizen of the City. This pushed the Sheriff into third place in the hierarchy that day. The Duke's first engagement was to climb aboard a steam launch, moored at the Norwich Yacht Station, aptly named *The Princess Margaret*. As the Royal party reached Fishergate, a specially commissioned fanfare sounded from musicians on Fye Bridge. Cheering schoolchildren, factory and office workers vied for a glimpse of the special visitor.

The landlord of the Woolpack pub in Muspole Street welcomed the Duke to his recently redecorated establishment, serving him with a tomato juice, presumably without the vodka. As he passed along St George's Street, students from Norwich Art School showered the party with ticker tape, worrying the Special Branch bodyguards. As the Duke prepared to enter Blackfriars for a sherry and buffet lunch, it was Joe and Jean's turn to shake his hand. Once the feasting was over, the Duke presented the city with the conservation award. He had spent the previous night aboard the Royal Train in sidings outside Norwich Station. During his speech he was less than complimentary about the view of the city's industrial area, visible from his carriage. A number of assembled dignitaries and guests squirmed a little at what appeared to be unwelcome criticism. At precisely two o'clock the Duke climbed into the pilot's seat of a helicopter of The Queen's Flight and flew to King's Lynn in the north of the county for further engagements. Joe had fulfilled his second official task as Sheriff.

There were plenty more to come.

Official Duties

'Joyce and I were good friends. We'd known each other for many years. She would sometimes say, "I've had this invitation and there is another one for us both, perhaps you would like to do this one?" We divided it up to some extent. She wouldn't turn down anything that was important either to the City or to her, but she also felt it was a job to be shared.'

Over the next eleven months, Joyce and Joe between them performed hundreds of official duties on behalf of the City of Norwich. Some were outdoors in all weathers, others requiring evening dress and a consort. It was not unusual to attend several short events over a day, with never enough time for refreshments, the official chauffeur rushing them from engagement to engagement. They were often hungry by the end of the afternoon. There was, however, no shortage of good food and wine at the British Pharmaceutical Conference Dinner held on 9 September 1975 at the Norwood Rooms in the Aylsham Road, a venue with which Joe was very familiar from numerous Lions functions. It was one of the largest conferences ever held in Norwich. Both the Lord Mayor and the Sheriff welcomed delegates from many countries.

On the evening of the final dinner the dress code was white tie and tails. The council hired appropriate outfits for both Joe and Gwilym. Arriving at 274 Unthank Road in the official car to collect the Sheriff and his lady, Joyce found Jean struggling to do up the buttons on Joe's starched dress shirt. The buttonholes appeared to be glued together. Joyce worked in fashion retail at C&A on a Saturday and immediately put her expertise to good use. In the back of the moving limousine, amid much laughter, the crisis was averted. The President of the British Pharmaceutical Society, James Bannerman, welcomed his civic guests to the Norwood Rooms. The guest speaker was raconteur, chef and broadcaster Clement Freud, Liberal MP for the Isle of Ely and Rector of the University of Dundee. Freud had won his seat at a by-election in May 1973, holding it with an increased majority in the February 1974 General Election. On that occasion Labour had been reduced to fewer than 10,000 votes on only 16.8 per cent. Eight months later in the October 1974 General Election, Freud received twice as many votes as the Labour candidate.

Aware of the local Labour presence in the room, including Joe, Joyce and Sir Arthur South, Freud had some fun with his speech, teasing them with his sharp wit and lugubrious style. Unfortunately his theme was not appreciated. Sir Arthur was incensed, his wife having to tug on his trousers to stop him walking out. The stress brought on one of Jean's migraines. Joe decided the best policy would be to take his wife home, as she was clearly feeling very unwell. Deciding not to disturb the speech, they quietly made their way through the tables towards the rear exit. Unfortunately, much to everyone's consternation, whilst the Sheriff was discreetly trying to escape, as the door was pushed open it set off the alarm. As it was clear there was no emergency, to the relief of all especially the Sheriff, an evacuation was not deemed necessary.

Formal civic or religious events revolved around City Hall, the war memorial and the Cathedral. Joe, thanks to his Army training, could remain poker straight for long periods of time, as rank after rank of soldiers and airmen filed past, often to the accompaniment of military bands. He and Joyce laid a number of wreaths that year, including on Remembrance Sunday in November. For those occasions he wore the Sheriff's gown, often thankful for the warmth it provided, but equally as often, a tailored suit with smart tie and polished shoes. But he always wore the chain, the symbol of his office.

One particular duty that Joe looked forward to very much was the traditional Annual Justice Service at the Cathedral in October, the only occasion when the Sheriff took precedence over the Lord Mayor. If at all possible, the historic civic coach was brought out to transfer these important visitors between venues. This was an exciting prospect. However, the *Eastern Daily Press* of 19 September broke a story with a disturbing headline, 'City Horses to be sold'. A team of eight horses, five Shires and three Truman Suffolk Punches, owned by Watney Mann Breweries, were always on stand-by to pull the coach on special occasions. But spiralling costs led Watney's to make the decision to sell. This was a blow for the City Council; the public loved the theatre and pomp of the black coach, dating from 1830 with its huge wheels, carved wooden perch for the brightly-liveried coachman, crimson silk upholstery and the arms of the City of Norwich emblazoned in brass. But the horses were essential. Joe's first outing with the Judge on 3 October was guaranteed but for those in January and April he might have to revert to the civic limousine.

It only took five days for Watney Mann to strike a deal with Essex farmer and businessman Leslie Mills. He bought the team for a price he refused to reveal to the press, agreeing that once negotiations on expenses were completed with the City Council, the horses would be available for County Shows and to pull the Civic Coach when required. Joe and the citizens of Norwich were delighted at the turn of events. In addition to the pleasure of wearing his regalia to meet the senior Judges in the coach, Joe was fascinated to find himself on more than one occasion seated on the bench in the Crown Court alongside the bewigged judge, observing prominent trials, including murder. Forbidden to speak, Joe silently formed his own opinion of the accused. Forthright and occasionally outspoken, Joe found it quite a challenge not to be able to pass comment.

Throughout his special year, Joe endeavoured to remain a committed member of Norwich Lions Club, scheduling his civic appointments so as not to clash with twice-monthly Lions meetings. His colleagues were immensely proud of Joe's achievement, delighted to accept an invitation to a private reception in the Sheriff's Parlour followed by a guided tour of the Guildhall from the man himself. On 6 May 1975, with less than a week to go before the next 'Mayor-Making', Joe and Jean joined Joyce and Gwilym at a cheese and wine buffet, held in the crypt and cloisters of St Andrews Hall. The event organised by the British Boot and Shoe Institute, marked the end of Norwich Shoe Week and the end of a civic partnership that would live long in the memory. Over her Mayoral year, Joyce was recorded as attending over 600 engagements, wearing her chain of office over 300 times, made ninety-six speeches and ate her way through 122 official lunches and dinners. No such figures exist for the Sheriff but it is suspected that his duties substantially boosted those statistics.

It was over. Joe admitted later, 'It had been a wonderful year, but a year is enough.' Although valuing the experience, Joe was ready to transfer his chain, hat and robe to the incoming Sheriff, ironically his old adversary Horace Rowley, the former City Engineer so central to the creation of the much-hated Magdalen Street flyover.

Joe could go back to work.

Aberdeen

'The local director of McDermott's asked to see me. I thought there must be something wrong but they were our biggest clients, bringing in more than the whole of our Norwich business. He said, "Mr Stirling, your Yarmouth people are giving absolutely superb service but I have some bad news for you. We've decided to move our Head Office to Aberdeen."'

This was serious. He was barely back at work full-time after his year as Sheriff and was faced with the news that McDermott's were pulling out of Great Yarmouth. The giant company had so far bought over £75,000-worth of air travel from the Great Yarmouth branch of Stirling Holidays. To lose those commissions would sorely dent the bottom line. The oilman went on, 'We shall still have an office in Yarmouth because of the gas industry, but all our main management and administration people will be based in Peterhead, about 20 miles from Aberdeen.' Joe politely wished them good fortune. But there was more. 'Now, if Stirling Holidays were to open an office up there, we can guarantee to give you all our business.' Joe was on the next flight to Aberdeen.

Joe was vaguely aware of Peterhead, a small fishing town much like Great Yarmouth before the oil and gas boom filled the tiny port with vessels servicing the rigs. Years before, with the Scottish fishing industry peaking at a different time from that on the East Anglian coast, teams of fisherwomen from Peterhead and Aberdeen travelled every year by train to Great Yarmouth to find work on the quayside, gutting and filleting tons of North Sea herring. Joe walked into the first estate agents he came across, explaining he was seeking suitable business premises to rent in the town. The reply was not encouraging. 'I'm sorry Sir, there is no property available, the Americans have taken up everything.' Seeing the disappointment on the face of a potential new client, he added, 'I'll just have a word with my manager.' An older man came through from the back with some information. 'There is no office space left, but our local council has had so many enquiries that they passed a resolution only yesterday to make it easier to give change-of-use planning permission from domestic to commercial. It only became effective this morning, the press haven't even reported it.'

Once again, by good fortune, Joe was in the right place at the right time. There was one house for sale in the High Street, just up the hill from the Port. The agent, rightly working on behalf of the seller, would have to contact his client to see if he was amenable to renting the property for commercial use. While the agent made the phone call, Joe explored the immediate area, anxiously awaiting the vendor's decision.

'He doesn't want to rent the house as an office, but he would be willing to sell it. He will need to apply for change of use, but doubtless he will get that and then he can sell it to you with guaranteed permissions.' Working on the premise of supply and demand, the local vendor increased the asking price considerably from when it was just a two-up, two-down terrace. At an emergency meeting of the directors on 5 July 1976 it was resolved that the company acquire the house in Peterhead. Joe had his foothold in Scotland. He could not wait to tell McDermott's. Local builders were found to fit out the downstairs with a counter, shelving and electrics, while Joe interviewed potential staff. Judith, by now the office manager in Great Yarmouth and IATA qualified, was flown up to Peterhead to train the new employees in the philosophy and practices of Stirling Holidays. As well as marketing heavily to the emerging oil industry, Joe found that the Scottish name 'Stirling' appealed to the people of Peterhead. Rather than dealing with Thomas Cook, the patriotic Scots turned to the newest travel agency in town to book their coach tours, package holidays to the sun or long-haul flights.

Within six months of McDermott's moving their Head Office to Peterhead, business had outgrown their premises. They moved again, this time occupying two floors of a contemporary glass office block dominating the skyline of Aberdeen. If Stirling Holidays were to continue working with them, then Joe would have to relocate into the city. Aware of the difficulties securing office accommodation there, McDermott's offered Joe office space in their new premises until he could find something more suitable. Once again the offer was too good to turn down. Unfortunately for Joe, at Peterhead there had been strong criticism of the Council's decision to allow residential properties to be used as office accommodation. There was a severe shortage of affordable housing for oil workers and the planning decision was reversed. Worse, any house already changed into commercial premises would have to revert back to domestic use. Consequently, Joe suffered a painful financial loss when selling the house.

During the hot summer of 1976 Judith once again left the balmy Norfolk coast to fly to the comparatively chilly Aberdeen. Her mission was to train new staff in the McDermott's building, essential to cope with the demand. At the same time Joe was flying to Aberdeen every two weeks or so, the additional demands on his time eased only by the reliable scheduled service from Norwich. He was anxious to secure a high street shopfront in the city. There was a limit to how long clients from other oil companies would tolerate visiting him inside the headquarters of a rival. After considering a number of commercial properties, Joe took on a long-term lease in the centre of the Aberdeen, creating a new comprehensive travel agency staffed by experienced people, under the name Stirling Travel. The contract with McDermott's generated interest from other oil-related companies. The good people of Aberdeen, their city booming, chose to spend some of their increased income on overseas holidays.

Stirling Travel proved successful from day one.

Lions Home and Away

'By 1978 Japan had the second biggest Lions membership behind the United States. In many ways it seemed very advanced. I took a group to Hiroshima. It was thirty-three years after the bomb but they were still rebuilding. I thought there would be more hostility towards Westerners, but there was none and people if anything were even more courteous and welcoming than expected.'

It felt strange not to be calling into the Sheriff's Parlour or going through his diary with the Civic Office staff. But the end of his term meant that Joe could once again focus on building his business empire and finalising arrangements for the 59th Lions International Convention, scheduled to open in Honolulu,

Hawaii in June 1976. Jean was excited: she had not forgotten her first tropical island adventure. Following the convention, it was estimated that the 45,000 Lions had left the islands better off by $20 million.

The mid-1970s brought a number of groundbreaking changes for Norwich Lions, each achieved with input from Joe. In October 1975 the Club held their first Antique Coin and Stamp Fair at Blackfriars Hall. The following April saw the formation of a second Lions Club for the city, known as Norwich North Club, covering Taverham, Drayton, Hellesdon, Catton and Sprowston. The local network was expanding. The Queen's Silver Jubilee Year of 1977 prompted the City Council to reinstate the annual Lord Mayor's Procession, an event dating back to medieval times when it celebrated St George's Day. Local Lions Clubs were invited to co-ordinate the collection and counting of thousands of coins thrown by excited onlookers into charity collection buckets, policeman's helmets and bedpans along the route. At first only agreeing to undertake it for five years, the Lions actually retained the responsibility for more than twenty-five. At the end of the procession the Lions shovelled pennies and halfpennies into sacks and loaded them into a van. A police escort led the van to City Hall, where the sacks were locked away overnight. On Sunday morning a team of Lions including Joe, spent many hours emptying the sacks, fingers sticky and black with grime from the coins, wading through mounds of copper as they attempted to reach a total sum. In later years the volunteers were helped by council staff in the Treasurer's office at City Hall, the task thankfully simplified by weighing machines and electronic calculators.

During 1977 Joe took on the role of Chairman of NOAH, the youth volunteer organisation he had supported since its inception in 1969. In the same year his committee were delighted to receive a Jubilee Fund award of £5,000. The money financed the appointment of a Youth Project Worker with enough left to pay for a small caravan, refurbished as a mobile marketing space. The young volunteers loved it, the caravan becoming a familiar sight in the city centre. An office move into the Charing Cross Centre improved the professional image. Requests for help came from larger voluntary groups as well as from individuals. Joe was determined that NOAH should become far more than a youth organisation, spending many meetings debating a change of name to one that would better reflect its wider range of activities. But he faced strong resistance from traditionalists. A decision was finally reached some time after Joe had stepped down as Chairman. On 31 May 1982 the Lord Mayor of Norwich, Eric Hartley, officially opened the refurbished office at the Charing Cross Centre with a brass plaque fastened to the outside wall. It read 'Norwich Volunteer Bureau'.

The announcement of the 61st International Convention, to be held in Tokyo, Japan in June 1978, created much interest. Joe had never been further east than Turkey. This was an opportunity to introduce the British Lions to the Far East. Joe made a 'quick dash' to research Tokyo, Taipei and Bangkok. He was aware that bookings could go one of two ways; either a huge response due to the curiosity value, or alternatively it could flop, with travellers wary of the distance, the language barrier and unfamiliar food. In the event, although the numbers were fewer than New Orleans, the people who booked were very different than previously, more adventurous in their approach to travel and prepared to take a risk on the unknown.

They found Japan a very different experience than previous summers. Very few Japanese spoke English, apart from a few working in international hotels, the street signs were indecipherable, menus confusing. But the people were welcoming, bowing politely at every greeting.

Merely driving through rural countryside left the British Lions feeling relaxed and invigorated. There was a spiritual stillness, a tranquil calm and clean, breathable air. Poverty was visible, but the small settlements consisted of sturdy wooden houses, raised slightly off the ground with traditional sliding doors, protected by thatched or tiled decorated curved rooftops, surrounded by neatly tended gardens. The farming villages were encircled by acres of lush green paddy fields, punctuated by the occasional Shintō and Buddhist temple or shrine. The local people were mainly elderly, their lined parchment faces watching with a distinct air of disinterest, weaving baskets or preparing vegetables as coaches packed with Westerners rumbled past their homes.

A relatively short 60-mile drive south of Tokyo took the party to Mount Fuji. As the coach, accompanied by their English-speaking guide, drove across the central plains, Joe and his party were stunned by the spectacular view of this dormant volcano, one of the most famous symbols of Japan. A further memorable experience was the ancient imperial capital of Kyoto, travelling the 300 miles from Tokyo on a high-speed Bullet Train, known as the '*Shikansen*'. Here they marvelled at cherry trees, Zen gardens, Geisha Girls, temples and tea ceremonies. However, the place everyone was most curious to visit was Hiroshima. However, Joe was concerned they would be mistaken for Americans, fearing abuse, even reprisals.

Joe's fears were unfounded. As in Tokyo, the people of Hiroshima were charming and welcoming, showing no signs of hostility. It was over 30 years since the American atomic bomb, but there were still signs of rebuilding work. In memory of the old Hiroshima and the 140,000 who died, the charred husk of the Chamber of Industry and Commerce building with its iconic dome, had been preserved.

It was here that Joe took his group to pay their respects to the dead.

Maggie, Madeira and Montreal

*'Joe used to spend a lot of time planning things. We could sense the professionalism.
He was very good at what he did on all the tours that I joined.'* (John Jones,
President of Norwich Lions Club 2014–15)

Britain was a miserable place to be during the winter months of 1978–9. Not
so in Gail and Peter's house in Norwich. She had given birth to their first
child, Christopher James, towards the end of 1978. Gordon was delighted to
be a grandfather and visited his daughter and grandson more frequently than
before, braving the arctic conditions. While pregnant, Gail had thought often
about her real mother, Beryl. During a visit from her father, Gail screwed
up her courage and asked him about his ex-wife. Instead of being upset or
embarrassed, Gordon laughed. 'You silly wotsit, I've been waiting for you to
ask for years.' He went on to tell Gail that her mother had been a lovely woman,
how much they had loved each other and how sad he felt that it had all gone so
wrong. 'If you want to meet her I could always get in touch with the Salvation
Army. They might be able to find her.' Gordon did exactly that. When the
letter arrived it read, 'We are pleased to say that we have found your mother.
However, she requests that you do not try and contact her again. She has a
new family now who know nothing about you or your brother. We ask you to
respect her wishes.' Gail cried and cried.

The snow arrived before the Christmas of 1978 with record low temperatures,
by mid-February the east coast suffering drifts six or seven feet deep. Labour
Prime Minister Jim Callaghan, in office since 1976, was using pay restraint
as one method of combating long-term financial difficulties. Britain faced a
'Winter of Discontent' blighted by striking lorry drivers and public sector
trade unions including waste collectors and gravediggers. Labour's poll
ratings plummeted, leading the way to a Conservative victory under Margaret
Thatcher in the General Election on 3 May 1979. Great Britain had its first
woman Prime Minister. Disenchanted with the Labour Party leadership, Joe
surrendered his membership card. It had been a watershed night for many
long-standing politicians, including Shirley Williams who lost her Labour seat
in Stevenage.

After the chill of the winter months, seeking some sunshine, Joe left the
office in good hands and took Jean on holiday. He always offered to take her on
business trips to overseas locations, but she normally replied, 'You are always
so busy, I won't get to be with you anyway.' This time it was just the two of
them. Benefiting from trade discounts, they flew into Miami in mid-April,
just before Easter. The drive to Clearwater in Tampa Bay was invigorating. Joe

was familiar with the area finding its string of small islands, like pearls in the ocean each linked by small bridges, very appealing. With the trip being very last minute, they took a risk on accommodation, Joe confident of finding the usual 'For Let' signs dotted along the seafront. This time with Easter falling in April, invariably the best month for the weather, everywhere was fully booked.

Joe and Jean crossed bridge after bridge, nearly giving up hope of finding somewhere suitable for a two-week break. They would give it just one more try, before heading for Miami and the high-rise hotels. Up ahead was a spot called Madeira Beach, with a brand new condominium block called Sandy Shore displaying a 'To Let or For Sale' sign. The one-beds were gone. But there was a two-bed they could view. The tour did not take long. They spent the following two weeks falling in love with the place. While saying goodbye to the manager Joe impulsively asked if their apartment might be for sale. Indeed it was, but the owners were already considering an offer. With further probing Joe learnt that the offer was $10,000 under the asking price. 'Then I will pay the asking price.' Within the matter of a few phone calls and a couple of signatures, Unit 207 was theirs. Having reserved his own apartment for three weeks in the coming October, he left arrangements for letting out the apartment over the rest of the year with on-site management. Joe had a bolthole in the sun and a new income stream. He returned home very happy indeed.

But for now it was back to reality. Joe was planning for the 62nd Lions International Convention in Montreal, Canada. It made a change to be north of the 45th Parallel. Amongst those booking for the trip, excited to be attending his very first International Convention, was Lion John Jones from Norwich Club. A member since 1973, John was a research scientist and passionate collector of Lions pin badges. He was particularly looking forward to finding badges commissioned by Clubs all over the world to commemorate this Convention. On 19 June 1979 two coaches of British Lions arrived at the hotel assigned by Oak Brook. Joe went in ahead to check arrangements, reappearing with the hotel manager. There had been a mix-up. A quick word with the drivers and the coaches were away, just 200 yards down the road to another tower-block hotel. Once again Joe went inside. It did not take him many minutes to decide that the standard was not good enough for his people. Joe guided the buses into the city centre, pulling up outside the official Convention Hotel, the world-renowned and heart-stoppingly expensive Queen Elizabeth Hotel with its 1,000 lavish bedrooms. The two busloads of Lions stared in awe as Joe confidently marched into the front lobby. It took a little while but when he emerged the drivers were instructed to open the luggage lockers, he had secured everyone a room. He would deal with Oak Brook later.

The ladies were intrigued to discover that it was in this very hotel in May 1969, during their tour of 'Peace Bed–Ins', that John Lennon and Yoko Ono had written and recorded their anthem, 'Give Peace a Chance'. The following day Joe placed himself near the front of the British contingent in the Grand Parade, his face beaming. He and Jean had also enjoyed their first night in the best hotel in the city.

In October 1979, Joe and Jean, keen to show off their new 'pad' in Florida, invited their good friends, Claude Zelley and his wife Joyce, to accompany them to Tampa Bay. As the hire car drew up at Sandy Shores, Joe was surprised to find bulldozers digging up the car park. The builders confirmed that with demand so high, they were building an identical block, this one even closer to the bridge leading to Treasure Island, with its superior shopping and restaurants. Joe, concerned that this might compromise his view of the ocean from Sandy Shores, took Jean and his friends to inspect the plans at the office of the developer. He liked what he saw. So did Claude. The two men discussed the property and the generous discounts for reserving early. Joe instantly put down a deposit on a fifth-floor apartment, Claude preferring the second floor. He had a fear of heights. After a wonderful, if a little extravagant, break Joe was back to work, with with a further property to add to his rental portfolio. He could see the investment possibilities.

And it was good to see Jean so happy.

Chapter 6

Employer and Grandfather, 1980–2000

Working for Mr Stirling

'I went in and immediately thought he was a completely fascinating character, full of life, extremely enthusiastic about the work. The office was untidy, with piles of paper on the desk, from years before. But I never thought I would get into travel, I had never been away before. The idea was exotic. Joe interviewed me himself. I think we hit it off.' (Ann Godfrey, Secretary, Stirling Holidays 1981–7)

Ian's wedding in January 1980 called for a new hat. Jean could not possibly wear the same one she bought for Jane's marriage to John Neville, her second husband, the previous summer. Her eldest son's bride was Judy Hyland, the ceremony held in the bride's home county of Hertfordshire. The house seemed peaceful but somewhat cavernous with her four children gone. Two of them married, Martin studying in London, Johanna at the University of Newcastle upon Tyne. Martin had never settled at school, leaving as soon as he possibly could, taking a job at Courts Furniture Store. Then one evening during supper he mentioned he'd just resigned. Joe looked askance. 'And what are you going to do now?'

'I'm starting to train as a psychiatric nurse on Monday.'

A correspondence study course linked to practical training at Hellesdon Mental Hospital, would lead to Martin achieving a degree in Social Studies. Johanna travelled north to study for an English degree. She always had been better at words than numbers. With a smile, Jean remembered Joe standing over her youngest daughter, offering unsolicited advice on maths homework while Johanna squirmed in her chair.

Joe needed a new secretary. It was increasingly difficult to maintain momentum on planning Conventions alongside so many other demands on his time. He was still flying to Aberdeen once a fortnight. Laker Airlines' Skytrain, opened in 1977 offering attractive low prices to the US, continued to pull in new clients. Joe was acutely aware that Jean spent far too much time on her own, relieving her boredom with language classes in Russian and Japanese, walking into the city, pouring over recipe books, experimenting in the kitchen and pottering in the garden. Something had to give. Early in 1981, Joe placed an advert in the newspaper. Ann Godfrey, early thirties, originally from London, trained shorthand typist, confident, feisty and on the dole, applied for the job. Despite never having travelled, she found the idea of working in the trade appealing.

Mr Stirling was in his upstairs office. Ann pushed open the door, looking around briefly, instantly aware of the most unbelievable mess. There were heaps of correspondence, guidebooks, invoices, receipts, timetables and brochures on the desk, shelves and floor. What if someone rang him with a query? He would need to search through that lot every time to find the relevant document. No wonder he was seeking a secretary. The interview went well. Ann asked all the right questions and Joe gave all the right answers. The job was hers. She would be helping to organise the Lions Conventions, a task that was now taking most of the year. Not that she was able to organise his mess for him; his room was strictly out of bounds.

Ann's desk was just outside Mr Stirling's office. She quickly learnt that if she needed a file she should ask and he would find it for her. Over the weeks she began to chat on the telephone to Doreen and Judith in Great Yarmouth. She would share a coffee with the staff on the front desk, including school leaver Clare Eastwood. The ladies compared notes about the inimitable Mr Stirling, how his footsteps on the stairs made them nervous, knowing their work would be scrutinised. Ann swapped tales of how contrary he could be, trusting her with huge amounts of cash one minute, yet standing over her while she typed an envelope the next, obsessively pedantic about layout and accuracy. But they agreed he meant well, it was just his way.

During May, only two or three months after starting the job, Ann had a whim to be radical with her hair colour, buying some shocking pink dye. The following morning she entered the office feeling 10 feet high. Joe looked at her, but not with the admiration Ann was hoping for.

'What have you done? They won't let you into America like that.'

'America?'

'I was going to ask you to help escort the Lions group to Phoenix next month but you will have to do something about your hair.'

Ann returned to the same shop, this time choosing a bottle of chestnut brown.

During the next few weeks Mr Stirling, along with Jane, experienced now at escorting groups overseas, put Ann through a strenuous training course. She could not have been more elated. There had been no mention of travel at her interview. This was a bonus. The experience in America was a massive learning curve, exhausting and frustrating, yet exhilarating. Numbers were particularly high, 120 people, as Bert Mason, a founder member of Belfast Lions Club and convention regular, had been nominated as Third Vice President, the highest honour yet achieved by any Lion from the UK. Ann accompanied a group to Los Angeles prior to the convention and afterwards to Las Vegas and the Grand Canyon. Joe escorted others to Yosemite National Park and Utah. Whilst in Phoenix, Ann spent much of her time locating lost luggage, taking sick travellers to hospital, accompanying wives on shopping or sightseeing trips. At two o'clock in the morning, the phone rang in her hotel room. A slightly worse-for-drink British delegate had just returned from a night out and discovered he had left his favourite hat in a restaurant. Could Ann retrieve it for him? Incensed at being woken, she made the call but they never did find the hat.

In January 1982 both Jane and Ian were officially appointed directors of Stirling Holidays, doubling the number around the dining table at formal meetings. Joe was gratified that his two eldest children were now able to contribute to and benefit from his expanding business empire. He once admitted to Jane that he only worked this hard in order to protect his children against any recurrence of events in Germany in the 1930s. If the worse happened again and they were under threat, he must be in a financial position, unlike his father, to buy his family an escape route.

After seven years of lucrative trading in Aberdeen, Joe was approached by the Norwegian firm Christian Salvesen with a tempting offer. This blue-chip company was operating in Aberdeen as part of the Offshore Support Industry. In 1913 Salvesen had been the first to bring King Penguins to Europe following their capture by whaling ships, donating several pairs to Edinburgh Zoo. Salvesen now wanted to diversify into the travel industry and needed Joe's trained and experienced staff to qualify them for IATA contracts. Jane was reluctant to travel to Scotland in the cold of winter so Ian took up the challenge, arranging the sale and transferring the lease. The Scottish period was at an end.

Bookings for the Lions Convention in Hawaii were brisk during spring 1983, with Ann once more called into service to cope with the high numbers. Having spent the whole of the first night arranging transfers from the airport, Ann dozed too long around the pool the following morning – the sunburn stung for days. With so many problems and queries to deal with, she managed just one half-day trip around the island.

But Hawaii was just the dress rehearsal.

Bert Mason

'There cannot be a Lion in Multiple District 105 who is unaware of the special significance of the 1984 International Convention. We shall see our own Bert Mason mount the highest rostrum and assume the office of International President. The eyes of the world of Lions will be upon OUR delegation. Our numerical strength, our enthusiasm, our involvement, will be taken as a measure of Bert's ability to "rally the troops".' (Promotional material published by Stirling Holidays for *The Lion*, February 1984)

In early spring of 1984, Norwich Lions Club asked Joe to be the Club President for a second time. Although honoured to accept, the timing was challenging. The Lions trip to San Francisco in July was bound to be well subscribed. Three years since he joined the International Council, Bert Mason was to be installed as International President. Bert and his wife Beryl had travelled with Stirling Holidays to each of the previous three conventions and the two men had become good friends. Everyone wanted to be in San Francisco to welcome Bert onto the stage for his big moment.

In anticipation of the interest in Bert Mason's convention, Joe produced an impressive eleven-page Official Tour Programme, offering seven different pre-convention tours, one to Northern California featuring the lesser-known communities of Eureka and Whiskeytown, others to Chicago, Denver, the Rocky Mountains and Yellowstone National Park. The post-convention tours, an unprecedented fourteen in total, included Yosemite, Disneyland, Las Vegas, Sacramento, Hawaii, San Diego and Lake Tahoe. There was even an opportunity to stay in the Stirling Holiday apartments in Florida's Tampa Bay.

Bookings rolled in from 247 Lions, including wives, the largest group Joe had ever dealt with. Some would be flying into Heathrow from Manchester, Glasgow, Edinburgh or Belfast. Joe would need more help than in previous years. Jane and Ann were asked to bring their partners John and Roger to deal with the suitcases. Joe generously booked the two couples into a top-floor suite at the prestigious Sir Francis Drake Hotel on Union Square in the heart of San Francisco, designated as HQ for Multiple District 105. The four of them felt very grand checking into the suite with its two king-sized en suite rooms and elegantly-furnished lounge, usefully serving as an office for Jane and Ann. There was little time to explore the city, the Golden Gate or the waterfront; they had excursions and individual itineraries to confirm.

It was estimated that 50,000 Lions arrived in the city, more than were expected for the Democratic Convention the following week. Ann overheard a comment from a local, 'One thing's for sure, the Lions spend money which is more than you can say for the Democrats.' In celebratory mood, the British contingent in the Grand Parade invested in splendid matching outfits, the men tidy in dark blue and green blazers, the ladies in white dresses brightened with multi-coloured scarves. Regional delegates from Wales, Scotland and Jersey wore national costumes. A Scottish Piper led the way with the group followed close behind by a bright red London double-decker bus. Thousands of feet tramped down Market Street to wild applause, the parade taking over four hours to complete.

Banquets, trips around the Bay, drinks receptions, business meetings, committees, plenary sessions on drug awareness and diabetes education, a Humanitarian award for America's First Lady, Nancy Reagan, barbequed steaks, ribs and beans at the Dixon Lions Club and finally the official introduction of the newly-elected International President. Every Lion from District 105, including Joe, entered the auditorium, waving the flags of the United Kingdom and Republic of Ireland, holding on high photographs of Bert and his wife Beryl, singing along with the band to 'Danny Boy' and 'Happy Days Are Here Again'. Songs, laughter and tears of pride were in abundance. From the podium, two Past District Governors read congratulatory telegrams from Queen Elizabeth II, the Prime Minister Margaret Thatcher and the President of the Republic of Ireland. On cue, Bert stepped forward, receiving a standing ovation. When he spoke it felt as if he was talking to each individual personally. His message was powerful, 'Answer the Call to Serve'.

Apart from the extended celebrations and farewells that evening, it was all over for another year. The contingent was split into groups, dependent on their chosen post-convention tour. John returned to work in the UK leaving Jane to escort a group to the sights around Los Angeles. Ann was to ensure that seventy Lions reached the Flamingo Hotel in Las Vegas for a two-night stay. The group, wilting in the intense heat, stood in line for check-in at San Francisco airport. Ann stepped forward.

'Sorry Madam. We received a call earlier today cancelling your seventy seats.'

'But that's ridiculous.'

Ann's body language indicated to the queue behind her that something was very wrong. Despite Ann's anguished protestations, the airline was not budging. She asked to ring her boss. The hubbub of imminent mutiny was reaching a crescendo.

Joe was still at the hotel gathering his people together for their tour to Hawaii. Within twenty minutes he climbed out of a taxi and swept onto the airport concourse, heading for check-in where he demanded to see the senior official. The two of them retreated into a private office. Joe gently reminded them of the business generated year after year by Lions International. The staff switched on the smiles and rolled out an aircraft exclusively for Stirling Holidays. The Lions were on their way to Sin City, buoyed by complimentary drinks and a crew determined to lift the mood. The entire adventure had stretched Joe and his team almost to the limit. But satisfied customers lead to referrals.

All the effort could only be good for business.

Moves and Murder

'I became friendly with Jane and Johanna and we used to have a giggle. We followed the office tradition of bringing in cakes when it was your birthday. We used to have bets on which one Joe would have. I would say he would have the biggest stickiest one that is oozing with cream. And I always won that bet.' (Ann Godfrey, Secretary 1981–7)

Joe celebrated his sixtieth birthday in October 1984. Although both Jane and Ian were managing different parts of the business and he could certainly afford to take early retirement, he was enjoying himself too much. It took energy to live out of a suitcase, continually on the move, but the business was exhilarating, there were so many incredible places yet to visit and he felt genuine satisfaction when clients thanked him and his staff for successful holidays or business trips.

During Joe's second term as President of the Norwich Lions Club a new fundraising initiative began. One of the businesses close to Carrow Road Football Stadium, Tibbenham House on Thorpe Road, offered its staff car park as a fundraising opportunity for local Lions Clubs on home match days. Inspired by this, Lion George Turner approached his old friend Charles Bussey, the owner of a number of motor dealerships including a garage on Thorpe Road, who readily agreed. Further companies followed their example, allowing more Norfolk Lions Clubs to 'adopt' a car park. Joe did his bit, working as part of a team, directing traffic and proffering a plastic bucket.

Joe's year at the helm had also seen the culmination of what many considered to be his most far-reaching success in his Lions career. The five-bedroomed property in Churchill Road, bought by the Club during Joe's first twelve months as President in 1966, was now surplus to requirements. The old mental institutions were closing down and there were no more patients needing to be rehoused. The Mental Health Organisation offered to return the property to Norwich Lions Club. Over the interim years house prices had risen and the property was valued at £50,000, realising a profit of over £30,000. President Joe, along with colleague Claude Zelley, father of young Lion Howard, set up a registered charity. Once the house was sold, the money would be held in trust and the interest used to fund charitable projects for decades to come.

In Great Yarmouth Joe and his staff had fun devising a one-off marketing campaign, offering a new white Fiat Panda car painted with the Stirling Holidays logo as a raffle prize. When the winner arrived at the showroom to receive her prize, Doreen and Judith had to stifle their amusement. Mr Stirling's eyes opened wide in appreciation at the glamorous lady with a deep tan, white halter-neck dress and matching stilettos, a blend of the fabulous Miss Shirley Bassey and actress Elizabeth Taylor. In fact her name was Marion Barron, a member of the famous Barron family, the first manufacturers of coin-operated slot machines in Britain at the turn of the twentieth century. In 1923 the Barron Brothers opened Britain's first purpose built amusement arcade and funfair on the Great Yarmouth seafront. Sadly, Marion could not drive and sold the car back to Fiat almost immediately. But the publicity photos had been eye-catching.

The office space above the showroom in Magdalen Street was becoming too small. Joe, Jane, and Ian all needed their own space. Ian was working on ambitious plans to offer escorted coach tours throughout Great Britain. He would require more staff. A decision was made. They would retain the shop and front desk staff at 73 Magdalen Street and rent new offices for the administrative staff. The letting agent suggested a building further down Magdalen Street, towards the city. Although it had been empty for some time, it would do until better came up. Furniture, files, stationery, brochures and office equipment were packed up and moved into Number 19a.

From day one Ann never felt comfortable. Something was not quite right. During the day she could ignore it, keeping busy while enjoying Jane's company, although she did miss gossiping with the girls at Number 73. Shortly after the move, Johanna joined the team. Having completed her degree she stayed living in Newcastle, but lack of job opportunities left her frustrated. When a place in a job creation scheme proved uninspiring, Joe persuaded his youngest daughter to return home and work for him. Unfortunately no one, least of all Joe, had the time to train Johanna in the complexities of arranging itineraries. She resigned after just six months. But for a time the three ladies enjoyed each other's company, giggling over a coffee break or taking lunch together. On birthdays the cake rituals caused further amusement when Mr Stirling was in the office.

With the volume of work, especially as Lions Conventions approached, Ann occasionally stayed late to catch up. It was during these evening hours that Ann became aware of thuds and creaking above her, bizarre sounds from a room that was almost certainly unoccupied. One evening her partner Roger arrived to work on some leaking pipes in the kitchen. He didn't stay long insisting that Ann leave with him. He never spoke of that evening again. They learned later that the building was said to be the most haunted in Norwich. Two decades earlier, shop workers began reporting phantom footsteps in empty rooms and objects moving of their own accord. Over the years many businesses rented the property but moved on within a few months. One evening during the 1980s an Ouija board session had been held on the premises. Allegedly, a female spirit calling herself Sarah 'came through', revealing that in 1872 the building was a public house, the Key Merchants Arms. It was known that the rooms above the bar were used as a brothel. One evening Sarah was drinking in the pub when a male companion mistook her for one of 'the working girls' and tried to force her upstairs. When she refused he overpowered and murdered her. Since then witnesses across the decades had reported seeing the figure of a young woman staring out from an upstairs window.

Joe had no time for such fairy stories. He was busy supporting Ian in negotiations to buy Sunrise Holidays, the touring side of a family business known as Norfolk Motor Services, based in Great Yarmouth. Throughout the 1970s, the two businesses had worked closely together. Norfolk Motor Services organised coach trips, for which Stirling Holidays sold tickets on their behalf. When Joe needed to hire a coach it was invariably them he approached first. After a time, transactions between the two companies became so frequent Norfolk Motor Services added a Stirling Holidays logo onto a number of their coaches. During the early 1980s, the proprietor Alf Blackburn was planning for retirement. His son was set to take responsibility for the coach hire work, but felt Sunrise would be just too much for him to manage. Before Joe and Ian could make him an offer, Alf had sold the touring operation to Trimdon Motor Services in Jersey.

Undeterred, Joe and Ian opened negotiations with the Trimdon family, securing ownership of Sunrise Holidays, along with the client list and use of office space in Great Yarmouth. In 1986, Joe announced a further office move. Ian had convinced his father that centralising the various operations was the way forward. Administration staff would transfer to the recently-completed St Mary's House, a three-storey office block with an eye-catching curved frontage in Duke Street.

For some, it was merely a relief to get away from that ghost.

Grandparents, 'George' and Gordon

'When I saw it I couldn't believe I was down as George Stirling. I went to the Civic Office and said, "Where did that come from?" They said, "We don't know.

The author on the platform at Cologne Station, September 2013, at start of 'Footstepping' journey.

The *Hintergasse*, Nickenich, 2013.

Hintergasse 10 in 2013. The garage doors would have been an arched entrance into the building.

St Arnulf's Church in Nickenich, with memorial wall.

Nickenich Memorial Stone to Alfred Stern, unveiled on 19 September 2010.

Memorial Stone to Ida Bertha Stern (*seitdem verschollen* translates as 'since lost').

View from the Stern apartment at *Görgenstrasse* 6, a branch of SinnLeffers clothing store in 2013.

Typical rustic half-timbered building in Koblenz dating from 1689, close to *Görgenstrasse*.

The Grammar School where in 1942 Alfred and Ida were held overnight before deportation.

The *Balduinbrücke*, the bridge over which the Jewish deportees were marched across the Mosel.

Railway tracks at Koblenz-Lützel from where Alfred and Ida left for Poland.

The Old Town in Cochem, 2013.

Bus from Cochem to Trier, 2013.

**The River Sauer at Echternach, Luxembourg, through which Günter waded
to freedom. The houses on the opposite bank are in Germany.**

Stolpersteine to Alfred and Ida Stern, placed outside Görgenstrasse 6 on 27 August 2011.

What is your name then?" So I said, "Well, my legal name is Gunter". They said, "When someone heard you were called Joe, they thought it might be short for George".'

Jean's final convention with the Lions was in Dallas, Texas in June 1985. Ronald Reagan had been the keynote speaker, the first US President to address the convention while in office. It had been very special to see him on stage alongside their friend Bert Mason, appearing as outgoing International President of Lions. But Jean would be sixty-five in August, becoming tired of the heat, the crowds and the interminable waiting at airports. As a woman brought up in the Brethren faith, she had never been completely comfortable with the self-indulgent behaviour she witnessed on Lions trips. Although admiring their generosity, commitment and energy, she came from a different world. She was glad of the good friends they had made, and the sights they had seen. She had no objection to Joe continuing to organise the trips as long as the Lions wanted him to. But for Jean life was about to be very different. Martin and Annemarie were expecting a baby.

In the space of three months from February to April 1986 Joe and Jean became grandparents three times over. Jean revelled in having her daughter Jane and two daughters-in-law all expecting at the same time. She counted down the months. First Martin and Annemarie, married in 1983, presented them with Francesca on 5 February. On 27 March Ian and Judy produced Rachel. Three months later on 24 June Jane gave birth to Claire. Three baby girls. Jean was ecstatic.

With his family rapidly expanding, Joe failed to notice the activity in the Guildhall. In May five wooden plaques, listing the names of 154 previous Sheriffs, were unveiled during a Civic ceremony. Geoffrey Goreham, former teacher, writer and local historian, Sheriff in 1985–6, had been disappointed that, despite the names of the Lord Mayors being recorded on wooden panels in City Hall, the Sheriffs did not have the same recognition. Taking charge of the situation, he secured the help of North Heigham Sawmills and collected a gift of ash timber from 150-year-old trees in Rackheath Park. Bowthorpe School volunteered the skills of three of its students to gild the names onto the prepared panels. Joe, his Past Sheriff badge depicting the Norwich arms of lion and castle hanging on a ribbon around his neck, arrived for the unveiling ceremony with Jean, looking elegant in her white linen two-piece suit. As the cloth fell away, it was impossible not to notice that his name had been mistakenly engraved as *George* Stirling. Joe was mortified, but maintained his equilibrium and said nothing. However the following morning he paid a visit to the Civic Office. The files at City Hall held the name 'G. Stirling'. No one had taken the time to check what the initial actually stood for. The board bears the incorrect name to this day.

Everyone loved the new babies. Gail often visited with her two boys Chris and Matthew, occasionally bringing Gordon to see his great-nieces. During the previous eight years, as an active member of the Magdalen Street Traders Association, Gordon had forged a reputation in the local press with his vociferous opposition to road closures and pedestriansation schemes. He once wrote to the Prime Minister claiming that left-wing fringe groups were infiltrating the ranks of Norwich City Council, creating a furore in the Norwich press. His carpet and furniture business Chandler and Skitmore opened in 1968, an additional store, 'St Benedict's House Furnishing Company', opening over a decade later. Although his role as a parent had an inauspicious start, over the years his relationship with both Paul and Gail developed, offering Paul a role in his business. In 1987 Gordon told the family he had cancer. Although it was a tremendous shock he appeared strong. He'd been brought up as Brethren and had faith in the afterlife, reassuring Gail, 'I will just go on to whatever the next thing is.'

Nevertheless, he did not want to die. He was not yet sixty. When doctors informed him they could no longer help, Gordon asked Joe to take him to Lourdes, in the French Pyrenees just north of the Spanish border. Joe was sceptical, why could he not simply pray for a cure from the comfort of his own home? But Jean was concerned for her little brother; they would all go to France. It was an extraordinary place of wide boulevards, statues of Our Lady, confessional chapels, a Disney-style castle atop two ramps to allow wheelchair access and hundreds of nuns in full habits and a variety of headgear. It was humbling to be amongst so many suffering people. The services, held twenty-four hours a day, were conducted in either Latin or French. In 1858 Lourdes was merely a small market town, until a servant girl called Bernadotte Soubirious claimed to see a radiant vision of a woman in white, the Catholic Church proclaiming it to be the Virgin Mary.

Gordon joined the ranks of the five million pilgrims who flock to Lourdes every year to seek a miraculous cure. Joe delivered him to the Sanctuary of Our Lady. The service over, Joe asked, 'Do you want to go back this afternoon?' Gordon replied, 'No, I don't think I can stand it anymore'. He retired to bed, declaring the following morning that he did not want to be there a moment longer. With flights booked not until some four or five days hence, there was no option but to drive a short distance, take rooms and explore the beautiful scenic views. Gordon was pleased to go home, losing his battle within the next few months in May 1988.

Gail was heartbroken.

Auschwitz

'The first thing you see is the writing high up in big metallic letters over the main entrance. "Arbeit Macht Frei". Work sets you free. In other words if you work hard you earn money to buy your freedom. But that was a lie.'

Towards the end of the 1980s, Joe accompanied a business group to a conference in Krakow, Poland. He was enchanted by the market square, its narrow alleyways and multi-hued historic tenement houses, virtually untouched by Allied bombing. While the businessmen were occupied in the Conference Hall, Joe showed the wives around the city, the open spaces of Planty Park, Wawel Castle and the fourteenth-century Cathedral, stuffed with Russian murals and eighteen chapels, each one more ostentatious than the last. His research had also turned up details of the tourist buses to Auschwitz, just over an hour away. Although much of the Nazi death camp had been destroyed after the war, a good deal of it was now maintained by the Polish Government as a museum, a moving tribute to those who perished there. Although he had no evidence, Joe firmly believed that this was the most likely place for his parents to have met their deaths.

Announcing his plans for the following day, he asked if anyone would care to accompany him. About six of the delegate's wives agreed. They had no knowledge of their tour leader's background. Joe kept that to himself. As the bus rolled past the main railway station for the camp, it became evident how immense the site was. It took another ten minutes to reach the main entrance, passing under ominous observation towers. The familiar gate, seen so many times on newsreels, books and newspapers, displayed its ironic message. It was almost overwhelming to pass beneath it, as so many millions of victims had, only they never left. In front of him stood a number of the original accommodation blocks, laid out in neat rows. Inside were wooden bunk beds, some standing three high, so many that it was almost impossible to walk between them. Joe passed through the museum, numbly gazing into the glass cases, each filled with relics from forty years before. Registration documents, striped uniforms, samples of hair, shoes, dentures, spectacles, combs, buttons, thimbles, artificial limbs and most distressing of all, monochrome images of little children smiling innocently at the camera. Joe thought of his grandchildren and shuddered.

An English-speaking guide took the group to view the remains of the death chambers and the canisters of deadly Zyklon B gas. She explained how the prisoners were duped into believing they were going into a shower, to be cleansed of any lice or infectious diseases. She told them of the incinerators where so many bodies were burned. She showed them where the mass graves had been. Joe felt the pressure but kept control. He had wanted to sense something of his parents. But he felt nothing.

He would not visit Auschwitz again.

Hospital Radio

'I remember saying to my mother, "That was amazing, but it's funny because he never talks about it." She said, "Oh, he thinks you're just not interested."' (Johanna Stirling in 2013)

Joe sat at the microphone. Around him the broadcaster and his assistant were preparing to interview their guest for a hospital radio show. In November 1989 he was invited to talk about his travel business. Bob Walker, the programme's presenter sat down. The red bulb over the door lit up.

'Welcome to Chatterbox Joe. I believe you've just had a rather frightening experience in Mexico.'

Joe explained how, when in Acapulco attending a conference of travel agents the previous April, he had been woken in the middle of the night by a tremendous roar, feeling pressure on his body. The bed shook, forcing him to grip the bedclothes to avoid falling out. Joe admitted he had been frightened, especially at first when unsure of what was happening. The earthquake, centred on Mexico City, measured 6.0 on the Richter scale, tremors felt nearly 200 miles away on the Pacific coast. Luckily for Joe there were no fatalities that night but thirty people were injured while trying to escape. Nonetheless, it was a disturbing experience, one he would not wish to repeat.

The interview over, Joe was rewarded with a cup of tea. For some reason, he spoke of his childhood in Nazi Germany. Bob was intrigued, inviting him to return to the little studio to talk on air about his early experiences. During that second interview Joe recalled the 1933 election when Hitler came to power, the horror of *Kristallnacht*, his walk across Europe, being stopped by the Dutch policeman. He spoke of leaving his precious violin behind and waving goodbye to his parents. Bob asked what had happened to them. Joe explained about the final letter he received as a schoolboy in Lydney, telling of their imminent resettlement in Poland. He confirmed, in his matter-of-fact style, his firm belief that they perished in Auschwitz. Just before the microphone was switched off, Joe spoke again.

'You know, I've never told anyone all this before.'

Burglars and Brisbane

'I said, "Look, I'm getting older and I want to ease off." They said, "Well, your family can take over; we know your daughter has worked for you. They could do it and ask you for odd bits of advice." I replied, "They are not Lions, it has worked because I am a Lion as well as a Travel Agent."'

It was late 1990. Joe and Jean had been to see a magnificent concert in London featuring the master violinist from California, Isaac Stern (no relative), on a seventieth-birthday world tour. Stern was popularly known for his solo work on the soundtrack of *Fiddler on the Roof*, but followers of more highbrow music including Joe, preferred the great violin concertos of Beethoven, Brahms and Mendelssohn. The programme had also included some exquisite chamber music from Haydn and Mozart.

But on returning home the following morning, the memories of the concert were eclipsed by the actions of overnight burglars. As Joe and Jean went through everything, listing the missing items, it became clear that all Jean's jewellery was gone, including handcrafted pieces from Thailand and Japan along with her gold bracelet with charms collected from around the world. Irreplaceable treasures, most painfully her mother's gold wedding ring. Jean was inconsolable. On searching further Joe realised that both his Past District Governor badge and gold-plated Past Sheriff badge were no longer in his drawer. That hurt. But it was done. The police took copious notes. However they were not optimistic about retrieving the items. They seemed more interested in advising Mr Stirling to fit an alarm and window locks.

The couple felt totally drained for days afterwards. It had been such a shock. The experience reinforced Joe's decision to retire from Lions Conventions. He had been considering it for some time if he was honest. Without Jean by his side, it was not nearly so much fun. Lions International announced the 74th Convention in June 1991 would be in Brisbane, Australia. It was the perfect place for his grand finale.

Jean was feeling unwell more often these days. It was such a shame she was not fit enough to join Joe at his final convention. Not having been to Australia, it was imperative he embark on a research trip before designing the programme. On return from a whirlwind tour Joe was brimming with ideas. The promotional pages in *The Lion* over Christmas 1990 laid out the options. The conversation with the Multiple District Convention Chairman became quite heated; he really did not want to lose Joe's services, with Joe adamant it was time for Stirling Holidays to withdraw. The decision was made. Brisbane would be his swansong.

He did not let the Lions down. His final tally showed 150 people signed up for the first-ever convention to be held in the Southern Hemisphere. Joe surpassed himself with extensive choices on offer for pre and post convention trips. Early in June the groups embarked on their preferred tours experiencing Singapore, Hong Kong, Perth, Cairns, Sydney and New Zealand. Having landed in Australia, some travelled to Ayres Rock and Alice Springs, others swam in the tropical waters of the Great Barrier Reef. In Sydney Joe arranged tickets for a performance of Mozart's *Magic Flute* in the magnificent Opera House. The sheer size of Sydney Harbour Bridge, familiar to most only from photographs and films, dazzled the British visitors. Who knew it was actually wide enough to take eight lanes of cars, plus two railway tracks, cyclists and pedestrians? Unusually, the convention was split between two venues with the official business, plenary sessions and ballots held on the Gold Coast, 15 miles from Brisbane. Delegates had a lot of fun on the shuttle buses. It was estimated that over 150,000 Aussies turned out to cheer the Grand Parade, saving the loudest roars for the contingent of Lions from 'back home'. Australian Prime Minister Bob Hawke was a key speaker with a Californian Lion, Donald E. Banker, becoming the new International President.

To mark his final convention, once business was over Joe threw a party on the Gold Coast, financed by Stirling Holidays. Over 120 revellers shared a first-class meal and danced all night to the live band. Joe was presented with a set of opal cufflinks as a thank-you from those who had travelled with him over twenty-one years. It was a tremendous feeling, a mix of satisfaction at a job well done, much pleasure from the hundreds of friends he had made and sadness that he would not be joining them again. But he was sixty-seven years old and his wife needed him.

There was no going back.

Acquisitions and Ailments

'George was quite a good friend of mine. He was a "gentleman's gentleman", didn't hide it, which in those days was a brave thing to do. He had learnt the trade while working for Thomas Cook, then setting up on his own in Charing Cross. He came to retirement in ill health, dying when he was only sixty. His brother and two sisters knew nothing about the travel business.'

The sale of Aberdeen meant Joe could consider purchasing further businesses nearer to home. His friend and competitor George Wortley had died leaving two shops, his Charing Cross main office in premises owned by the City Council and another in the Prince of Wales Road. The family members who inherited were inexperienced and less than enthusiastic. Stirling Holidays obliged, taking over the showroom and staff in Charing Cross, a far more central location than 73 Magdalen Street. It was now thirty years since the Civic Trust refurbishment and twenty since the flyover had opened. The street, at one time so pivotal in the commercial landscape of the city, once again appeared neglected. In Charing Cross, the sign writers removed the name of Wortley, replacing it with Stirling Travel.

At around the same time, the couple owning the only travel agency in Sheringham were considering retirement to Majorca. They approached Joe, offering to sell both their main branch and a smaller shop in Cromer. Having scrutinised the accounts, the directors agreed the deal. There were now five retail branches in the Stirling Holidays portfolio, although Cromer, yielding poor figures, was closed in 1994. Satisfied with these new acquisitions and no longer responsible for Lions travel every summer, Joe believed this was the right time to ease back and allow Ian and Jane to drive the family business forward. Ian went on to purchase Anglia Holidays from Air UK and Warner Fairfax, a coach tour company in the West Country. For a while, Stirling Holidays Limited was the largest tour operator in East Anglia.

Despite Jean's recurrent stomach problems giving concern and Joe beginning to show signs of painful angina, the couple continued to escape to their apartment in Tampa Bay, particularly over the winter months. By 1992, the area was becoming increasingly sought-after with prices rising at an unprecedented rate. When an American buyer made him a great offer for Sandy Shores, the first of Joe's two properties, he did not hesitate to accept. They could concentrate on enjoying their more spacious Beach Place apartment. Over the early 1990s, Joe and Jean took full advantage of the reduced fares for those in the travel trade, flying to Florida every October, returning during December for Christmas in Unthank Road. Once the New Year festivities were over, they escaped the British cold and damp by spending a further six weeks or so in the sun. They made friends, explored the region and ate well. While Jean remained relatively fit it was a good life. But as the decade passed, now well into her seventies, she was becoming increasingly frail.

Joe gently explained to his family, that although he and Jean loved spending the festive season with them, travelling back and forth across the Atlantic, twice every winter was increasingly exhausting. Between 1989 and 1992, Joe and Jean had been blessed with three further grandchildren; Martin's boys Joseph and Charlie, Ian's son Julian arriving in between his two cousins. The little ones would adore the three-mile stretch of beach, Disney and burgers on offer in Florida. For the following few years, Joe and Jean remained there over Christmas and New Year, their children taking turns to visit with their families for festive breaks.

In 1995, beleaguered by ongoing health problems, Joe offered his two eldest the opportunity to take over the business completely. After much heart-searching and consideration, Jane decided this was not how she saw her future. In February she resigned as a director of Stirling Holidays, choosing instead to further her marketing career with the University of East Anglia in Norwich, developing opportunities for outside organisations to use the campus facilities, particularly during the summer months. There was now a gap on the Board. Martin stepped up and was appointed as a director a month later. In July the family celebrated Paul's marriage to Sarah King from Ely, Cambridgeshire. As a wedding present, Joe gave the happy couple and their children, Jake, Henry and Benjamin, the use of his Florida apartment.

On 21 May 1996 Joe and Jean reached their fiftieth wedding anniversary. It was half a century since the couple, both in army uniform, had exchanged vows inside an Anglican church, witnessed by a Brethren congregation. Five decades together was well worth celebrating and close family gathered to offer congratulations at an extravagant meal in the city. Joe gave an emotional tribute to his wife, causing a few, including Gail, to wipe away some tears. Everyone loved Jean. She had an aura about her. It was that same year that Jean's doctors diagnosed her bowel cancer.

In her usual selfless and stoic fashion, Jean had concealed the true extent of her suffering from everyone. For rather too long it seemed. By the time she did ask for help, her tumour was too large to be operable. After a course of painful radiotherapy and surgery, followed by love and care from family and friends, her condition improved, so much so that she was able to fuss over her husband following his hip replacement later that year. He had been suffering pain and mobility problems for some time. By November they both felt ready to return to Florida.

The sunshine would do them both good.

Selling Up

'Ian came to me and said, "Blakes have approached me. They say you are thinking about retirement and wondered if I would be willing to sell them the tour operating side."'

During 1997 it seemed that all eyes in the local travel business were focussed on Stirling Holidays Limited. Joe was over seventy years old; surely his company was now ripe for the picking? First to step up was Blakes, a family group trading since 1908, originally focussed on boating holidays on the Norfolk Broads and now planning an expansion into coach tours. Joe was happy that his son should negotiate terms, advising him to be sure to secure himself a position with the company with a long notice period. Joe had the security of his grandchildren to consider. Ian was offered a role as a director of the foreign travel division, offering him new horizons.

During that year improvements were underway to the runway at Norwich Airport to accommodate the increasing number of large passenger jets using their facilities. The board of Norwich Airport Limited was busy formulating a major transformation of the existing terminal building with a new business lounge, improved check-in facilities and most significantly a travel agency. The company would need a presence in the centre of Norwich. Stirling Holidays, with its four retail outlets covering the city, Great Yarmouth and Sheringham was of great interest. Joe was experienced enough to recognise a good deal. Jane had moved on, Ian was negotiating his own future and both he and Jean were feeling their age. In discussions with Norwich Airport Limited, Joe insisted that his shops would continue to trade and that existing staff, including Judith in Great Yarmouth, would remain in post. Over a period of months the facia of Stirling Holidays shops morphed into that of Travel Norwich Airport. The transformation was complete. By the beginning of 1998 all visible signs of Stirling Holidays on the high street had gone, the family business now a property management company.

Joe was officially a retiree.

Chapter 7

Retirement

Crisis Overseas

'One morning I woke up and thought, "That's funny, I feel as if I've been walking a lot." Anyway, I got dressed, had my shower as usual and sat down for breakfast. I couldn't get my breath or finish my food. I sat at the computer but the feeling didn't go away. It got worse and worse.'

Jean was too poorly to visit Florida in October 2001. But by the beginning of 2002 she felt a little improved, agreeing to attempt the long journey once more. Her doctor gave his blessing with the proviso that Joe was always there to monitor her chemotherapy medication and ensure that she rested. Joe was so much more alive in the sun. He had missed the apartment. They would go.

That morning in Beach Place Joe felt very odd, his angina coming on as though he had taken a vigorous walk. Jean was concerned. A quick call to a doctor, a few tests and he was in the hospital. The doctors were not reassuring. 'Mr Stirling may have had a mild heart attack'. He was scheduled to undergo angioplasty to check for any blockages in his arteries. Waiting for his appointment, Joe suffered a far more serious attack. A specialist surgeon was called in from 20 miles away to perform an emergency triple by-pass heart operation. They had very nearly lost their patient.

In Norwich Jane took the telephone call from her distressed Mother. Jean was plainly in shock. It was clear that someone must fly out to Florida that very day. On calling her sister to break the news, Johanna's reaction was incredulous. 'But he can't be ill. He's looking after Mother.' Ian drove Jane to Gatwick. If it looked like she'd be there for some weeks, then her siblings would take turns at caring for them in Florida. Jane was appalled to find her father in an intensive-care ward, unrecognisable and delirious. But he was alive. Jane stayed at the apartment, driving her mother to the hospital every morning. Joe was slow to recover; his near-death experience taking its toll both physically and mentally. He wouldn't eat, despite protestations from Jean and Jane. His memory was poor. He sat in a chair, head in his hands. This had not been in the life plan.

One by one Joe's children flew out, staying for a short period before returning home to work and families. Four weeks after the attack it was Johanna's turn to relieve brother Ian. Almost overcome on arrival at Beach Place she vowed, 'If they keep this apartment, I'm never coming back.' Two weeks later Joe was much improved, the medical staff prepared to release him to rest at the apartment before travelling back to England. Joe gave Johanna authority to instruct the bank to sell the apartment after twenty years of ownership. There was no problem finding a buyer. But there were issues with the exit visas, the authorities refusing to give permission for Joe and Jean to leave the United States until the huge medical bills, in excess of $10,000, had been settled. Since his angina was diagnosed, a condition considered as high risk by insurance companies, policies were extortionately high. He began to take the risk of travelling without insurance. On this occasion his strategy had backfired badly. Anxious telephone calls crossed the Atlantic, Jane fearing her parents' journey home could be further delayed, or even that they might be arrested.

Fortunately Joe had been shrewd enough to have some savings in an American bank. The account was emptied, with further funds transferred from Norwich. The hospital administrators were satisfied. The situation resolved Johanna was now able to fly home to attend to some urgent business of her own. The morning of her flight she drove both her parents to the clinic for Joe's check-up. It was good news; he was showing good progress. With Martin unavailable to travel, his wife Annemarie flew to Florida to accompany her parents-in-law to Norwich. Two weeks later the couple arrived home to a hero's welcome.

The year didn't improve. Jean grew weaker. Her oncologist examined her test results, breaking the bad news that her cancer had returned, spreading quickly to bones and both lungs. There was little he could do to help her further, even pain relief would be challenging. He suggested that Jean be moved to the Palliative Care Unit at the Colman Hospital, directly opposite their house. Jean was adamant. 'I know about that place. I don't want to go there, people go there to die.' She much preferred to stay at home. The doctor agreed that if she needed specialist help they would arrange for nurses to call at the house.

Joe proved to be a conscientious carer, much to his children's amazement. All his married life Jean had been the foundation of the home, fulfilling all domestic chores, happily keeping house for her husband and children. Jane could not ever remember her father even making a cup of tea. But now, despite concerns that his angina might be returning, he did everything to make Jean more comfortable, getting up several times in the night to help her to the bathroom. When she was unable to climb the stairs, Joe made up a bed in the living room. But Jean hated sleeping down there.

The only answer was to invest in a stairlift.

Rhein-Zeitung

'When no further letters came I became 99.9 per cent certain that my parents were victims of that dreadful business. But that was something that grew slowly. Okay, so you don't get another letter. Maybe they didn't have enough money for postage. Maybe the train had crashed, it was wartime after all, or maybe they were too ill to write. It was not like the normal way when somebody dies. The family grieves and there is a body. In my case I had no knowledge at all.'

The usual selection of mail dropped through the letterbox. Bills, circulars, a couple of get-well cards for Jean, a credit card statement. Most intriguing was the large brown envelope with a Koblenz postmark. Joe had no idea what it might be. He would take a look while Jean was still sleeping. Inside was a folded German newspaper, the *Rhein-Zeitung*. An explanatory letter was signed by his old friend and fellow Lion, Dieter Dierkes from Vallendar, a suburb across the Rhine from Koblenz, the Lions Club also twinned with Norwich. The newspaper was dated 20 March 2002. Dieter suggested Joe might take a look at page 20. A black and white photograph of a disused railway line leading away towards wooden buffers dominated the page, beneath the headline '*Keiner hatte auch nur den Hauch einer Chance.*' Joe's head instantly translated this into 'None had the slightest chance'.

Listed in alphabetical order were 337 names. By now his mind was racing. What did it mean? Instinctively his eyes went straight to the list under the letter 'S'.

Salomon, Sabine (56), Koblenz
Stern, Alfred (52), Koblenz
Stern, Ida (46), Koblenz

He read the names for a second time. His father, his mother and step-grandmother. He read on. Friday 22 March would be the sixtieth anniversary of the first Nazi deportation of Jews from Koblenz. The chairman of the local friendship association was quoted saying, 'We want to honour those who died. They lost their names to become mere numbers. We want to remember them by name.' Could it be that after all this time, at seventy-seven he might actually learn what happened to his parents? The article was spread over six pages. As he processed the information he thought of his mother and father, his imagination filling in the gaps as he considered how they would have coped.

Alfred and Ida were prepared for the knock on the door of *Görgenstrasse* 6. Two small suitcases packed, a photograph of their son Günter tucked amongst Alfred's shirts. Two young lads in Nazi uniform jostled them down the stairs and into an open jeep. Having collected two other couples from nearby addresses, the vehicle raced through the streets, pulling up at the gates of the Grammar School on *Steinstrasse*, in a northern suburb of the city. Dozens of official lorries and trucks were parked up outside the building, each unloading groups of pale and exhausted people. People just like them. They were corralled into the exercise hall, to their horror the floor covered in straw. With so many of them the crush was almost unbearable. There were no toilet facilities or water. The doors were locked from the outside.

In Joe's mind he could see Alfred and Ida sitting with mother-in-law Sabine sharing stories with Wilhelm and Jenni Kahn. The couples had much in common. Before her marriage Jenni was also a Salomon. She had married Wilhelm in Kruft, the village next to Nickenich. Their daughter Margot and son Rudolf were a similar age to Günter. All three children had escaped on the *Kindertransport* nearly three years earlier. They exchanged news of their youngsters' new lives in England; relieved they were being spared this dreadful indignity. That night David and Hedwig Liebert, both in their early sixties, terrified of what was about to happen to them, committed suicide in the privacy of the shadows.

The following morning was a Sunday. Still reeling from the events of the night before, the 300 were deliberately marched through the most Nazified parts of the city, passing the homes of previous neighbours, friends and colleagues. Down the length of *Steinstrasse* followed by a left turn into *Moselweisserstrasse*, where the windows of the elegant pre-war apartments were filled with onlookers, shouting abuse and shaking their fists. Stones, eggs and tomatoes frequently hit their targets. If the elderly or infirm fell behind, Gestapo officers kicked and dragged them back into the main body. They passed Jews Square, a fenced area built specifically for Jewish children to play once they were forbidden from going elsewhere. There were no children playing now. The group reached the foot of *Balduinbrücke*, the fourteenth-century stone footbridge over the Mosel. From here they caught a final glimpse of *Deutsches Eck*, Alfred recalling happier times spent there with his young son. The Prussian fortress of *Ehrenbreitstein* stared down upon them from its elevated position on the east bank of the Rhine. The group crossed the road near to *Brenderweg*, Sabine's street where Ida had fled with her son that dreadful morning in 1938. As they stumbled up the incline towards *Lützel* freight station, Ida prayed that this really did mean resettlement in Poland, as the authorities had promised. With Alfred's skills at growing vegetables and keeping livestock, they could eke out a living from the land and make a home ready for Günter's return after the war.

The line of wooden goods wagons was a terrifying sight. The instructions were to fill up the trucks from the front, leaving suitcases on the platform, from where they would be put on a wagon at the rear. But in fact the luggage was taken away, the contents destined for auction. The guards were threatening, violent, vile. Joe knew his father; he would have protected Ida from the worst of it. He would most certainly have ensured they travelled together. The journalist explained that the Koblenz Jews had fallen victim to the Nazi plan named 'Action Reinhardt', resulting from the Wannsee Conference in January 1942, a meeting in Berlin of fifteen senior Nazi officials, held to co-ordinate the 'Final Solution of the Jewish Question'. The Jewish centre of Izbica, once an important centre of trade and crafts in eastern Poland, had been identified as ideally positioned between what would become three major death camps. It also had a railway line, the town designated as a 'way station' for trains, carrying human cargo travelling between the camps. By March 1942 it was the turn of Koblenz to endure a mass deportation, first to the holding camp of Izbica, before onward transit to Belzec, Triblinka or Sobibor. Joe read to the very end of the article. But there were still so many questions. What had happened in Izbica? In which camp had his parents died? None of this was clear from the article.

Joe folded the newspaper. He has seen graphic cinema footage taken at death camps towards the end of the war. He knew how this story ended.

Jean might be awake. He would put the kettle on.

Saying Goodbye

'I remember Mother saying to me, "I don't think I could have looked after him as well he is looking after me."' (Johanna Stirling, 5 March 2013)

The cardiology department at Norfolk and Norwich Hospital had concerns over Mr Stirling's heart scans. They referred him to Papworth, near Cambridge, the largest specialist heart and lung hospital in the United Kingdom.

'We hate to tell you this but you need another bypass operation.'

'But I've already had a bypass.'

'Yes, but it didn't go as well as it might have.'

Joe was less than impressed with the consultant surgeon assigned to his case. His offhand attitude and lack of respect meant he lost his patient's confidence from the initial consultation. It was to decline further a few weeks later, when, lying in his hospital bed prepped for surgery and already feeling drowsy, Joe was informed that the surgeon would not, after all, be performing the operation that day. Joe's X-rays had revealed abnormal deposits in his lungs. He would need further tests. It wasn't so much the prognosis that upset the patient; it was the consistently poor bedside manner. Resolving to go elsewhere, Joe discharged himself from Papworth. His letter of complaint resulted in the hospital offering their top man to perform his bypass surgery. With alternative hospitals too far for Jean to visit, Joe reluctantly agreed. The operation carried out in March 2002 was a success. When Jean and Johanna visited him the following day, fearing they may find him poorly as in Florida, they were relieved to see him sitting up in bed eating a hearty lunch.

Joe received a letter during late May, this time from Judith, still working for Norwich Airport Travel in his old Great Yarmouth shop. Her new bosses would not be extending the lease in Great Yarmouth, instead moving the office into Castle Mall Shopping Centre in Norwich. The closure date was set at 28 June 2002 with inevitable redundancies. As one disappointed customer wrote to Judith, 'It seems that Yarmouth is becoming a ghost town'. It was thirty years since she had joined Stirling Holidays. Joe sent his sympathy. He had been unaware of that decision. He would need to find new tenants.

Chemotherapy kept Jean's deterioration under control for a while, but the treatment was withdrawn, the decision made to attempt an operation on her chest in late May, hoping to ease the pressure on her lungs. Joe, unable to delay any longer, underwent a hernia operation in June. Barely recovered, in September he was back under the knife for a second hip replacement. Once back home, Joe was glad of that new stairlift. November was a distressing month. Bedridden, Jean suffered hallucinations in the day from the high levels of morphine, nightmares disturbing her sleep at night. Joe continued to share her bed before the family made him see reason. He needed his sleep in order to care for Jean during the day. He reluctantly moved into the guest bedroom, allowing Marie Curie nurses to take over her personal care, letting themselves into the house several times throughout the day and night to administer pain relief and patiently attend to her needs. Jean's trusted doctor visited more regularly as November drew to a close. During one evening visit, he took Joe aside, gently suggesting that close family might wish visit Jean the following afternoon. Hopefully she would be awake to see them. He could not, however, offer any guarantees.

On the 29th Jane, Ian, Martin and Johanna arrived as arranged. As they gathered around their mother's bed she appeared to be sleeping. Within a few moments she opened her eyes, unusually alert, greeting each child by name before stretching to give Joe a kiss as he sat on the edge of her bed. Laying back she visibly relaxed, passing away a few moments later.

They had been together for fifty-six years.

Return to Nickenich

'I met Johannes some years ago when he arranged a reunion of the surviving boys from school in Nickenich. There had been 18 boys in the class. Six had died in the war, six had died in the normal way and six had survived. Those six came. We recognised names but of course, we didn't recognise each other, an 80 year old from a 14 year old, you wouldn't expect that.'

Joe and the family supported each other through the difficult weeks and months after losing Jean. His commitment to Lions charitable work kept him distracted. In 2004 members of Norwich Lions Club visited Vallendar near Koblenz. Joe was able to thank Dieter personally for sending him the life-changing newspaper two years earlier. Since that day Joe had made many enquiries with the German authorities, attempting to discover details about the fate of his parents. Despite the Nazis being renowned for their meticulous record-keeping, no one seemed able uncover to which death camp they had been deported. Through a series of coincidences while in Vallendar, Joe was put in touch with lifelong Nickenich resident and local historian Johannes Andernach, as a boy a year ahead of Günter in the village school. Johannes was arranging a reunion of surviving school friends and Joe was on his invitation list for 15 September 2005.

Johannes arranged a full itinerary including lunch at the *Waldfrieden* restaurant, on the road to Maria Laach. They were six elderly men from all over the world brought together after sixty-seven years; five born Catholic, one a Jew. They had much to discuss while strolling around the lake and savouring the local speciality doughnuts in the timbered *Café zur Linde*. Joe heard details of the lives and deaths of boyhood *Schulkameraden* (school friends) and how everyone, including Johannes, had been called up for the armed services during the war. Not everyone had made it. Joe was saddened to learn of his two special friends, Toni Fuchs and Rudi Pauken, both killed in action. Some remembered Joe's parents, sharing memories of Ida's legendary sponge cakes, potato pancakes and matzah biscuits. To finish this wonderful day Johannes arranged for the *Ortsbürgermeister* (Mayor) to welcome his old friends back to Nickenich.

The Mayor was honoured so to do.

Finding Family

'He gave me the contact of a man called Gerald Stern with an address in Newcastle. He said, "Gerald has built up enormous records of his relatives and he may be able to tell if you are from the same family." I got in touch and Gerald wrote back saying, "I am actually related to you. At Great-Great-Great Grandfather level we are from the same person."'

In retirement, Joe developed his fascination for genealogy. Researching his German family tree was particularly challenging. The majority of archivists were helpful and sympathetic, especially once Joe told them the fate of his parents. Most progress resulted from emailed enquiries to the records office in Meudt, his father's birthplace. They suggested he contact a genealogist in the United States who specialised in tracing Holocaust survivors. He in turn gave Joe the contact email of Gerald and Monica Stern from Newcastle upon Tyne in England. Gerald's parentage had been traced back to Meudt and it was possible that the two Stern families could be connected.

This proved a major breakthrough. Gerald, a Jewish businessman and avid genealogist, was born in the same year as Joe's son Martin. He confirmed that the two of them were indeed related. Moreover, Gerald informed Joe that his own father, Alfred Stern, known as Freddy, was still alive and living with his wife Gabriella in Newcastle. Freddy was Joe's third cousin, a year older than Joe, born in Montabaur. This was a tantalising link to the past. In February 2011 Gerald drove his elderly parents to Norwich to meet the cousin from Nickenich. Freddy spent much of his time debilitated by haunting memories of his early life, clinging to sadness and regret. The optimist in Joe found it sad that Freddy seemed unable to let go.

Gerald's intensive research resulted in a further significant discovery. There was a third cousin, Pete Loewenstein, born in South Africa in 1947, now living in Nottingham, England with his wife Stella. Within the space of a few months, Joe had gained two relatives, albeit distant. He looked forward to meeting Pete and Stella, inviting them to visit Norwich on 2 April 2011. Joe's children gathered in Unthank Road to welcome them.

Before leaving Nottingham, Pete emailed to mention that they would be bringing Meagan, their Welsh Border Collie. If Joe had a problem with dogs, or maybe had an allergy she could always remain in the car. Joe appreciated this concern, relating the incident with the Nazi boy and his dog, when he was forced from his bicycle in the Hintergasse. Meagan slept in the car while Pete and Stella became acquainted with the Stirlings. But over the following few hours, with patience and perseverance, combined with the dog's gentle nature,

Joe's newfound cousin succeeded where so many had failed. Joe watched the dog at first from the safety of his living-room window as she exercised in the garden. Then he spoke to her through the window of Pete's car, reluctantly agreeing to her getting out, as long as she was on a lead. Within a short while Meagan became the first dog to enter Joe's house in over fifty years. Pete wrote later, 'From the outset Joe and I felt like kindred spirits. We share so many things that are important to us, not just a shared German Jewish heritage; also a humanitarian rather than a religious approach to living; a sense of humour and a sense of the ridiculous, a love and interest in other people; a love of classical music. He is the brother I never had.'

Visiting Joe became an annual event. The following summer Joe threw tennis balls for Meagan on Happisburgh Beach on the east coast of Norfolk. Sadly, this special dog died of liver failure a few months later at less than five years of age. In 2014 Pete and Stella arrived with another collie Elsa, even more relaxed and responsive than her predecessor. Joe took to Elsa instantly, able to settle with her on his sofa. He was some way towards overcoming his anxiety. The Nazi youth had not won after all.

Monica Stern proved instrumental in Joe joining the Association of Jewish Refugees (AJR). He had been aware of this national support group, but assumed it was a religious organisation with membership open only to 'observers'. Monica was a committee member, able to reassure Joe that there was no such requirement. At the regional meetings in Norwich he would meet others who fled Nazi Germany on a *Kindertransport*, maybe survivors from the camps, along with their children, known as second generation Kinder. The monthly magazine for members, *AJR Journal*, was always an absorbing read. Towards the end of 2012 Joe signed up, joining his first gathering at the Synagogue in Earlham Road to enjoy a lunch of rye bread, schmaltz herring and home-baked quiche. He found himself relaxing with these people, encouraged to share his story. Joe's tale caused quite a stir, prompting member Frank Bright to write to the editor of the *Journal* in January 2013.

> Not only were there eight for Myrna's lunch get-together, but one of us was a complete newcomer, hailing from Koblenz, who had been in Norwich all his adult life and had only just heard of the AJR. As a fourteen-year-old, impatient to get on a *Kindertransport*, he had tried to reach England by himself, without any papers, by crossing the Dutch frontier after a long walk.

The interest in Joe's story was growing.

Music

'Music touches me and speaks to me, commanding my attention. When I was in Birmingham, on leave from the Army, we wanted to hear the Birmingham Symphony Orchestra play but couldn't afford to pay. But once bombing destroyed the main concert hall, they played outdoors in the park, in a fenced-off area. But we could hear it just as well from the other side of the fence. One of my very good friends would bring the sheet music along and we followed it as they played. I could read it then but since that time I have never looked at music in terms of reading it. I couldn't hear it by reading it.'

Throughout Joe's life, classical music has remained a constant thread, providing entertainment, solace, intellectual fulfilment and the society of like-minded enthusiasts. His mother sang songs from the operettas, in Birmingham he had been transported by his guardian's duets for piano and violin. In the Army he introduced unsophisticated servicemen to the wonders of Beethoven and Mozart. The organised trip from Bramley Camp to hear Schubert's song cycle *Winterreise* had been significant in his courtship with Jean. Later in life when travelling to the great cities of the world, Joe always hoped the dates might coincide with inspirational concerts. Content to listen alone at home, he prefers DVDs rather than CDs, enabling him to fully appreciate the skill of the violinists, the cellists and the conductor. For the same reason when attending live concerts, he chooses to sit near the front. Previously prepared to travel long distances to indulge his passion, in retirement he is more regularly seen at Norwich music venues such as the John Innes Centre, St Andrew's Hall and the lesser-known Park Lane Chapel.

Some time after Jean's death, Joe began to attend evenings held by Norwich Music Society in the Friends Meeting House in Upper Goat Lane where Norwich classical-music lovers gathered together once a week, to play favourite 78s for everyone to enjoy. Having become enthusiastically involved, Joe was asked to become their President, a role he relished during 2014.

Joe arranged musical evenings at his home in Unthank Road, playing DVDs of symphonies, ballets and operas to invited guests. With the added attraction of home-baked cakes and biscuits, provided by expert baker Annemarie, still living just a few doors down, these events became legendary. Roger Rowe, a regular attendee, retired from his international career as a Chartered Surveyor, had been the Programmes Organiser of Norfolk and Norwich Chamber Music Club since 1986, initially holding concerts in the Assembly House, later moving to the John Innes, near to the University, taking advantage of the excellent acoustics. Roger gained a reputation for his imaginative and innovative programmes, attracting well-known international musicians as well as supporting talented young people.

But there was more to come. A unique opportunity arose for Roger to buy a disused chapel, conveniently situated just outside his home in the city. The miniature church was built in 1900 by Norfolk members of a little-known Christian sect known as the Swedenborgians, originating in Stockholm during the mid-eighteenth century and once counting poet William Blake and Helen Keller amongst its followers. Since then the Chapel had served both Mormons and Congregationalists. Roger thought it might make an excellent rehearsal facility for his widening list of musical contacts. Far more than that, with a few adjustments, it became an intimate venue for small concerts, seating up to seventy people. Roger began to encourage the same quartets and soloists appearing at the John Innes, to give a follow up performance in the Park Lane Chapel. Joe loves this venue, attending almost every event, taking advantage of rare opportunities to speak with the musicians, seeking their views on a particular piece or composer, sharing his thoughts on the performance, or relating a story from many years of concert-going. He is often seen there accompanied by his good friend Joy Croft, with whom he shares similar tastes in music. Roger loves the chapel too. It is very much his 'baby' and he will often walk down the path to indulge his love of playing the piano.

On most occasions he has only the stone angels for company.

Stolpersteine

'The more people walk over a Stolperstein, *the greater the honour to the person who lies there'.* (Günter Demnig, Artist and Initiator of the *Stolpersteine* Project)

The brass plates known as *Stolpersteine* (stumbling or pavement stones) are just four inches square, set on concrete blocks into pavements outside the last known address of victims of the Nazis. By 2014 there were over 40,000 in 600 cities and towns throughout Germany and other once-occupied European countries. The requests for the stones continue to grow. Engraved by hand, the inscription on each plate opens with '*Hier Wohnte . . .*' (Here lived . . .) followed by a name, a birthdate, and when known, place and date of death.

In June 2011 Joe opened an email from Hans-Peter Kreutz, the secretary of the Christian-Jewish Society in Koblenz. Earlier in that year Joe had welcomed Koblenz academic Doktor Margit Theis-Scholz and her twin teenage daughters, Marie and Sophie into his home. Marie, researching the Holocaust, had learnt of Joe's life from an article in the Norwich *Eastern Daily Press*, available in Koblenz library. She was determined to include Joe's testimony in her dissertation. On return to Germany Margit, much moved by his story, made enquiries about acquiring two *Stolpersteine* to commemorate Alfred and Ida. The email to Joe confirmed her success. The ceremony was scheduled for Saturday 27 August at 10 a.m. and would form part of an annual reunion of Rhineland Jews, now living all over the world. The Lord Mayor of Koblenz would attend the *Stolpersteine* ceremony outside *Görgenstrasse* 6 and Joe was invited to be an honoured guest.

More recent research by journalists and academics had shed light on the story of Alfred and Ida's final months. Early in 1942 the occupying Nazis offered a deal to the Jewish population of Izbica. They could remain living in their simple wooden homes as long as they played host to at least one incoming Jewish family. The town was transformed into a ghetto within a matter of weeks. A permanent Gestapo command was established, headed up by SS Officer Kurt Engels, a man notorious for his cruelty. Food became scarce. Locals and incomers, young or old, rich or poor, were forced to work on Nazi building projects. Exhaustion, disease, beatings and shootings became commonplace.

Every week a list was published, giving the names of those to be immediately transported to 'work camps' further into Poland. For those with the means, bribery became the only chance of avoiding this fate. On 24 March, just before the convoy of trucks from Koblenz arrived, the first deportation of Jews left for the extermination camp at Belzec, creating space in Izbica for deportees from the west. It is likely that Alfred and Ida survived in Izbica in unimaginable conditions until the middle of May, only then taken by train to the recently-opened death camp close to the Ukrainian border, outside the village of Sobibor.

Berlin-born artist Gunter Demnig began his ambitious *Stolpersteine* art project in 1995. Although aware that he could never hope to honour each of the six million victims of the Holocaust, he began by placing, without permission, fifty-one stones in one Berlin street. Three months later a building company complained to the local authority that the blocks were impeding some construction work. Out of respect the labourers refused to remove them. Council officials carried out an inspection and the memorials were retrospectively legalised. Demnig, inspired by a quote from the Jewish Talmud, 'a person is only forgotten when his or her name is forgotten', intends his stones to be read by the casual walker, powerfully reminding them of those who once lived nearby.

Joe's relatives from Montabaur are also remembered with *Stolpersteine* honouring Willi and Betty Stern and Aunt Rega, Alfred's elder sister. On 10 November 2013, the 75th anniversary of *Kristallnacht*, Gerald Stern unveiled a memorial to the Jewish citizens of the town, including his grandparents Willi and Betty, who had fallen victim to the Nazi regime. This was a culmination of many years campaigning during which he had succeeded in arranging *Stolpersteine* for his family. Over 300 people, many of them relatives of the dead, packed the civic meeting room in the Town Hall to hear speeches by both Mayor Klaus Mies and Gerald. When thanking the Mayor he added, 'Now my family has a place to grieve.'

There is no stone for Uncle Alex from Düsseldorf. Although no evidence exists, it is probable that he and his wife drowned when a German U-boat torpedoed the ship carrying them to a new life in America during the early years of the war. Alfred's younger sister Meta was more fortunate, reaching the United States with her husband Leopold Rosenthal where they had five children. Meta died in Los Angeles in 1980.

In Koblenz, the inscription on the stones for Alfred and Ida's adhere to the standard format.

HIER WOHNTE
ALFRED STERN
JG. 1889
DEPORTIERT 1942
IZBICA
ERMODET 1942 IN SOBIBOR

Joe respectfully declined the kind invitation from Herr Kreutz. At eighty-seven he preferred to sleep in his own bed. But he could assure him he would set the time aside to reflect on his parents' memory. On the morning of 27 August, Jane thoughtfully called at Joe's house to see how he was coping. As she glimpsed through the living room window on her way to the back door, she could see her father sitting alone, head bowed, cradling the framed photograph of his father and mother.

Jane quietly turned around and drove away.

Humanism and Prison Visiting

'Humanism is a positive statement about a human attitude to life. Atheists say, "I don't believe in God". Humanists say, "I believe in the one precious life we have."'

After Jean died Joe approached a funeral director for advice. She had disconnected from the Brethren even before meeting Joe. There was no question of her joining her parents in Attleborough cemetery. Although enjoying hymn singing at school and occasionally since, Joe had always been a 'doubter' and had effectively left the Jewish faith on arrival in England. In his heart Joe knew that the traditional Christian service would not be appropriate for Jean, himself nor his family. The funeral director advised they had access to Humanist celebrants who could design a service reflecting Jean's life and beliefs. As with so many concepts new to Joe, he was intrigued. It was a personal and touching service, held at Earlham Crematorium, every seat filled and each of their children sharing memories of their mother or reading poems of consolation.

Through this experience, Joe was inspired to learn more about the Humanist approach to life and death. Over time, through background reading and attending meetings of the Norfolk Humanists at the Friends Meeting House, he recognised that the values and ethics were in alignment with his own, questioning the origins of the world through science rather than accepting the biblical story; respecting individuals' ability to judge right from wrong based on reason and personal experience; finding meaning in this life without the need for an afterlife. He joined the British Humanist Association, discovering new friendships through lively debate and fellowship.

His inquisitive nature, eloquence and 'hands-on' approach led him to contribute to the establishment of a 'Sunday Assembly' for Norwich, formally launched in September 2014. These monthly non-religious gatherings to celebrate life, offer those who feel the need the ability to join a like-minded community, singing secular songs and listening to talks on topical subjects followed by cake, including some from Annemarie's Norwich Tea Lounge, donated by Joe for everyone's enjoyment.

Early in 2009 Joe applied to work with Age Concern as a volunteer visitor at Norwich Prison, one of only two in the country to have an Elderly Lifer Unit. It was these older and often infirm prisoners, receiving few if any visits from friends or relatives, who benefitted from stimulating company from the community outside. Joe's view was emphatic; whatever the prisoners had done, these men were shut away with no hope of release, surely that was punishment enough? Two notorious prisoners were resident on Mousehold Heath at that time; serial killer Donald Neilson, serving five life sentences, together with Ronnie Biggs, the Great Train Robber, interned in Norwich since 2005, resuming his sentence following thirty-six years as a fugitive in Australia and Brazil.

Joe regularly played Scrabble, dominoes and cards with Biggs, never discussing his crime or time on the run. He found the man pleasant company, respectful, quick to shake hands with the team of visitors on their arrival and departure and a competitive games player. During 2009 Biggs' health deteriorated, spending two periods in Norfolk and Norwich hospital. In August following pressure from his son Michael, Justice Secretary Jack Straw released him on compassionate grounds. Biggs' final remark to Joe was 'I shall miss our Thursdays.' In poor health, he was transferred to a nursing home in Barnet where he rallied, writing a second autobiography. He died in December 2013 aged eighty-four. Joe was a volunteer prison visitor for four years, until pressure of commitments forced his resignation.

Besides, he was beginning to feel his age.

Man in Demand

'I have a busy week. Monday Lions Club. Tuesday Sunday Assembly committee meeting at my house. Wednesday afternoon catch up with my biographer(!) Evening Theatre Royal ballet, Thursday Humanist meeting and Wymondham Lions Charter dinner. Next week equally busy, lots of live music.' (Email from Joe Stirling to author, 13 April 2015)

Joe has been consistently in demand since his first public appearance at the Forum Library during Refugee Week in June 2009, directly leading to him volunteering for Human Library events under the title 'Refugee from Nazi Germany'. This gentle man in the grey suit invariably challenges people's expectation of a 'refugee'. His audience, whether it be an individual or a group, sit spellbound as he relates the story of his early life in his gentle, candid and direct style. He is regularly invited to visit classrooms where he engages with primary school youngsters (he prefers to speak only to those over nine years old), speaking in terms they can understand, about the difficulties and consequences of being a Jew in Nazi Germany. Joe takes it all in his stride, seeing himself as an example of 'Living History' with a serious message about the dangers of discrimination and prejudice. The children love him, afterward sending him simple drawings with thank-you notes. Older students equally respond to Joe's simple delivery and open honesty. During a recent Human Library event, commissioned by a Further Education college in Norfolk, one particularly challenging young man was permitted to speak with the 'refugee' as long as he was on his best behaviour. The one-on-one conversation lasted over an hour, the teacher remarking later, 'That is the most engaged that boy has been with anything, since he joined us.'

Local feature writers Rowan Mantell, Keiron Pim and Derek James have each published a number of articles about Joe's life, resulting in him appearing on local radio and television stations, including twice in August 2014 on BBC

Radio Norfolk as guest of broadcaster Matthew Gudgin. When asked to select musical pieces to intersperse the conversation, some choices reflected his childhood, *Der Lindenbaum* by Franz Schubert, one of his mother's favourites, 'When the Rabbi Sings' and '*Kindertransport*', an unpublished piece for solo cello composed by close friend Frank Pond. His musical heroes, Beethoven, Mozart, Johann Strauss and Vivaldi also found a place. The listeners wanted more.

Lions rarely retire. In August 2012 Joe and his colleagues celebrated his fifty years in the Lions Club. It had been an auspicious half-century, recognised by Oak Brook near Chicago with a Certificate of Appreciation 'in celebration and recognition of fifty years' dedicated humanitarian service'. The engraved metal plaque is proudly displayed in his home, alongside his much-coveted Melvin Jones Fellowship award, a rare honour rewarding Joe for his personal financial donations to good causes supported by Lions International. Joe's continuing generous philanthropy has benefitted, amongst others, UNICEF, Marie Curie Cancer and the Philippines Disaster Fund.

As his reputation has grown, Joe has been invited to speak to a variety of groups including Norwich Synagogue, the Out and About Group, the Civic Association, the Strangers Club and Norwich Soroptimists. Every individual reacts in their own way to his story, some crying openly when he talks of his final goodbye to his parents. Others simply cannot keep their eyes off him, this diminutive figure who has actually lived through a time that most people think of as distant history. Joe was especially pleased in April 2014 to address the annual dinner of the Civic Association, the so-called 'Chain Gang', a fraternity of those who have held civic office. Since his time as Sheriff he has rarely missed a Mayor-Making, Battle of Britain flypast or Remembrance Sunday parade.

The seventy-fifth anniversary of the first *Kindertransport* to enter England was commemorated in December 2013. Throughout that year an innovative and energetic professional drama group, devised and directed by Ros Merkin, performed 'Suitcase', an original mix of promenade theatre, music and dance, held at ten railway stations throughout the United Kingdom, re-creating the true stories of those refugees. The penultimate event was at Harwich Parkeston Quay on 29 November. Friends drove Joe to Harwich. Dr Merkin was informed that a genuine member of the '*Kinder*' would be present. He sat on his fold-up chair, muffled against the cold, on the same platform where he had arrived on 19 July 1938 as an exhausted and disoriented child, with no idea of what his future might hold. Joe watched the young actors played out his story, engrossed in every word.

At the opening reception of 'Anne Frank Week' in January 2014 at the Millennium Library in Norwich, Joe was introduced to Anne's stepsister and Auschwitz survivor, Eva Schloss. They had much to discuss. Three nights later it was Joe's turn to give a public presentation of his story. The library staff set up forty chairs in amongst the bookshelves. Before long over 100 people were struggling to squeeze into the space. Forum management agreed to open The Curve, the purpose-built auditorium with tiered seating for 120 people. An estimated 150 eventually settled down, including a group of schoolchildren obliged to sit on the floor. Joe spoke for over an hour, holding the attention of every person in the room.

Most men fortunate enough to reach their late eighties rarely venture out, instead spending their days pottering around the garden, wrestling with a puzzle book, dozing in front of daytime television, content to be slowing down. Not Joe Stirling. At ninety he remains loyal to his past interests and commitments, yet happy to be challenged by new adventures, finding joy in discovery, passionately supportive of education and the younger generation and willing always to engage in lively and intelligent conversation. He lives alone in the family home with only a few hours' domestic help each week. There are occasions in the year, such as Christmas evening and Paul's birthday in June, when the family traditionally gather at *Opa*'s house. Joe becomes a 'guest in his own home', relaxing in his favourite armchair while the ladies prepare food in the kitchen, grandchildren, and more recently great-grandchildren, fussed over and admired.

Although accepting his travelling days are over, he still drives his car, albeit only locally and no longer in unlit areas after dark. Mobility can be a challenge, one of his hip replacements showing signs of deterioration, but he manages his own shopping, pushing a trolley around Sainsbury's picking out easy-to-prepare meals. His love of something sweet is still there, with cakes and biscuits kept in the larder in anticipation of visitors. No longer a shareholder in his own company, he retains an interest in the activities of the family property business, endeavouring only to offer advice when his experience and views will be helpful.

Every day, a copy of the *Evening News* is delivered to his home. Maintaining a keen interest in current affairs, he reads every page. A well-thumbed diary lives in his back pocket, pencilled contents revealing a busy and productive life. Joe is frustrated when dates clash. He finds it difficult to hear clearly on the telephone, preferring to communicate by email. He checks his inbox every morning and several times during the day for messages from his many correspondents worldwide, lost when the computer or broadband lets him down. An ancient radio is kept permanently tuned to Radio Norfolk, specifically for listening to Norwich City matches, his support for the club as passionate as it ever was. He misses Jean every day.

Each year 27 January is set aside as Holocaust Day, an important date in the Jewish calendar. In Norwich the Council of Christians and Jews bring together representatives of all faiths into the Anglican Church of St Peter de Mancroft to share a deeply moving service, conducted in both Hebrew and English, to remember the victims of the 'Final Solution'. Joe has been an invited honoured guest for many years, welcomed in the opening address and much sought after following the service by friends and well-wishers. In 2015, three months after his ninetieth birthday, Joe was invited by the Holocaust Memorial Day Trust to light one of seventy nationally commissioned candles outside the Forum in Norwich, as part of a larger initiative throughout the country, marking the seventieth anniversary of the liberation of Auschwitz–Birkenau.

As ever, Joe Stirling was more than happy to oblige.

Epilogue

For his ninetieth birthday on 18 October 2014, Joe's family arranged a surprise party at the Georgian Assembly House in Norwich. Over sixty guests were invited, representing many facets of his life. Judith Lubbock, the Lord Mayor of Norwich and Bill Armstrong, the Sheriff, attended in their official capacity, civic chains of office worn in honour of the former Sheriff. Sadly, Norfolk was too far for octogenarians Hazel and Barbara to travel. Hazel Brown (née Allsopp) wrote to Joe from her home on the far west coast of Wales, happy to inform him that her son was the new Vicar of St. Mary's Anglican Church in the Welsh town of Fishguard. Joe knew how very proud Christopher's god-fearing grandmother Doris would have been. Brenda Vedmore (nee Hyde), still living in Lydney and back in touch with her Günter after seventy years, sent him love and birthday wishes.

Kathleen Bidewell, in her ninety-sixth year, sent a birthday card from her Care Home for Retired Christians in the Norfolk town of Dereham. Her nephews Andrew and Michael were happy to pass on her best wishes in person. Paul and wife Sarah flew from their home in the mountains of Southern Spain, where they had moved with their five children in 2004. Gail arrived with her newfound half-sister Diane, the daughter of Beryl and Elias Williams. Some months after her mother had died in 2001, Diane stumbled across some documents, hidden under a false bottom in a bedside drawer. Included amongst them was a birth certificate for one Gail Skitmore. Fate decreed that at about the same time Gail, now divorced from Peter, was taking lessons on her first computer. After years of searching, Diane contacted Gail via email, tentatively asking if Beryl might have been her mother. The two women immediately became great friends; Gail was now able to ask all the questions about her mother that had so far gone unanswered. In adult life Gail also became closer to Pauline, her stepmother, earlier rifts long forgotten.

Party guests were curious to know the identity of the two ladies from Germany. Jütta Hansen is a life long resident and village historian of Nickenich and close friend of Johannes Andernach. She travelled from the Rhineland with daughter Jessica, bringing greetings and gifts from the Mayor of Nickenich, Herr Gottfried Busch. In 2010 he had unveiled memorial plaques, affixed to the wall in front of the church, just a few hundred yards from the *Hintergasse*. The inscriptions honoured citizens of the village who perished at the hands of the Nazis, including Pastor John Schulz, members of the Egener and Marx families and Alfred and Ida Stern. Joe's family is still held in high regard in Nickenich. The gifts from the villagers included a circular glass 'sun catcher' hand-painted with the village crest. In his acceptance speech, Joe was visibly moved by this touching gesture from the past.

Johanna, acting as Master of Ceremonies, included in her speech words that will resonate in all those who truly know Joe Stirling.

What is amazing is not so much what he did (that was out of desperation) but the way he chose to let it affect the rest of his life. He sees the good in people who helped him rather than focusing on the terrible things he witnessed and fled from and letting those stultify him. He chose to give up his personal dream of going to University and do what he felt was right and that sense of 'rightness' has persisted throughout his life.

Bibliography

Most of the stories and information in this book are taken from interviews conducted especially for it, but the following books and websites have been exceptionally informative and inspirational:

A Tale of One City at www.ataleofonecity.portsmouth.gov.uk.

Ancestry.co.uk (web).

Andernach, Johannes, website on history of Nickenich at http://buggy.homeip. net/wb-andernach/

Bard, Mitchell G., *48 Hours of Kristallnacht* (The Lions Press, Connecticut, 2008).

Berry, P,. and Bostridge, M., *Vera Brittain, A Life* (Virago Press, London, 2008).

East Anglian Film Archives at www.eafa.org.uk.

Fergusson, A., *When Money Dies* (Old Street Publishing, London, 2010).

Goodrum, P., *Norwich in the 1950s*, (Amberley Publishing, Stroud, 2012) _____, *Norwich in the 1960s* (Amberley Publishing, Stroud, 2013).

Goreham, G., *The Sheriff's Tale* (Crowes of Norwich, c. 1986).

Harris, M. J., and Oppenheimer, D., *Into the Arms of Strangers* (Bloomsbury Publishing, London, 2001).

Hoffman, H., *Moselland* (Verlag Heinrich Hoffman, 1942).

The Lion magazine, British and Irish Edition, various issues between 1971 and 1992 (Lions International Multiple District 105).

Martin, P., *We Serve. A History of the Lions Club* (Regenery Gateway, Washington D.C., 1991).

Memories of the Forest of Dean at Sungreen.co.uk.

Middleton, V., *British Tourism. The Remarkable Story of Growth* (Butterworth and Heinemann, Oxford, 2007).

Nickenich Jewish History at www.alemannia-judaica.de.

Norwich Heart at www.heritagecity.org (web).

Palgrave-Moore, P., *The Mayors and Lord Mayors of Norwich* (Elvery Dowers, 1978).

Rendell, B., and Childs, K. (eds), *The Tin Platers of Lydney and Lydbrook* (Review Graphics, 1950).
Stalcup, A., *On the Home Front* (Linnet Books, Connecticut, 1998).
Stirling, J., *Aller Angfang is Schwer* (unpublished memoir, 2002).
The British Way and Purpose (Directorate of Army Education, 1944).
United States Holocaust Memorial Museum at www.ushmm.org.
Williams, S., *Climbing the Bookshelves* (Virago Press, London, 2009).

Index